P9-EDU-134

THE PERMACULTURE WAY

Practical steps to create a self-sustaining world

Graham Bell

Illustrated by Brick

Foreword by Bill Mollison

Preface by David Bellany

CHELSEA GREEN PUBLISHING COMPANY
White River Junction, Vermont

A Permanent Publications Book

Published by:
Permanent Publications
Hyden House Ltd.
The Sustainability Centre
East Meon
Hampshire GU32 1HR
UK
Tel: (01730)823 311
Fax: (01730) 823 322
Email: enquiries@permaculture.co.uk
Web: www.permaculture.co.uk

Published in the United States in 2005
by Chelsea Green Publishing Company
www.chelseagreen.com

Published in 2004
by Permanent Publications, UK

First Published 1992
by Thorsons an imprint of Harper Collins

© 1992 Graham Bell

Graham Bell asserts the moral right to
be indentified as the author of this work

Illustrations © 1992 Brick

Cover photographs Photos.com and Nova

British Library Cataloguing-in-Publication Data
A catalogue record for this book is available from the British Library

ISBN 1 85623 028 7

All rights reserved. Apart from any fair dealing for the purpose of study, research, criticism or
review, as permitted under the Copyright Act, no part of this publication may be reproduced,
stored in a retrieval system, rebound or transmitted in any form or by any means, electronic,
mechanical, photocopying, recording or otherwise, without the prior written permission of
Graham Bell, Hyden House Limited or Chelsea Green Publishing Company.

For my father
Jim Bell
and for all fathers
that we may give with compassion,
and receive with joy.

The contents of this book and the word Permaculture© are copyright. The word permaculture can be used by anyone adhering to the principles and ethics expressed herein. The only restriction on use is that of teaching; only graduates of a Permaculture Institute can teach 'Permaculture', and they adhere to agreed-on curricula developed by the College of Graduates of the Institutes of Permaculture.

AUTHOR'S ACKNOWLEDGEMENTS

I would like to thank my partner Nancy Woodhead for her creativity and support during the production of this book. I am grateful to Andy Langford for his hard work in establishing Permaculture in temperate Britain over many years, and for the large number of ideas he has cheerfully given myself and others.

I am grateful to Andy and Nancy for reading the script and also to others who did so, notably Diana and Jay Woodhead, and Ian Lillington whose prompt and detailed comments were much appreciated. I thank my colleagues Kate Cox, Andy Foreman, and Caroline Leckenby who also read the manuscript, but more importantly kept daily business turning over whilst I was absent from my desk, idly writing this book.

The following people, knowingly or unknowingly, provided help, ideas and information on specific points:

Eoin Cox (landscape), Chris Dixon (wilderness), Ian Flindall (energy), Ken Hennessy (species), Verity Langford (work), David Leigh (water), Jim McGurn (transport and community), Stephen Nutt (maps), Lon J Rombough (US varieties and references), Dorothy Shipp (midwifery), Bernard Quinn (geotextiles).

Permaculture in the UK has benefited greatly from three senior growers whose gentle momentum in the face of official indifference is exemplary: Robert Hart, Arthur Hollins and Bruce Marshall, please take a well deserved round of applause. I am conscious that there are many more creative and visionary people throughout the world who shine in their achievements in greening the planet, and that you may be one of them. I look forward to this minority of souls becoming the majority, and hope that this book makes some modest contribution to that change.

Many more people who are unnamed have contributed to my thinking, and I particularly thank all those who write for *Permaculture News* for their free input to expanding our understanding of the planet. The authors mentioned in the booklist have all added dimensions to my vision of a sane future.

The final manuscript is my responsibility, but would not have been possible without the enthusiasm of all these people, and the support of my household. I also thank John Button for his tireless commitment to advancing green thinking and John Clark for his drawings, which help show that planet-repair can be fun.

FOREWORD

by Bill Mollison

This major effort by Graham Bell of Scottish Permaculture may be added to the slim library of those who teach or practise integrated design. The book deals with cool climate, and more specifically with plants and animals for the British Isles and Europe, but the principles and philosophy hold good anywhere on Earth.

I suspect that this book is the precursor to others which will arise to elaborate specific techniques for specific places – we need similar books for tropics and arid lands, and even for specific methods of production. Permaculture, as a system of design for people in nature, has come a long way since 1974 when it was first proposed by myself and David Holmgren.

There are now more than 54 international teaching centres and over 80 teachers at work; student numbers and projects (some 6000 students by the close of 1991) are expanding exponentially, and will need to do so if we are to offset the damage done to soils, forests, air quality, water and basic nutrition by an uncontrolled materialism. This is obvious to all of us as unethical monetary and monopoly supply systems under the guise of 'free market'. Our only real freedom is to choose those areas where we can act responsibly in relation to conserving and regenerating the earth's resources – and this is mainly achieved in our homes, but also in our work.

Many local regions are now organising to increase self-reliance. In a real sense the current recession differs profoundly from the previous recessions of over-production (1928-35) or financial mis-management (1890s). It is a recession of wealth, of natural resources, caused by overuse and wastes, and may well continue for the foreseeable future; natural assets are our only real wealth, and may have been devastated for that ephemeral and unreal substitute – money.

As the numbers grow of those who, like Graham Bell, consolidate their knowledge in real projects, so wasteful systems will change, and we can only create widespread change by cooperating to create our own future. Work-netting, not networking is the way to do this. Each of us need do very little to create a sustainable future; it is only the sum of all our small efforts that changes society and land-cure ethics. Graham outlines the way forward. Good luck to all of us.

Bill Mollison

PREFACE

by David Bellamy

I have four books in my library which form the cornerstones of my hope for the future: Marcus Porcius Cato's *Treatise on Agriculture,* (circa 160 AD); Robert Sharrock's *History of the Propagation and Improvement of Vegetables by the Concurrence of Art and Nature* (1660); Hans Jenny's *The Soil Resource* (1980), and Bill Mollison's *Permaculture* (1988). I can now add this book to the collection, for it is of great importance. This is a spring-board text, which relaunches the wisdom of almost twenty centuries into the arena where it is most needed and from which it can be most effective – the rich countries of the temperate world.

With more than a third of the world agricultural and pastoral lands already threatened by erosion and desertification, with an estimated 100 000 people dying every day of conditions relating to malnutrition and environmental pollution, and with the human population exploding through the 6 *billion* barrier, this is not the time for more research and more international conferences: it is the time for action.

The research has already been done, by Bill Mollison and the teachers and students of 54 teaching institutes across the world. The success of their practice and expertise is on permanent display, from window-box-sized plots in urban heartlands, through co-operatives revitalising urban sprawl, to new working communities in vibrant living landscapes.

Permaculture is the conscious design and maintenance of agriculturally productive systems which have the diversity, stability and resilience of natural ecosystems. It is the harmonious integration of the landscape with people providing their food, energy, shelter and other material and non-material needs in a sustainable way.

This is both handbook and workshop manual, a *vade mecum* of hope which will allow the rich nations of the temperate world to put their own houses in order, by giving them a firm base from which they can preach and fund the new ethic of sustainable development.

Permaculture simply asks people to put as much into life as they demand from it. Is this too much to ask to save the world? Please buy this book; do not place it in your bookshelf or on your coffee table, but use its principles in your everyday life. Teach your children, lobby your governments – local, national and international – with the wisdom it contains.

Thank you for caring.

David Bellamy
Bedburn 1991

CONTENTS

Acknowledgements   11

Foreword by Bill Mollison   13

Preface by David Bellamy   15

Introduction   17
What the reader should expect to gain from this book. Where is Permaculture?
How the book is organised. How best to use it. Useful definitions. The way
ahead.

1 Why Permaculture?   25
What is wrong with present practice. Resource destruction. How Permaculture
offers an ethical approach. Intrinsic worth of life. People care/land care. Give
away surplus. Aesthetics as by-product of good design. Design vs technique.
Can we afford Permaculture? Resource development.

PART I WHERE ARE YOU NOW?

2 The Value of People   37
Human needs and resources. Health. Skills: correct valuation, sharing and
development. Work and pollution. Children as people. The age myth. The
global village. Leadership. Fresh approaches.

3 Real Capital   45
What capital is. What it needs. Fair exchange. Money. How to create capital.
How to access the capital you have. Alternative money sources. Alternatives
to money. Risk management.

4 Make a Personal Stocktake   **57**

You. Your skills. Your needs. Your physical assets. Possible co-operators.
Any shortfall? Any surplus?

5 Looking at Nature   **63**

Physical patterns. The core model. Wind and water patterns. Microclimates.
Sun sectors. Spirals and flows. Biotechnics. Going with the flow. Edge
and ecotones. Maximise edge. Niches. Predators. The spiral of intervention.

6 Universal Aims   **73**

Theoretical patterns. Patterns of thinking. 'Timeless Way of Building'.
Minimum intervention. Maximum useful relationships. Liabilities into assets:
'Everything is a gift'. Diversity of elements; duplicity of function. Minimum
effort for maximum effect. Stacking (multi-dimensional). The flywheel effect.
Start near. High yield. Design element template.

PART II WHAT CAN YOU DO?

7 Your home   **83**

Purpose. Siting. Neighbours and extramural amenity. Water provision.
Sanitation (1). Access. Sun side and shade side. Fire. Winds. Frost topography.
Zones and sectors. Labour saving. Energy efficiency. Natural materials.
Construction ideas. Retrofit ideas. Furniture. Stoves. Waste usage.
Greenhouses. Home as garden. Living structures. Fences and boundaries.
Security. Viewpoints.

8 Your Community   **101**

What is community? Historical and international examples. Designing for
people. Co-operation. Communication. Trade. Decision making. Community
banks. Community transport. Opting in. Benefits. Culture. Resources and
needs. People with special needs. Security.

9 About Towns   **109**

Urban gardening. International examples. City farms. City-country fingers.
Farm link-ups. City culture.

10 About Wilderness 115

Why wilderness? Regeneration techniques. Wild harvests. Species.

11 Working with the Landscape 120

Maps. Symbols. The map is not the land. Contours. Water tables, water flow. Prevailing and other winds. Climate (cold/warm?). Rock and soil structure. Dam sites. Wind sites. Slope management and erosion resistance. Sun/shade. Changing landscape: earthworks, water storage and forest. Temperate vs Arid.

12 Managing Energy Flows 129

Entropy vs availability of energy. Conservation. Primary vs Secondary uses. Food as energy. Sun power. Energy cycles. Maximised flow from source to sink. Water, wind. Passive vs active systems. Plant/animal cycles. Biomass. Transport. Cultural interchange. National/personal vs local/communal. Water/land/air. Public transport. Draught animals. Pedal power. Alternative fuels.

PART III HELPFUL TECHNIQUES

13 Gardening 147

Minimum tillage. Mulching. Rotations. Bed types. Perennial vs annuals. Fruit/vegetable/fibre crops. Crops as fertiliser. Maximum ground cover. Use of all layers and seasons. 'Weeds'. Salads and herbs. Indigenous vs exotic species. Companion planting. Seed conservation. Growing under glass. Integrating stock.

14 Orchards 159

Tree techniques. Fruit and nut varieties. Small fruit. Stock integration. Forest gardens.

15 Agriculture 171

Minimum tillage. Natural soil feeders. Erosion avoidance. Foggage. Stock vs arable. Thinking again about stock. Biogas and other energy cycles.

Rotations. Trees in broadscale farming. Designing for climate. Diversity and stacking. Fukuoka/Bonfils. The independent seeds merchant. Added value products. Stock/aquaculture system.

16 Aquaculture   181
Fresh and salt water environments. Food chains. Plant/animal/fish/crustacean/ insect/bird species. Zones around and in water. Feeding. Manures. Minerals. Erosion control. Flotsam. Design features. Water power.

PART IV UNDERSTANDING RESOURCES

17 Fertility   189
Patterns of enrichment. Definition of true yield. Cycles of growth. Soil development techniques. Species list.

18 Water   202
Where it is. What it does. Hydrological cycle. Capturing it. Using it. Recycling it. Sanitation (2). Pumps. Reed beds. Aquaculture/Mariculture. Sacred water.

19 Endpiece   209
Design sequence. Design checklist. Commitment to succeed.

Appendix: Species Lists. Trees, Perennials, Annuals, Stock.   215

Booklist   229

Useful Contacts   233

Index   235

INTRODUCTION

This book is about taking control of your life. It's also about creating wealth without environmental damage, using a systematic approach called Permaculture.

What is Permaculture?

Permaculture is a way of arranging your life to be happy and abundant. You can meet your own needs without making anyone else's life less pleasant. Human habitats can be made highly productive with much less work than is taken to make them destructive under present systems. By making conscious decisions in designing our lives we can manage our resources well, reducing wastage.

The term was invented by an Australian, Bill Mollison, to imply **Perman**ent **Agriculture**. In 1978 Bill and David Holmgren wrote a book, called *Permaculture 1*, outlining a vision for rebuilding sustainable and ecologically benign human settlements.

They wrote to give vision to a society which, in pursuit of high standards of living, was losing its sense of proportion. Bill and David outlined ways of meeting human needs whilst increasing the planet's fertility. For over eighteen years

Bill Mollison has been writing and teaching all around the world. His latest work, *Permaculture – A Designer's Manual*, is an incomparable catalogue of skills and insights built on the worldwide experience of thousands of practitioners of his early bold vision, and his own unrivalled knowledge.

What Will This Book Give You?

This book is an introduction to Permaculture for people living in cool climates. It gives a starting point from which people can begin to practise Permaculture. It suggests practical steps for taking responsibility for your own needs.

It is addressed to those who believe there's a problem, who admit that we have gone astray. If you ever felt that sense of urgent and painful distress which goes with the question 'But what

17

can I do about it?' then this is the place for you. Although there is no one answer, there are positive actions we can all take. This book offers a framework, a structure – a way of thinking. You can adapt the approach to your own life, starting now. This book is an invitation to accept your own role as a leader in the greening of the planet.

Rather than work ourselves into the ground we need to learn to see better. By careful placing of each human construct and each living thing we can let their natural characteristics give us greatest benefit. The alternative approach, of bending nature to our will, is too energy-consuming to last.

It would be nice to think that the solutions offered in this book encompass all of life. They don't – no book can do that. I hope these examples will show you patterns which you will want to use and adopt as second nature.

Doesn't It Mean Giving Up A Lot?

It does ask you to limit your personal consumption. It does encourage you to accept and demand responsibility for your own life. Where it suggests you put aside high consuming habits Permaculture offers other ways of working which should be fun as well as sustaining. If it feels painful, then it's not creating abundance and it needs rethinking. You should gain more than you lose.

Permaculture doesn't mean, for instance, abandoning technology. It means that every time you choose to use technology you do so because you really want to, and because it's the best way to accomplish your task.

You will find parts of this book which are important to you, personally. I find gardening the best example. In Permaculture you agree to garden, not just because it enables you to eat good food, and to understand the processes by which basic necessities can be made healthy and available, but because gardening exhibits all the qualities of planet-care in a possible way. It is small scale, local, and something for which you can take personal responsibility. It is also found world-wide amongst all peoples, and brings together all the strands of our relationship with nature. It is a great symbol for an appropriate level of work and reward.

If you accept Permaculture as an ethical system, then you will no longer be able to differentiate between work and leisure. Your goal will be to make all life a relaxed, constructive way of behaving.

Where Can I See Permaculture?

Everywhere and nowhere, because it is a way of thinking, not a tangible object, and you can never see 'all of it'. Local Permaculture groups in your area will have lists of sites and projects which show the principles in action, but aspects of it can be seen all around you. There is no such thing as a 'complete Permaculture', because it is also a process of development over time.

Permaculture is a name given to a very old process. Ancient native cultures understood if you ever squandered a resource, you would some day run out of that supply. So there are remnant examples of Permaculture in practice all around you. Some people are members of the Permaculture Institute, and consciously study the subject as a design discipline. Some people do it just for pleasure. Many more have never heard the word, but practise it through common sense.

The Permaculture Institute is a world-wide body which teaches people the art of seeing in this way. The aim of qualified designers is to develop inter-dependence with the immediate com-munity, rather than 'self-sufficiency'.

How Is This Book Organised?

It is in four parts:
Where Are You Now?
The first part asks you to look at yourself as a valuable element in the world. It describes some overall con-cepts, and explains the theory of Permaculture. You need to read this section to understand the underlying theories in the practical sections.
What Can You Do?
This section moves out from you as the centre to the successive circles of community around you. It also looks at how you can manage the flow of life through those concentric communities.
Helpful Techniques
Part three is a suggested list of tools for personal action.
Understanding Resources
The final part is a look at managing our most essential resources, land and water.

You will find some answers here that suit your personal circumstances, others you will have to create to fit your own needs. There are some 'Shining Examples' included in boxes through-out the text – to encourage and remind us all that ordinary people have the power to do great things.

What Can I Do?

You can complain about nuclear power stations and adulterated food, or you can start your own energy system and grow your own food. Anywhere. Now. It doesn't matter if you don't get it all right straight away. It doesn't matter if you don't produce all your own energy needs today. What matters is that you are reducing your own net consumption.

If we all move in the right direction it's a start. Whether we are too late to stop the hostile reactions of a damaged planet, I don't know. I find the

21

possibility that we can reverse our destructive impetus more palatable than assuming that 'the end is nigh'.

Some Essential Definitions

Work

Permaculture is about reducing the amount of work needed to meet a given end. There are different concepts of work which it is important to distinguish here. Physicists talk of work meaning 'energy expended', and we also talk of work as the paid or unpaid jobs we do. In an ecologically kind society we need to minimise our energy expenditure, and to maximise the creative and rewarding nature of our personal work.

Systems which pollute are wasteful, not just financially, but in that they create unnecessary work. Nature does not waste, it is a complete system in which each element produced by one part of the process is indisputably needed elsewhere as a resource. Humans work far more than other creatures in nature, setting greater demands for their satisfaction, and creating yields for which they have no uses. Each plant, animal, bird and micro-organism is placed within the natural system at a point where its needs can be met and its wastes supply someone else's needs. By

conscious design we can improve the situation.

Sun Side/Shade Side

On a shrinking globe we can no longer say 'north and south' and be understood by everybody. In the northern hemisphere north means shade side, and south means sun side, from the position of the sun at midday. In the southern hemisphere the situation is reversed, south being shade side, and north being sun side. Throughout the text the terms sun side and shade side are used to enable a global understanding of specific points.

The Way Ahead

I have no pretensions towards objectivity. I believe that all of us have a very personal view of Life and of Death. This book indulges my personal knowledge and prejudices. I do not expect anyone to agree with all of the text. I hope that it is provocative in a constructive way without being offensive. I hope you are provoked into confidence in your ability to take remedial action. The world needs you to do that.

This book should be tolerable reading in any temperate climate. The precise details will be more pertinent the more your climate is like south-east Scotland, which is where I live. For those in such exotic locations as eastern Canada or industrial Belgium, I rely on your judgement and enthusiasm to translate my advice into local realities.

I am heavily indebted to many previous thinkers and doers, and know that very little in these pages is original. I see my role as that of the early 'natural scientists', to report on observed findings, where observation implies minimal disturbance of the subject. The style suggests sketches from life, rather than dissected carcasses. I have decided not to interrupt the text with detailed references, but there is a full booklist at the end of the book and personal sources are given in the Acknowledgements.

It is customary when apologising for stealing everyone else's time and talent to admit all the errors are your own. Personally, I blame them on history. What is offered here is a template that is now, and always will be, open to improvement.

I believe it is the conversation you have with your neighbour over the garden fence which saves the world. And if you want to know what the news is, go outside and look.

I hope this book helps you realise your power to change the world from your own doorstep.

Graham Bell
Coldstream 1991

1 WHY WE NEED PERMACULTURE – FACING THE MUSIC

Unless we accept there's a problem, we'll never see the need for the solution.

What Is Wrong With Present Practice

The power of human creativity has outstripped our ability to govern, or even know, the results of our actions. World governments, often the blindest form of life, have noticed something is wrong. 'Help! The world is polluted!' They are forming commissions daily, to study it.

Politicians face a rising gale of Green awareness, claiming never to have worried about anything else. 'Our policies have always regarded the environment as our most important asset'. 'Hurrah!' we say, and ask: 'What are you doing about it?' Ominous silence, or a crackdown on litter louts. The biggest litter louts are, of course, the companies who use disposable packaging.

Are the voters reassured? It appears they're worried too. 'Slightly less dirty everything' from petrol to toothpaste is selling in western supermarkets as if we consumers could save the environment by being a little cleaner in our wasteful habits. These are small steps in the right direction, but they are not solutions. And it's not just the capitalist West that's affected. Citizens of Eastern Europe feel concerned and powerless in the face of overwhelming environmental degradation.

The phrase 'like there's no tomorrow' springs to mind and takes on an ominous significance. Myself, I am concerned every time I empty a bowl of washing-up water down the sink. Could I have used it better? When will I turn on the tap and find filth, or nothing at all? What a waste! How worrying. What can I do? Our society is based on the assumption that the ownership of property is desirable. It is materialist and also consumerist. This is the tendency to consume and discard essentials and luxuries. It comes from a belief that it is a desirable object in life to have a 'better standard of living'. In a consumerist society standard of living is associated with disposable income.

Is this the best measure to use? After all, there is no formula for determining how happy people are. Is there? Attempts to form numerical models to measure how healthy people are have been received with great lack of interest or active mistrust by politicians. In 1980 the British government suppressed the Black report, which had been commissioned by Parliament, and showed that poverty causes ill-health. The arithmetic of money remains the only intelligible standard of what people need as far as politicians are concerned.

Ethically concerned people have always challenged the 'values' of monetary wealth and asserted the need to find a 'higher' non-disposable purpose to life. It is individuals who have values, not society itself. In tending my personal garden (in the figurative and literal senses) I do that which is immediate and within my control. This is the first and essential step to world-wide rejuvenation of natural justice . . . accepting responsibility for making your life harmonious with the needs of the planet.

The Earth has the ultimate power to cleanse itself of tiresome infestations. You do not need to be a worshipper of some mystical 'Earth Mother' to believe this. Our global home can be God-created if you wish, but it still has all the charms and inevitable habits of a living organism, and as such it has its own immune system to eradicate threats to its survival. As James Lovelock points out in *Gaia*, how else could life have survived on planet Earth for 3500 million years, 'against all the odds?'

Respect for the planetary ecology is ancient. Our present materialistic/consumerist fetish is a mere sneeze in the deep breathing of time. So we see that the term 'alternative' is outfought by the very history of ecological awareness. This book is not about an alternative, but about that which is appropriate.

We can return to managing our massive knowledge and capability for construction, not destruction, in a way which accords with natural processes. I do not suppose any previous golden era to which we should all return, nor that we should reject out of hand modern technology. However, there are plenty of old ideas worth assimilating into our lives, alongside useful current discoveries. The future is what we make it. The only certainty is that things will always change.

I'LL TAKE IT IN SPIRITUAL HARMONIES, EMOTIONAL FULFILMENTS AND SMALL DENOMINATION SMILES...

anti BANK

Resource Destruction

Although no climatologist can say that 'this year' displays the symptoms of the greenhouse effect any more than any other, one thing is clear . . . everywhere, throughout the world, people are experiencing extraordinary climatic conditions. Soil erosion is accelerating. Forests are being destroyed wholesale and deserts are growing. We have increasingly poisoned water supplies owing to the excesses of an agricultural system dependent on chemical inputs in the rich parts of the world, and increasingly scarce or salted water supplies in the poor parts.

To ignore the risk and wait for more famine, pestilence, drought, storm, or civil conflict caused by any of these, to drive us to seek better ways of doing the business of living would be foolish. The world news tells us that if we seek now for co-operative and creative strategies that liberate people and planet, we may be in time. Any delay increases the risk that change will come too late.

How Permaculture Offers an Ethical Approach

At different times in history people have formulated many ethical approaches to life. I live in a Christian culture, which I respect, yet I can also find strength in Buddhist or Taoist literature. I believe that all religions and codes of conduct stem from the needs of people at given times and places. One of the great beauties of the Islamic culture is that it is not a religion, it is a way of life. In Christian Europe our understanding of mathematics, geometry and astronomy, and consequently our ability to build and navigate, were greatly enhanced by absorbing scholarship from the great thinkers of Islam. Science, beauty and God could never be perceived as separate, but as different aspects of the unknowable infinite.

Permaculture is not a cult or religion – it is a system for designing which can be adapted to any culture or place, but it asks you to see yourself as one with the universe, and to measure its wonder for your mutual benefit. You and the rest of creation have the same interest at heart – survival – so you should look after each other. Looking after yourself first has a ring of 'selfishness' about it, yet it can be a highly ethical approach.

This understanding of connectedness indicates that whatever you do to the world you affect every other aspect of life to some degree. Fritjof Capra (*The Tao of Physics*) tells us how physicists have discovered that simply measuring one particle of energy causes instant changes to another, possibly millions of light years apart. The act of measuring alone has been proved to cause physical changes. The ethic is to do nothing unless we have to, and to read the consequences of all our actions.

An appealing aspect of Permaculture is

27

that it might be the basis for agreement amongst ordinary people the world over that they have a common goal, and that this makes a good basis (and pre-requisite) for world peace. But why do we need ethics at all? Conflict and strife are the result of more and more people fighting over fewer and fewer resources. Fighting is not only painful and bad for the health of individuals and nations, it is also a one-way trade – massive resources are wasted in pursuing the conflict, and there is no end product to pay the bill. The yield of other productive processes (agriculture, industry, wage labour) has to be diverted to fund war. Agreement on a common code of conduct, which we call ethical, can avert this wastage.

People today are increasingly aware that our present wasteful ways are threatening not only our planet's beauty, but the fundamental natural systems that make our planet work. The standard of living to which we are accustomed cannot be maintained. Millions of people in the developing world stand little real chance of ever achieving Western standards of living. To do so would involve a mind-boggling expenditure of non-renewable resources. There are women whose lives are consumed in endless journeys in search of water or firewood. There are children whose rosiest prospect is carrying a rifle in the wars which have lasted all their lives.

Permaculture is possible under any culture, in any climate, by people with any skills. The real danger in the rich North is that we will not get productive food, energy and fibre systems in place before the poor people of the South stop us bleeding them dry. In this case we are facing anarchy, disease and starvation in the industrialised world. No amount of 'democratic' history will save us.

This is not pessimistic 'environmentalism': it is clear from world population figures. In 1977 the world had a population of 4116 million, and this was increasing by about 1.5 million a week. The world at this time had 1440 million hectares of farmland, that is land under plough or permanent crops – just over a third of a hectare or just under one acre per person. By the year 2000, at present rates of growth, the world will have 6397 million people to feed and only one fifth of a hectare, or around half an acre, per person to do it with. Or it may be even less as present agricultural practices, war and a more extreme climate continue to degrade, erode and desertify our agricultural land.

Hands up, who wants half as much to eat in ten years' time? Or should we rely on AIDS to limit population? And remember that if we're lucky enough to reach the year 2000 healthy and fit, there's no magic formula to say that the problem stops because the date is a round number. There could be 20 000 million people by 2020 AD. Where would they go? How could they eat? Clearly a working system of birth control is a pleasanter prospect than genocide or plague. A system of resource management other than war is vital.

Intrinsic Worth of Life

A system only becomes Permaculture when its design is shown over time to produce no harm to any other system. This reminds us that nature has no hierarchy. The lion is not more important than the ant. The magnificent Kauri pine does not make a blade of grass unnecessary. All have their place and an intrinsic right to life, without having to fulfil some human need. Our business in designing our lives efficiently is not just to feed and clothe ourselves better, it is to take as little as possible of the Earth's space for the production of those needs, and to return as much as possible to wilderness.

Wilderness is a precious resource. It gives us the vast undisturbed forests and oceans needed to make the Earth's atmosphere rich in oxygen by trapping carbon in living matter, and thence in soils and rocks. Without this system we couldn't breathe and therefore couldn't live. It gives us a huge reserve of species, so that if any of our present economically useful species fail through ecological disaster, others are available. These are also the building blocks of a natural economy – a system of exchange and wealth operating without human control. More importantly, we are reminded that creation is a thing of beauty and complexity beyond our understanding, and that it is ours to treasure and pass on, not simply to exploit and exhaust.

People Care/Land Care

Not till the fire is dying in the grate,
Look we for any kinship with the
    stars.

George Meredith 1828-1909

29

Permaculture invites you to care for yourself, to care for your family and immediate community, to care for your neighbours in the widest possible sense, all around the globe. It is rooted in strong historical evidence that such care cannot work unless we also care for the land. Implicit in this is the understanding that we duly respect the waters and air of the Earth as well.

All our resources are derived from the land on which we live. Even that great bugbear of the Green movement, the motor car, is a natural product. The body and chassis are made from metals mined from rocks in the ground. The tyres use rubber tapped from trees. The petrol is refined from oil found underground, which may also be the source of the plastic seats, and so on. In time natural decay and erosion will return all the automobiles on Earth to ash, bedrock or particles scattered to the wind.

At present, however, the Earth cannot keep up with our rate of production and consumption. We must deepen our understanding of the land and our relationship to it. This doesn't mean that we all have to give up everything else in life and become peasant farmers. Much as that might be an instant solution to global conflict, it could also be a life of grinding, unremitting toil, and Permaculture seeks more rewarding paths to Paradise.

You cannot have sustainable land use, unless the whole cycle of energy production and consumption within your culture is designed to respect the land (and water and air). In 1989 Comic Relief on British TV showed a hapless native of Burkina Faso explaining in French how twenty-seven years previously he had hacked a path through the forest at the point where he was then sitting on a log in an arid semi-desert. Soon we shall see scenes like this from the Amazon basin. With 3 per cent remnant tree cover in Britain, we have little to crow about.

Everywhere that humanity assumes power over the elements, the elements retaliate without mercy. It is only a matter of time. Our global climate is giving us very strong hints that time is running out. We need Permaculture: culture consciously designed to provide all our necessary resources and consume all our wastes forever.

Give Away Surplus

Every superfluous possession is a limitation on my freedom
                    Henry David Thoreau 1817-1862

Giving away surplus should be a comfortable process, as it means passing on what you don't need. If your hens lay more eggs than you need, give them away. Obviously you don't do that if selling eggs is your vital source of income. Visions of purity of soul achieved through noble poverty are fine,

> A marvellous flow of transmitted surplus is created around the world in the passing on of baby clothes. Delicate small garments knitted or sewn by hand are made by relatives and friends the world over for new babies, who soon outgrow them. Parents pass on the clothes in good condition to other new parents.

and are realistically achieved by some, but not by anyone with the job in life of caring for others – children, the sick, people with disabilities, others with no source of income, or a partner who has been hard at work all day and wants a decent supper. In the real world, that means most of us. Tailor the idea to your specific circumstances. Maybe your surplus is in skills, not possessions or money. Teaching a neighbour needle-work, or minding a friend's child, are just as much ways of surplus sharing. We can all learn to share our skills, too. The point about this pattern is that we are offering something for nothing, and we are creating a world in which it becomes *normal* to do this.

Aesthetics as By-product of Good Design

A visitor to our yard last summer said: 'I can tell you're really doing Permaculture because it's a mess!' I didn't actually feel flattered by this remark. He explained that there were lots of things going on, and that he could see that the piles of building materials over there were obviously for some purpose, and the vegetables growing in that heap looked pretty edible, and so on.

People often react to a Permaculture plot this way. It's part of our prevailing culture that we think things in straight lines and tidy boxes are 'neat' and therefore in some way more productive. Farmers talk about 'nice clean fields' when there's bare earth without a weed showing. In fact all of these things are highly dysfunctional. Nature is random and prolific. It generates as fast as it can in three dimensions an array of living and decaying outputs, which form rapid successions of adaptation. The one uniting factor in natural systems is that nothing is constant.

When you get that feeling that something looks a mess, think about function. Think of the great beauty of mature woodland, or true forest if you've ever seen such a thing. Everything has a place, and the beauty increases as your understanding of what that is increases.

You can still plant flowers. You can still paint your front door the colour you like. It's fine to design your own world to be beautiful. But in designing a productive habitat for humans which meets the ethical needs we've just discussed, being aesthetic doesn't count

31

as a use. Every living thing has its own beauty. Putting it in the right place can only enhance it, and putting things together in the right place at the right time is the essence of Permaculture.

Another first reaction to contact with Permaculture is 'What's different?' The answer becomes more obvious the more you think your way into the discipline. The core of the matter, however, is that Permaculture is about well-directed energy flows. And again this kind of functionality has its own beauty.

Design Versus Technique

Permaculture is *not* a technique. There are lots of useful ways of doing things that can be highly productive, which may be great tools. Within this book you will find ideas for action on a wide range of topics – appropriate energy, community finance, perennial vegetables, and even cultural transformation. None of these in themselves, or even together, constitute Permaculture. That term describes the way you think when you put all these things into a design for sustainable living, systematically.

For example, organic growing can be very energy demanding, and provide few of its input needs, or it can be well-designed as part of a wider strategy. The same is true of any technique. People who choose to practise Permaculture spend a lot of time collecting, understanding and learning helpful techniques, but the real secret is how effectively they are placed together.

Can We Afford Permaculture?

'It isn't economic' is a quick way to see off 'the conservationist lobby' if you're a profit-minded industrialist. The argument often works, only because conventional economics fails to count the true cost of pollution. Permaculture insists that you design to include all outputs as well as all inputs. When you do this and discover the cost of cleaning up the North Sea, the Great Lakes, and the acidified and dying forests and lakes of Northern Europe and America, the resurfacing of all the stone buildings in all our cities and the health bill for dealing with all the sick people, suddenly it isn't profitable to pollute.

And this is before we start to measure in anything other than money! When it comes to real values like health and happiness, the balance sheet weighs even more heavily against waste and pollution. The question becomes: can we afford not to have Permaculture?

In fact, as we shall see, Permaculture is a system based entirely on sound economics.

Resource Development

Permaculture is largely a plan for developing resources. In effect it is a way of learning to be your own government. It is no longer any good blaming 'the farmer', 'the Water Board', 'the government', or any other remote blamable agent. Although any or all of these may have degrees of responsibility for the degradation of our environment it is only you and I that can put things right again. A century's worth of bleating that we have the 'wrong government' will not patch holes in the ozone layer. No amount of protest at the doorstep of petro-chemical companies will reduce the amount of poison that has already been poured on to our agricultural land. Only we have the power to affect the future, by acting creatively for the good of ourselves and others.

'Think globally, act locally', is a slogan which reminds us, not just of a duty, but of our personal capability to effect change for the better. It's time to face the music.

PART I

WHERE ARE YOU NOW?

2 THE VALUE OF PEOPLE

Our central concern is designing for people.

What Do We Have, And What Do We Need?

There is one resource which we consistently undervalue – people. Have you ever looked at the annual reports produced by public companies? Pages of information about numbers, profit, stock turnover, maybe a couple of photos of star projects and a page about the retiring chairman, but hardly ever any information about their thousands of employees or customers.

I have never met a bank note that could sew well or a computer system that could sing a baby to sleep. Let's revalue the people resources we have. Start locally by thinking of yourself and working outwards.

You are a resource, and like any other part of a living system you have needs, outputs and inherent characteristics. What do you need? Air, food, drink, shelter, warmth, clothing, affection, company, stimulating work, freedom

from stress, health. Anything else? Add it to the list.

What are your outputs? Useful work can be divided into three areas: that which is directly creative to meet your own needs, or indirectly contributory, by bringing home wages to buy in those same needs. Lastly there is the vital work of nurturing others in the social grouping, be it as a parent, nurse or other carer. You may produce edible food, clothing, shelter or other artefacts. You certainly produce waste gases (carbon dioxide and methane, for instance), urine and faeces. A large part of household dust consists of the dead cells from our bodies. We also support parasites in huge numbers, although most of them are microscopic. On a social scale we completely alter the landscape, and we all make some contribution to that as part of our outputs. We may have other social outputs, such as artistic creativity or socially responsible sharing of the burden of running our community in some way.

There are human characteristics which are general, and others that are particular to a culture or to us as individuals. We like to group socially, preferring to sleep at night and wake in the day. We tend to wear clothes, at least in public. We then have a widely differing set of customs and habits which go with our own national or tribal culture, or the sub-cultures to which we belong. All sorts of people celebrate Thanksgiving in America, but an accountant's family may do so very differently from a group of young students. Christmas may mean a lot in your family, but not if you prefer to observe Diwali in the Hindu calendar. At the most personal level we have all those idiosyncrasies which make us ourselves, but which are also character-istics rather than needs or outputs.

This variation is very normal, and only lightly conceals an underlying pattern which is constant. We all have needs (met by inputs) and produce outputs as part of the process of living. We all have characteristic ways of organising and conducting the flow of getting our needs met. Our ability to perform this cycle effectively is governed by some essential freedoms. The first and most basic freedom is to be healthy, and sadly, it is often the first freedom we lose.

The Health Issue

This word, health, is based on some rather large assumptions. Like 'natural' it gets used so often it is easy to lose sight of its significance. Health is presently a major concern: in the United States it is the key issue in consumer pressure group campaigns. It's a major worry in Eastern Europe where forty years of economic endeavour have led to massive pollution of the urban environment. In Britain it has become a battleground between the left and right wing in politics as to whether it's a 'right' or a purchasable commodity.

The word *health* comes from the Old English *hœlth*, which simply means wholeness. Indeed the modern English word *whole* is derived from the same root. So *to heal* is to make something (or someone) whole, to be healthy is to be whole, and the best word to conjure up the essential meaning is probably *wholesome*, implying something pleasant and desirable, rather than just an absence of disease. Another surviving derivative is 'hale', as in 'hale and hearty' which has a marvellous sense of joy as part of its expression of what constitutes health.

Britain has a very special approach to health, with its public access to a free National Health Service. It has often been suggested that the NHS is succeeding because of the increased case load which it has carried over the years. This is debatable – a successful 'health' service would treat *fewer* people as the population got healthier. The NHS is a major asset to Britain, but not by making us healthier as a nation, rather as a necessary tool for people divorced from a wholesome way of life. If people are valuable (and they are) then health is their most important asset. The whole design system described in this book aims to make us healthier.

Skills

'Tis God gives skill,
But not without men's hands: He could not make
Antonio Stradivari's violins
Without Antonio.

George Eliot 1880

We need to appreciate how valuable we are individually and collectively. Sometimes it seems that society puts out messages telling us the opposite. There is some strange hierarchy of skills in the world. Some particular abilities are somehow 'less' or 'more' important than each other. There will be changes between different cultures, but it's noticeable that, globally, agricultural workers, clothing makers, sewage and refuse disposal workers, cleaners, and carers for the sick, elderly and children are on low pay scales, compared to industrial workers or 'professionals'. All the people in this list of low paid workers are providing skills that deal with our basic necessities in life. We can live without cars; we can't live without food, but a car manufacturer earns more than a food manufacturer. Pay scales do not indicate the true importance of someone's work.

A second falsehood in the myth of skills valuation is the concept of 'the expert'. These are the people who can be identified by their 'otherness' and their specialism. 'Experts' are expensive people who have some highly specialised skill which is usually couched in jargonistic language. They have special etiquettes about the way they do things

to ensure that amateurs don't get a look in.. Some of this is wholly justified – I wouldn't want to visit an amateur brain-surgeon, or have my house wired up by an unskilled electrician, but all too often experts are simply protecting their own territory. They do not use their skills to enable others.

So an important aspect of enabling us to see ourselves as the resourceful people we really are, and to act accordingly, is to practise sharing our skills. This is a plea for anyone with a skill to train everyone they work with to some degree. It asks experts to talk in plain language, or at least explain technical terms. It requires a mature judgement of how much the lay person can do.

Architects can involve the community in their design process, without expecting the client to learn all the building regulations, or how to calculate stresses. Doctors can explain physical symptoms in terms that patients understand, without expecting them to have the same level of physiological or pharmacological knowledge. Mechanics and engineers, indeed, any skilled person, can share their valuable understanding. No one will get put out of a job – we'll all value each other more.

Which of us . . . is to do the hard and dirty work for the rest – and for what pay? Who is to do the pleasant and clean work, and for what pay?

John Ruskin 1849

The essential ingredient in this equation is that we all value the skills that are so often thought of as 'unskilled'. People with caring skills, the cleaners, cooks, receptionists, drivers, and shop assistants of this world become seen as people without whom none of us can manage. The great majority of human work revolves around these unsung skills. Start to value them in yourself and others today if you do not already do so. In a well-designed and balanced society resources will be available for the training, support and pay of all these skills, which are in themselves an invaluable body of expertise quite as important as the 'professions' or 'trades' which presently eclipse them economically.

Because most work is unpaid doesn't mean it's not work.

Work, Pollution & Self-Esteem

It's a major Permaculture principle that work is something to be avoided. Here work is used in the sense that physicists use it, to mean 'energy expended'.

Limiting our expenditure of energy is the main way of controlling pollution. If we can find ways of conserving energy, or using natural self-replicating energy systems to provide our needs, then work is minimised. Work is only required in the first place because we have an unmet need. If we design our system well then we have most of our needs provided by outputs in the system. If outputs in the system are used then pollution is eliminated. The system becomes a closed energy cycle. We are emulating natural ecosystems successfully, because we live by harvesting the output of other elements in the system, and our own outputs meet others needs. The Garden of Eden found!

When work *is* necessary it is always more efficient if carried out with ready access to trade skills. Self-employed business people can only flourish if they understand how to manage their money, their craft and their customers. Being self-employed they may only have themselves to carry out all these functions, and are therefore brought into direct contact with the need to have trade skills. In fact, any undertaking requires the same mix.

A joiner is efficient at turning timber into artefacts because s/he knows the way to handle grain, which timber to choose for which job, and how the tools will do their work for the least expenditure of effort. A weekend DIY carpenter may curse at how difficult the job is – because they don't have the trade skills. Taking time to acquire trade skills makes the whole job easier in the long run, and reduces the work needed to achieve a given objective.

There are not five thousand million human inhabitants of Spaceship Earth each able to provide all their own needs and use all their own outputs, starting tomorrow. The ideal is a target. It's our direction of change which is important. Our present pattern is one of increasing population and increasing consumption, and cannot be sustainable. Once we are on a path of decreasing consumption, the Earth's own healing mechanisms will have time and space to catch up.

Work and Children

Whilst reducing consumption we can still see meaningful work as a desirable human need. One of the great Victorian social aims was the reduction of the working week. If you accept the premise that most work is unpaid (and a lot of that, women's work) then the wisdom of this can be seen in a new light. At the time it was seen as undesirable that children and women should be carrying out paid work in industry, and desirable that men should be entitled to their wages from a shorter working week. It's another developed world myth that children are not useful members of society, that it's exploitative to 'make' children 'work'. The implication is that free will suddenly develops at the age of majority.

I do not have any easy answer as to how we can open our society to children, give them a just status, and a fair measure of their talents. I have a very uneasy feeling that we don't do it now. With a booming world population it is less and less possible to keep children in a suppressed role. The millions of children forced into action in the economies of Asia and Latin America belie the developed world tendency to see children as 'innocents' to be 'protected'. At the same time I do not wish my own children to be exploited as cheap workers or deprived of their opportunities for education. What roles for children as constructive individuals can you see in your own community?

Gold Age, Not Dotage?

This same question of inclusion should be addressed to the age myth. We talk of 'retirement'. From what? From being useful? A society obsessed with consumerism sees youth as a virtue and age as a hindrance. The slim, fit, athletic stereotypes of advertising join together to preach inadequacy to the motley majority who are subliminally persuaded that they need whatever product is the subject of the image to rejuvenate themselves.

In traditional societies which have preserved their ability to endure, the generations are the continuum and therefore the meaning of existence. Age is valued for its experience, and elders deserve respect. So they do indeed, wherever they are. Not as 'frail old folk', but as people with a meaningful role to play. Societies like those in peasant

China cannot understand how Westerners tolerate 'old people's homes'. The statistics bear out our neglect – there is a terrifying tendency for men to die soon after retirement. It's as if they cease to exist, having become bereft of meaning when their 'job' ends. By defining and limiting people by age we are neglecting a great resource.

The Global Village

Modern communications, television, radio, jet-powered flight and the internal combustion engine have shrunk our

---

Age Exchange aims to improve the quality of life of older people by emphasising the value of their reminiscences to old and young, through pioneering artistic, educational and welfare activities. Based in London, the group brings older people together to talk about their past, and these activities are taken out into schools and youth groups where children learn from their elders and create drama around the stories they hear. The generations work together, adding meaning to their experience, and history is preserved by the ordinary people who experienced it.

---

planet and brought us all closer together. This is a great opportunity for those of us privileged to live in multi-racial communities. We have a vast varied wealth of culture and experience to draw upon.

In a shrinking world, cultures are brought closer together. No matter where you look, at pop music, clothing, or gardening, facets of design are understood and shared around the world. The Japanese admire and emulate Western culture. The Europeans admire and emulate Eastern culture. Different languages, religions, climates and latitudes, and different flora and fauna all serve to enrich people's cultures in different ways.

The wonder of the present age is that we can share these things to our mutual benefit. Every country also has its racists: people who fear the 'global village' which is developing because they feel disempowered within their own cultures and cannot contemplate competition. In all of these difficult social areas into which we have looked, roles of age, youth, men, women, and mixed races, the future holds enormous challenges which demand change. Change is threatening for all of us. It demands that we rethink and alter the habits of a lifetime. It also means we step into unknown territory, and the unknown is the most fearful thing with which we can be presented. For change to be successful and rewarding, strong leadership will be needed.

Leadership

For the triumph of evil it is only necessary that good men do nothing.
Edmund Burke 1729-1797

Many people feel that leadership is in some way bad. These feelings are probably completely justified by personal experience based on bad leadership. Leadership is good; not only that, it is vital. But it is not the preserve of a chosen few. Nor is it an opportunity for the few who get the chance to direct things to lord it over the rest. The best skill of a good leader is to bring out the leadership qualities in others. For we are all leaders. Every parent is a leader, and every child can become one. We all have skills of leadership, and in appropriate circumstances are the right person to take charge. We can all develop these skills, and it's healthy to do so.

Too often in large-scale modern societies we are made to feel that we are not important, that we are only followers, or worse still consumers. The message to give yourself today is 'if you can see that something needs doing, give yourself permission to do it'. Permission giving is the key. We feel restricted by hierarchical systems and by current rules of 'what is acceptable'.

This is terribly destructive to our creative potential. If you see someone taking a leadership role, support them. If you take a leadership role yourself, demand the loyal support of your co-

43

workers and expect it. I often think our creative potential is only limited by our own expectations.

So . . . expect the best!

Fresh Approaches

This book has started not with the key concepts of Permaculture, but with the needs and outputs of people. If the people care ethic is not foremost in all our minds, then any designing we do becomes academic and amoral.

Our global environment and our social structures are badly damaged. We need fresh approaches to people care issues. Perhaps this chapter has raised more questions than it has provided answers. Remember the solutions to problems of creating good human interpersonal relationships can never be solved by the individual. They require the input and support of each and every one of us.

The British Green Party used to have a pamphlet entitled 'Where the Wasteland Ends'. A nice use of words, this, combining the sense of the profligacy of the materialist society ('the waste land') with that drab image of the earth as a rubble filled building plot (wasteland). After years of debate Green politics has not created the next stage – 'After the Wasteland'. Maybe the fault has been in relying on the competitive strategies of debate to create a solution.

In practice I am as competitive and unforgiving as the next person. We need to appreciate the skills of synthesis, that is, borrowing and blending the best of all worlds. We all need an atmosphere of encouragement if we are to flourish and be creative. In a society which preaches success, failure is a pretty unpalatable deterrent to being creative. We can, however, do better than this, and we must.

To get to the place and time which is truly 'after the wasteland', we need to develop methods of exchange between us which stop wasting our own potential. We need to see and promote the many good things around us which are positive and creative. We need to remember that every dawn chorus carries on regardless of which government is in power, and to make of ourselves a human dawn chorus.

3 REAL CAPITAL – WE ALL HAVE WHAT IT TAKES

Capital is the investment we make at the start of any enterprise. Every experience in life increases some part of our capital. We are all 'rich' in some things, and we can all improve our ability to succeed by developing our capital.

What Is Capital?

This section needs a health encouragement, rather as the opposite of government health warnings on cigarette packets. It would read something like this: **'Do not panic – we have discovered money is a useful tool. Understanding all your potential resources can seriously improve your health.'** If the mention of capital or money instantly turns you cold, then read on, as this is directed at you. If you like and understand the stuff, we need you to help out on the voyage!

Capital is the fund of resources which enables you to carry out your work. Most people understand capital as the accumulated wealth of an individual or company, measured in money.

Consider someone newly out of a job, with last week's wages clutched in their hands, who is determined they are never going to be a wage slave again. They invest their hard-earned money in some stock to become a market trader. You would say that their capital was the amount of money they invested. Even when that money is spent on stock, their capital investment remains the same, because the stock has a value as an asset. They can cause their capital to grow by investing more money, or by leaving money in the business when they make a profit.

In conventional accounting the sums get more complicated as time goes by, but that is the essence of capital. It is, if you like, yield from one time and place which is not distributed to meet individual needs, but is stored to make possible future yields. The hypothetical market trader, for instance, can't make a profit unless they have stock. Farmers, on the other hand, need land and tools to grow food. We can widen the definition of what is considered capital.

If you don't have capital and you want to create yield, you will need to beg, borrow or steal capital from someone

45

else. This is what happens to tenant farmers. They pay rent to landowners, and maybe borrow money from the bank to finance their machinery, and even seed. The people who own the capital – land and money – will make a contract with the tenant farmer, because they can get a *return* on their capital because of the work the farmer does, as rent or interest.

Return on capital is very important. Imagine I invest a million pounds, dollars, or whatever in a farm. The project has net costs of one thousand units, and sales of two thousand of the same units, so I make one thousand units profit. On one level this is very good – 100 per cent profit! But as a return on capital it's very poor, only 0.1 per cent. So we see that return on capital is important as a measure of whether or not that capital is enabling useful work to produce yields.

In Permaculture we are always interested to make yield as large as possible. Yield, like capital, can be measured in more ways than money, and non-monetary yield can also be returned to the system to make the next cycle of productivity. So what other assets do we have to launch our Permaculture enterprise?

We are all highly skilled people, aren't we? A trick question that, as most of us spend a lot of time feeling that we *aren't* up to the task in hand. Whilst the feelings are real enough, the fact is often different. Bringing up children is, for instance, one of the most demanding jobs you can have. 'But I'm only an unskilled manual labourer'. You will find, if you list your skills, that they are many and various. They may go from something as simple as 'a good sense of humour' (an invaluable asset) to 'strong arms', which are useful when engaging in Earth repair work. If you don't have enough of these sort of skills personally, then they have to be borrowed too, just like money.

There are all our other assets. If you decide to start a smallholding, and are a keen gardener, you'll find you have many of the tools you're going to require in future, sitting in the shed. They're part of your capital.

Some assets don't serve the purposes for which we need the capital now. They're still valuable. You could trade in your priceless complete collection of Led Zeppelin albums to your local dealer for money to buy tools. Even if you have nothing other than the clothes you stand up in, you still have the asset of your own abilities to tap the many other available sources of capital that exist – capital in the broadest sense.

What Does Capital Need?

It needs faith, that people believe it is of value. Modern English 'fee' and 'pecuniary' are two words derived from different sources relating to money. Fee comes from Old English 'feoh', and pecuniary from Latin 'pecu'. In late usage both words meant 'wealth', but in the early part of those two cultures, the words meant 'cattle'. A person's status could be measured by the size and health of their herd of cattle. The cattle-wealth system would not work if someone did not believe in it. Vegetarians are unlikely to accept cattle as payment, nor would Hindus who believe in the beasts as sacred, and,therefore beyond ownership.

Sometimes capital assets are perceived as valueless because their value is mistakenly missed. One friend is making some fine mahogany furniture from old school laboratory desk tops. The demolition contractor was going to burn them as rubbish. All of us have valuable skills and personal attributes which we don't know about, or don't quite believe in. We sometimes need outside help to recognise what we have, and this goes for communities as well as individuals.

Capital also needs to be protected from predators. If your cattle die of disease, or your tools go rusty in the rain, their value is diminished. 'Currency' as a word for money reminds us that capital can also have a 'use-by date'. Victorian pennies may be nice to own, but they won't buy any sweeties in the corner shop. In the same way you may maintain your tools to a fine standard, but they may become outmoded and worthless if someone invents newer, better ones enabling your competitor down the road to do the same job in half the time for half the price.

Capital is also worthless, in one sense, if it is not used. If you own ten houses, but they all stand empty, then you are as poor as the person with none, because you have no return on your capital. If you have a fine brain, but don't use it, your asset is wasted. Capital which isn't working is usually losing value.

Fair Exchange Is No Robbery

Any ethical system will assume that people are going to engage in fair exchange. Parties agree that what one gives and the other receives are equitable. It doesn't necessarily mean that the opposite sides of a deal are of equal value in a monetary sense, for either side may accept an uneven bargain.

It also means that where one party has the upper hand in some aspect of exchange, such as setting the prices, and having secret knowledge of the profit involved, or holding a commodity in scarce supply, they do not take advantage of the other party.

The way of Permaculture is to develop all use of special expertise in a collaborative way. The community architecture movement has sought to redress the poor deal of the 1960s high-rise building boom by building to specifications arrived at by consultation with the community. Although all parties to this process would probably agree that community design has a long way to go yet, it is a healthy trend, and a typical reflection of Permaculture thinking at

work. Expertise is a resource to be shared, not used to ransom the client.

Is Money Bad?

'Filthy lucre', 'the root of all evil' – doesn't money have a lot of nasty names?

Many people feel disadvantaged because they have little free (or 'disposable') money. Without capital to increase the yields available for their usage, they feel tied to their present way of life, although they would like it otherwise. Many people also feel disadvantaged because they do not understand money and the way it works. Anyone can learn to understand money, and can make money work for them. The hard part is to look at our distress around money, see why it arises, and deal with it in a positive way.

Accepting these statements is a good start:

1 Money is not bad, it is completely neutral, being just a tool. People can use it well or badly, and create fair or evil things with it, but money itself is without motivation, and can therefore be neither good nor bad.
2 Money is a complete confidence trick. That is, as long as we all believe in it, it works fine. The moment there is a mass movement of disbelief it fails to work.

Coinage has existed for thousands of years. Our present money system has its origin in promissory notes issued by Venetian merchants in the Middle Ages. The traders of the Mediterranean relied on gold as a standard of value to enable trade to break out of the physical limitations of barter. If you wanted a commodity, you could offer something valuable you had in exchange, or pay in gold 'to the value of' the commodity, agreed by negotiation. The vendor then took your gold, and spent it elsewhere, either on personal needs, or on further trading. The object wasn't necessarily to make a profit (although that was desirable), but to trade something of which you had a surplus, for something which you lacked.

Merchants at sea were always at risk that their gold would be stolen by pirates. The first bankers were people who set up strong vaults and offered to guard gold for the merchants. They pointed out that risk could be lessened by paying with 'promissory notes'. No gold would be moved by the merchants. They would 'pay' with a note giving the recipient the right to collect gold from the merchant's banker.

In time the notes achieved identical value to the gold, as the recipient could simply pay someone else with the same piece of paper. High security was maintained when banks were sited in powerful city states who would defend the stable trade on which their wealth depended.

If no-one was taking the gold out of the vault, the bankers could quietly lend it elsewhere, and charge interest. In other words, they could make a profit lending something that wasn't even theirs. Soon they realised they could just write promissory notes for the loans, as long as everyone didn't come knocking at the door at once to ask for their money back.

Banks had learnt to create money out of nothing, and charge people for the privilege of having it. They could also charge people who did have it · for looking after theirs. This all sounds too easy – but rest assured that it is long accepted throughout the world as fair. It was regularised in Banking Acts in the early nineteenth century. Thus today all clearing banks can lend money up to eight times the value of their deposits. They make money from nothing.

Now I don't want you to run down the road and withdraw all your money from the bank. But we should all understand that money is a system of lubricating commerce, it is not a god, good or evil, and it should not control our lives. Try inventing your own money. Take a pad of paper, some coloured crayons, and half an hour, and make all the money you have ever dreamt of – it's very liberating. There is no more or less substance to yours than any yen, dollar, penny or rouble that was ever minted. It's just that people believe in theirs – not yours.

Animals which fear fire never learn to

use it as a tool. It's the same with money.

How to Create Capital

The capital which precedes all others is that of knowledge. Many people in our dislocated times feel that they don't have what they want, but they don't quite know what that is. One way to find out is to train. Read books, go to evening classes, listen to people talk, or even just go touring in search of people who are working on projects which appeal to you. Staying in other communities as a working guest is a great way of seeing your own life from a new perspective.

Industrial society is based on a reductionist view of science. That is, the workings of nature were understood by reducing everything into components. Many valuable lessons were learnt by this technique, and hugely powerful tools, such as railways and a global telephone system are its technological results. The disadvantage is that it leaves us with a culture where everyone is supposed to specialise, and we feel out of our depth and isolated if working 'outside our field'. By putting aside this specialist attitude, we can blend all possible knowledge back to a growing understanding of the whole.

Even if it's only doing the washing up, the most basic skills can be swapped for knowledge. With knowledge, you have something to trade. That might be for wages, or it might be for a business partnership with someone who has money, but is ignorant of skills to pursue a chosen ambition, which you understand.

Capital can always be attracted by making a financial proposition to someone else. The world is perilously short of people with creative vision. Put together your personal dream in words and/or pictures and go selling the dream. If it's sound enough, and if you've thought it through well, people will back it.

In a money system based on make-believe, the generation of faith is a great producer of success. It's nonsense that one minute the world is in recession, and the next there's a boom. World resources are being depleted comparatively constantly. People's needs are pretty steady – at least by comparison to the violent swings of world stock markets and bank rates. Believe in your objective and keep your eyes and ears open, and the right time will arrive.

Don't worry, Permaculture isn't a faith, religion or belief system. There are some more strategies coming up soon, to help it all happen.

How to Access the Capital You Have

Access has been a word of growing usage in recent years. The computer revolution showed that we could 'access'

information fast and in huge quantities to make more informed decisions about resource management. Radical programmes of action by people with disabilities showed that because something was there it wasn't necessarily accessible. New structures need to be built in our society to open up resources which are barred by physically inadequate environments or by restrictive public attitudes. A closed mind ('Oh, they're disabled') can be as big an obstacle as a flight of stairs to someone in a wheelchair. Many adults who had poor experiences of education as children are able to make good their disadvantage by accessing skills and knowledge through special retraining schemes.

The first step is to recognise what you have. Often our individual resources are under-used. Making a list of our assets can help us remember to use them. Next we might list the capital we require to achieve our aims, and any shortfall will give us a 'shopping list'. By applying the principle of giving away surplus, we can often swap things in plenty for things we need. In Permaculture circles we operate 'offers & requests' bulletins for people to do just that. Local papers and radio, shop windows, and community centres are all great places for this kind of exchange. You access part of the capital you have to free up that which you don't.

Make sure you maintain, monitor, mend and update all your capital periodically. In fact, part of the 'budget' of any household should be repairs and maintenance. Often there are people who love to use these specific skills if you don't. My father-in-law is a retired doctor, and he's the best I know at sharpening knives. Whenever he visits the bread knife is lethal for weeks. I'm not sure I ever repay him properly, but then on a global scale I'm sure he shares the benefit of some kindness I do elsewhere in turn.

Sometimes we're frightened to use our capital, because it's kept in reserve 'for that rainy day'. Maybe that way we earn a little interest, but one of the best ways we can help each other is to stop investing in anonymous banking systems, and to put our money into

51

practical schemes with measurable results. Ethical investment has a great future, and the day is not far off when we will see big companies recognising that they are a common part of the movement to make our mark on the planet a little more benign. Meanwhile all the small direct contributions that are made to free rainy-day savings from the money markets are doing a great job of lubricating innovative and socially enhancing projects.

Alternative Money Sources

The first recourse of most people seeking money beyond their own means is the bank. In practice there are many other sources of investment. A growing body of ethical investment organisations offer funds for approved projects. In the United Kingdom The Ecology Building Society, Mercury Provident, and the Friends Provident Stewardship Trust all fulfil this function. They all have different policies for lending, both from the point of view of the project itself, and also relating to interest rates.

A growing idea is the development of loan trusts. These are community banks which accept deposits from local people to develop specific projects beneficial to the area. Investors can either throw their money into the general pool, or ask for it to be directed to specific enterprises. Credit unions are another form of this idea.

Then there is the gift. There are many charitable institutions who will consider worthy enterprises for partial or complete funding. This may be in the form of 'seed funding', that is, small sums adequate to pay the costs of assessing the viability of the idea, or to start a 'snowball' effect by drawing other investment to it. Other times grants will be conditional on funding being raised elsewhere for a specified proportion of the budget. This last requirement may apply to commercial borrowing, too. There is always the private benefactor, and this leads to the third possible source of funds.

Your 'affinity group' might broadly be defined as those contacts who are pursuing similar objectives to your own, or who feel strong ties because of family links or friendship. This is the most likely place to find private benefactors. More often money will be lent at low or nil interest rates, by sympathetic subscribers.

Another way is to look for shareholders in your idea. These people or institutions will lend money, not necessarily for fixed interest, but for a share of future profits. It is usually desirable to avoid this kind of arrangement if it gives your backer a controlling interest. Responsibility and control of any community development should always remain with the people it is designed to benefit. There are quite informal investments possible along these lines, but the investment may be

The Centre for Alternative Technology at Machynlleth in Wales has raised a million pounds on a share issue to ethical investors. By turning into a public company the centre is able to fund demonstrations of more water and wind powered machinery to educate its annual 75 000 visitors.

taken along various legal paths as far as creating a public limited company.

In Britain the Industrial Common Ownership Movement (ICOM) has worked on a number of such projects, raising large sums to fund environmentally sound ideas.

You can also raise funds by pre-selling an enterprise. Take a restaurant as an example. We want to start a café, both to be a good place to eat, and to act as a focal point in our community for like-minded people to meet and discuss things. We do all our sums and find we need £20 000 to get going. The bank tell us we can borrow £10 000 as long as we raise the other half elsewhere. Pre-selling means getting people to buy our products and services before they're ready. So we print twin meal tickets worth £20 each, redeemable within the first two years' trading. When we sell five hundred, we've raised the other half of the cash. You can add refinements such as giving a discount (make the tickets worth more than people pay), but

however you do it, the system has two great advantages:

1 A proportion of people will never redeem their tickets.
2 If no-one will pre-buy, then it's likely the project is doomed to failure. If the tickets go like hot cakes, then it sounds like you're on to a winner. You have tested the market.

You could probably sit down for half an hour and brainstorm a list of twenty other ways of raising money. There is a wide range of options available, and no-one need feel that some worthy cause is impossible because 'there isn't the money'. There is a grave shortage of worthwhile investment opportunities for people who want their money to do useful work. A proper business plan will always yield help in the end if the venture is workable. There is not space here to describe how to make a such a plan. Historical and forward accounts need to be combined with a written review of all your resources, and planned products and services. Enterprise agencies will help, and many banks issue guidelines for good business plans.

Alternatives to Money

Systems have always existed which by-passed money. New sophisticated ones are now being developed. Barter predates money, and it's still possible: if

53

I dig your garden, will you give me half your crop? The problem with barter is that it's one to one, and the desirable system of exchange isn't always that simple.

How do we work barter if there are three or more of us, each wanting something from one person, and having something that another different person would find useful? Set up a local exchange trading system (LETS) is one answer.

This is how an ideal situation works. Anyone can trade, and can specify that they want to be paid a proportion of their trade in either hard cash or 'green' pounds, dollars etc. This enables people to be realistic. A builder, for instance, could be paid materials in 'real' money and labour in 'green' money. The green money is in a centrally administered account. If I do £100 worth of building work for my neighbour, he writes me a 'green' cheque which I 'bank' with the administrative office (which could be in another neighbour's kitchen). This is entered in both our accounts, but not directly connected. In other words LETS owes me, and my neighbour owes LETS.

The neighbour may, in turn, go baby-sitting for a local doctor, two nights a week, for which he earns £20 per week, all in green money. In five weeks he'll have paid off my bill. The doctor buys vegetables at the local greengrocers, who takes 50 per cent green money. She spends £30 a week there, so she's got to take £35 a week in 'green' money just to meet the rate of her outgoings. The doctor charges £20 an hour to private patients, so she doesn't have to do much to pay off her investment, does she?

This is the first problem. LETS systems soon uncover the gross difference in earnings between various types of work. And indeed some people don't like to put a price on everything they do. The doctor could make the whole system easier by dropping her prices, and that's exactly what happens where the system works – the 'haves' start to see how life is for the 'have-nots', and moderate their demands. Secondly, some people are spenders and then don't feel they have anything to trade, so they run up big bills. These people are short in trade skills, so the system must also develop a management 'eye' which can spot these

The first LETS started in British Columbia, Canada, when the school bus service was threatened with closure. The response of the community was to establish a system whereby community trading provided all the resources necessary to provide and maintain the bus, and pay the driver. Such a simple matter as not being able to get the kids to school presented a great threat to the community and then helped establish its integrity.

situations, and offer trade skills training to get people out of debt. Everyone has something useful to offer.

People who sell and refuse to buy are the biggest threat to the system. They build up big balances, which at first seems great, but actually they're freezing the system by failing to return their wealth to the community. Their capital isn't working. The easy solution is to charge interest on positive balances: 5 per cent per month should ensure we don't hang on to our money too long. The interest deducted goes to meet the costs of training and administration. Interest charged for having money in the bank? The world turned upside down for everyone's good! There's also a small levy on each transaction to meet costs.

The last headache in the system is the administration. However, there are now packages available for micro-computers to run the whole show.

LETS is not the only way of making your own money. Social Credit is an older system whereby the community invests in itself the power to create money, in much the same way as banks have done. In the Channel Islands, the States Parliament of Guernsey made its own money issue to raise funds for the provision of public buildings. This meant that the community paid for its services with money which was redeemable against services offered by itself.

There have been strong Social Credit movements in New Zealand and Canada in the past – indeed, British Columbia had a Social Credit government at one time – but all attempts at making the system work have been undermined by central governments. It awaits a stronger public sentiment that the power to create credit should reside with the community, not that small section of influence, the banks, before we can expect to see a change of heart.

Risk Management

The best laid schemes o' mice an' men
Gang aft a-gley
                    Robert Burns 1759-1796

All these things will be as nothing if we are not prepared for the worst. This is what is meant by risk management. Before setting on any venture there are three measurable levels of consequence:

1 what you would really like to happen
2 what would be the least happy result you would find tolerable (the break-even point)
3 what could really go wrong.

It is important to plan for each of these three eventualities.

A great tool for this is the 'no-lose scenario'. When the armies of the world train their military leaders, they give them no-win scenarios – how will they react when everything goes wrong?

Reverse the process, by listing everything that can go wrong, and then ask yourself 'If such-and-such happens, what will be the benefits?' No matter how dire the consequence there is always some benefit, even if it is to have learnt never to do that thing again. The things that do go wrong are often not what you expect, but by looking failure and fear in the face in this way, in advance of taking action, you are much more calmly able to deal with set-backs, and also to feel a measurable success at the end of the day.

The advantage of knowing your break-even point (where expenditure and income match) is that once you know you are past this point, everything is a success. You know you have succeeded, now it's just a question of 'how well?' The other advantage of this measure is it gives you a first target. 'This is how well I have to do to be OK. Anything better than this is great!' You should also know what you really want, because otherwise you will never have the ultimate to aim for in life. As life is full of failure, the way to get what you'll be happy with is to demand the Earth.

If you can make one heap of all your
   winnings
And risk it on one turn of pitch-
   and-toss,
And lose, and start again at your
   beginnings
And never breathe a word about your
   loss.

             Rudyard Kipling 1865-1936

. . . the chances are you're slightly crazy. 'Know thyself' (Anon. c500 BC) would be a better stricture, and one which we shall now undertake . . .

4 MAKING A PERSONAL STOCKTAKE -- YOU ARE YOUR BEST ASSET

Our success in meeting our personal needs and creating a surplus to share with others is crucially dependent on knowledge and faith in our own ability.

I and many others, known and unknown to me, call upon you:

To celebrate our joint power to provide all human beings with the food, clothing and shelter they need to delight in living.

To discover, together with us, what we must do to use mankind's power to create the humanity, the dignity and the joyfulness of each one of us.

To be responsibly aware of your personal ability to express your true feelings and to gather us together in their expression.

Ivan Illich 1967

You

A stocktake is made when a business wants to know how much it's worth, which it has to do every so often to satisfy the accountants and the tax authorities. This also gives valuable information to the managers of the enterprise, telling them what they have in store. It also tells them how much of their capital is tied up in stock, and gives them a chance to review whether it's doing useful work or not. Too much stock, and they can't move in the warehouse, and they can't pay the bills. Too little, and they have nothing to trade with.

We're going to do the same thing now, but turn the spotlight on ourselves. In a world where it's scientific to be critical, very few of us grow up with a real understanding of our worth. Consequently, the world is largely peopled by individuals who do not believe in their own capacity to affect the future of the planet. In reality there are only individuals like ourselves, no supermen and women lurking in corridors of power with vast brains dwarfing the rest of us mere mortals. We are the best people to decide our future.

Change is Dangerous

The acceleration of change does not merely buffet industries or nations. It is a concrete force that reaches deep into our personal lives, compels us to act out new roles, and confronts us with the danger of a new and powerfully upsetting psychological disease.

Alvin Toffler 1970

There are many tools to help us. Here are a few I recommend. After Freud came psychoanalysis, an inexact science at the best of times. In the early 1960s a new school of thought formed around Eric Berne in the United States, dealing in 'Transactional Analysis'. Berne's book *Games People Play* and Thomas A Harris' book *I'm OK – You're OK* were both international best sellers (read them if you want to know more). The essence of 'T.A.' is that our characters are very much decided in the first five years of our lives, and they consist of three parts, Parent, Adult, Child. The words have very specific meanings in this context.

Your Parent is the stored memory of all your early authoritarian experience, and leads you to repeat patterns of managing yourself and others which were practised on you. Your Child is largely non-verbal and records the feelings of early life. Repeat situations may bring up strong feelings in later life based on infant experiences. Your Adult develops from the first year on, as your own ability to interpret experience and make conscious decisions. All three aspects are vital to managing our lives. We release our Child when we play and have light-hearted fun, and when we are curious about new possibilities, as much as when we are frightened by situations we cannot control. We need our Parent to protect us from danger ('Don't step in front of moving traffic!'), as well as to guide us in situations where we need to take charge. We need our Adult to make us individual and inform our judgements.

It's a very important concept to understand that our needs are being met on each of these levels. Understanding these different aspects of ourselves can help us see where we're vulnerable and where we're strong, and plan accordingly.

Co-counselling is another healing process which recognises that our natural clear intelligence can become clouded by hurt, 'since human beings do not think in a sensible, rational way while they are being hurt' (quotations from *Fundamentals of Co-Counselling Manual*). It encourages participants to 're-evaluate' their experience and to release their pent-up 'discharge' over subjects that cloud their thinking. Weeping, sighing, laughing, scratching, shaking, and shouting are all ways in which human beings 'release the tensions which the experience of hurt placed upon them'. When this process is understood we start to welcome these discharges of emotion as signs that we or

This manual is not an attempt to help people 'find themselves', but it is inevitable that anyone who chooses radical Permaculture solutions to designing the community in which they live will have to deal with discharge brought on by change. People are in general very unhappy about money, ownership, power, and great changes to their patterns of living. This is as true of people with plenty of money and possessions as it is of poor people. It's important that as individuals we are ready to separate our discharge from the reality of our ability to act as warm, intelligent, loving human beings. To deal with the stressful process of change, we need, as individuals, to be prepared.

another person are clearing our minds of past hurt to find intelligent solutions to present situations.

If the relationship between two people can be made more creative, fulfilling and free of fear, then it follows that this can work for two relationships, or three or one hundred, or, we are convinced, for relationships that affect entire social groups, even nations. The problems of the world – and they are chronicled daily in headlines of violence and despair – essentially are the problems of individuals. If the individuals can change, the course of the world can change. This is hope worth sustaining.

Thomas A. Harris 1967

Your Skills

This is an exercise for which it's worth getting a very big sheet of paper ready, and some bold writing implements will help. We're going to make a list by 'brainstorming'. That is, don't worry about whether your thoughts are true or not – just write them down. There are many blocks to thinking creatively. Removing self-censorship is the starting point of unleashing our creativity. Now, write on the piece of paper all your own skills – nothing is too silly or unimportant. Don't dismiss anything because you 'don't do it very well'. Millions of people are great cooks – even if very few get top ratings in French restaurant guides!

59

Feel free to discharge like crazy while you do it: giggling, screaming, getting angry may all be very appropriate responses to recognising that we are highly skilled people, no matter what we've been told by the conventional educational models, our parents, the boss, our partner . . . or even ourselves.

What did you get on your list?

Does it include your language skills? Does the list include your domestic skills: cleaning, cooking, organising, sewing? Do people skills feature: child-care, good listener, like explaining things, loyal friend, good grand-daughter, and so on?

Have you included numeracy? Being able to count is one level, being a qualified accountant is another, but they're all skills. What business skills did you list? In most households someone does the shopping every week year in, year out, and develops a keen eye for prices and the skills of dealing with suppliers, as well as managing a budget which is never quite large enough for the demands made on it. We all learn sales skills to some degree or other.

What manual skills did you list? There are the things in which you've trained, and then the skills you've acquired through having to do a certain job. That might be anything from cycle maintenance to carpentry, digging through to building micro-circuits.

Then there's the whole area of knowledge. You know something about many different areas of life, even if

| Take a little while to admire how skilled you are. |

you've never 'done' the thing to which it refers. That will include the natural world and the way it functions, basic science and technology, and any array of amazing facts and practices.

I hope you didn't forget your emotional skills: your sense of humour, your loving nature, your ability to protect when necessary, and so on.

Your Needs

Make another list, and this time include what you need in life. Remember that we have physical and emotional needs, and that the latter can be as real and as important as the former.

Food, drink, shelter, clothing, companionship, learning, love, respect, useful work, warmth, and so on. Don't be afraid to be more specific. If you and your family need a three bedroom house within walking distance of all amenities with central heating and a fine view, then put that. You know what your needs are, and no-one else does.

Your Physical Assets

To help you meet your needs there are also the physical assets which you possess, or to which you have access. This includes personal possessions, such as home, garden, car, as well as personal assets, such as two strong arms, good eyesight, and so on.

Include here all the land access you have, rented as well as owned, and the tools of trade which you can use. Remember it's immaterial whether you 'own' everything in this list. If there's a welding set in the community workshops, and you're free to use it, then it's a physical asset. Everyone immediately has any available public library network at their disposal, so their book resources are huge.

Possible Co-operators

Society is a co-operative existence. There may be things you need in life which aren't provided by your personal resources, be they skills or physical assets. One of the saving graces is that there are others who can help. Neighbours, relatives, the like-minded person that you find by chance meeting – all are a rich potential source of co-visionaries. It's often the case that life-long friends reveal their unbearable defects to you when engaged on your first combined venture. What has actually happened is that you have changed your expectations

8 We all survive by having useful relationships with many individuals

of each other, and that the new role does not fit the old admired virtues. Strangers can be entirely free of these prejudices in each direction. Do not discount any avenue for help.

Any Shortfall?

At the end of all this list making you will find out what you want, what you need, and any shortfall between the two. Do the sum now, and see how it works out. This is what stocktaking is all about – a realistic appraisal of where you are now.

Any Surplus?

The other probability is that you have some things in surplus. They may take many forms, from possessions acquired earlier in life, which have lost their importance as your values (and waist size) have changed, to personal skills which you feel are under-used. Maybe your own garden is completely under control and you'd like to take two hours a week to look after someone else's. Maybe your sense of vision, good humour and incredible range of skills is just looking for some worthy community that needs developing. If so, it starts at your doorstep.

5 LOOKING AT NATURE

Understanding how the physical world is patterned is essential in getting the planet's energies to work for us.

Physical Patterns

All living things belong to an endless food chain; all live by feeding on something and die at the hand of something else. This is the proper order of living nature. Matter and energy on the earth's surface are also in a constant state of flux, passing through continuous cycles without birth or death. Such is the true image of the universe . . . This must not be seen as a world of intense competition for survival, or of the strong eating the weak, but as a united family of many members that live together in a single harmony.

Masanobu Fukuoka 1985

To practice Permaculture well it is not necessary to store a vast quantity of facts. It is better to understand underlying patterns. This gives much more flexibility, for rather than know the specific remedy for each and every situation, the elements of many different situations can be easily adapted to a pattern we know to be worth repeating.

Observation shows us that the Earth never stores energy in living matter in straight lines. The natural flow of all energy is in curves. Trees which grow apparently straight have gentle tapering curves of form, and spiral in the grain. It's the same with sunflower seeds on the head of the flower. And galaxies, shorelines and muscles.

This cyclical character underlies all natural energy flows and is part of the constancy of the Earth's corporate life. Living organisms flourish, not as individuals, but as elements in this flow, which is planet-wide and of manifold variety. To relearn our place on the planet, not as masters, but as a life-sustaining component, we need to study and emulate the physical patterns of nature.

The Core Model

The core model offers a template on which the variety of natural shapes in a seemingly simple object can be seen to be marvellous. Take an apple core, and imagine it seen from different angles. If it were sliced from top to bottom, we would have a set of concentric circles. Cut at one angle, it makes a parabola. Draw round it while moving upwards, and you make two spirals.

This shape is a useful one to bear in mind when looking at living objects. Ask twenty people to draw a tree. How many will draw a trunk with leaves on? Yet a tree has all the characteristics of the core model, having roots which occupy

a similar volume to the part above ground. The core model reminds us to look beyond what we can see to seek the whole of life.

Wind and Water Patterns

We know that the power of wind and water is immense. They have eroded and remade the rocks of our biosphere many times over. And yet in one sense they are very gentle energies, tending to go round things, rather than through them. They do this in distinct and predictable patterns. All the patterns of nature can be seen at both the 'macro' (large scale) level and the 'micro' (small scale or local) level.

Macro movements of wind and water make up the weather. Cool climates vary from continental to maritime. Nearer the centres of large land masses the temperature reaches greater extremes of coldness in winter, and heat in summer. Nearer the seaboard the climate is moderated by the effects of the sea as a great heat store in winter and cool store in summer, so the range of temperature is less. Maritime influence extends further inland on coasts which face prevailing wind directions. These coasts also tend to be wetter, as more moisture is brought inland and precipitated from evaporation over the sea.

Living in a temperate climate is a great joy. We see such huge variations in colour and texture of the landscape. The

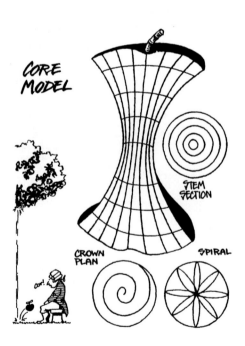

CORE MODEL

CROWN PLAN

STEM SECTION

SPIRAL

end of winter gives us the ground nearly bare, high summer, a lush humidity, and autumn the very special smells and colours of deciduous flora, and an earth reclaiming nutrients for the next growing season. In spring new buds push up through earth and bark and there is promise of the whole cycle repeating. What drives this cycle?

Climate is historically predictable because the Earth has constant wind patterns. The globe heats unevenly. Since the molecules of anything warm tend to expand, the substance becomes less dense. Warm air is less dense than cold air, and so differences of air pressure are caused. The air moves as wind from high pressure to low pressure regions. Between 40 and 60 degrees North or South of the equator, which means the majority of the habitable cool lands of the Earth, the pressure is predominantly low, drawing warm winds from the sun side, and cold winds from the shade side. Polar and equatorial regions tend to be at higher pressure, and so their prevailing winds blow away to the temperate areas. The cycle is maintained by air warmed in the tropics rising and being taken at high altitudes to fall, cooled, over the poles, and (warmer) at around 30 degrees North and South (the Horse or desert latitudes).

The rotation of the Earth affects the pattern. The prevailing winds in the Northern hemisphere temperate zones are South-westerly, and in the Southern hemisphere, North-easterly. In the

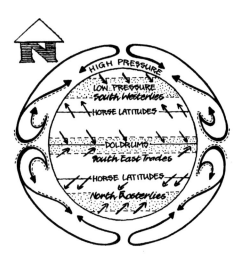

Northern hemisphere West coasts are comparatively wet, and East coasts dry, and the reverse in the Southern hemisphere. Where warm equatorial air and cold polar air meet, depressions form, bringing changeable stormy weather.

Local geography distorts this overall pattern. Mountains and valleys divert airflows and cause moist air to rise in some localities, releasing rain, and thus making less rainfall in areas 'in the rain shadow' of these high rainfall areas. Large land masses increase extremes of climate by holding large low-pressure air masses in summer, and high-pressure masses in winter. This gives rise to the characteristic constant chilly winds of great plains in winter, and their short hot summer growing seasons which are so productive of heat-loving crops, like maize and tomatoes.

On the micro-scale, water or air flow over and through the landscape. At low velocity there is little friction, and therefore the patterns of flow mould gently round any obstruction. As speed increases eddies form in the leeward of the obstacle, where circulation occurs in an area of lower pressure. At greater velocity these eddies are 'cast' into a stream flow, making repeated turbulent patterns. This matters because air or water behind a shelter can be very turbulent. At torrential speed the patterns disintegrate, drawing the stream closer in to the obtruding body and storing highly turbulent flow in the leeward.

Microclimates

We may have an overall climatic reference for a site, yet the detail of the site may alter the general climate to cause especially warm, cold, still, or windy areas. It is essential in any circumstance to know the location and how it functions through all the seasons in relation to its surrounding environment before applying a generalised solution.

Sun Sectors

The sun rises in the East and sets in the West only in poetry and on two days of the year in cool latitudes. The rest of the time it changes its relative position daily as the Earth rotates at an angle around it. So in midsummer we have the longest day and in midwinter the shortest day. The nearer the pole you live, the greater are the extremes.

The extremes are more noticeable in the Northern hemisphere because the land masses extend nearer the poles. Tierra del Fuego, the renowned spot for inhospitable climate and last landfall in South America, is only at the equivalent latitude to Moscow, Newcastle (England) or Edmonton (Canada). The southernmost town in New Zealand would be the same latitude as central France or Toronto in the Northern hemisphere.

Wherever you are, you can manage the sun sector most effectively by measuring it. Work out where the sun rises and sets at midsummer, and the same for midwinter. Your best growing land will be in the area that receives full sun all growing season. The areas that only have partial sun will favour shade tolerant crops. To achieve a high level of solar gain in a building, position it where receives sunlight throughout the seasons, not just in midsummer. This does mean knowing your site well.

Shade measurements for proposed structures or trees can be measured by holding a tall pole, and measuring the shadow cast. There are also solar charts, and instruments through which to view solar effects. Better still, visit your local planetarium and ask for a demonstration! Also take into account the different zenith of the sun, that is its high point, which is roughly at noon (depending on your time zone). This is important because it affects angles of reflection, and means that neighbouring features, such as hills, houses and trees may shade your building in winter when the sun is lower, although they don't in summer. Most people house-hunt in the warm weather. You learn much more of a site's limitations seeing it in mid-winter.

Spirals and Flows

The flowing nature of natural energies should be observed and used for its beneficial characteristics. Gardens which flow with the landscape have a special quality to them, which is partly to do with their abundant nature. Straight line growing achieves lower productivity within a given area. Spirals, in particular, maximise the useful area for yield by offering increased 'edge' effect and many more micro-climates, and therefore more possibilities for variety than rectangular shapes.

Natural shapes also have interesting effects as regards tessellation. This is the ability to produce shapes which fit well together (from the Latin for 'tiles'), and can be seen in snakeskin, dried mud, tree bark, seed heads, rock formations and leaf structures. It appears that the evolution of tessellated shapes has come about to enable efficient energy flows to take place within organisms. This is worth repeating in human constructs.

Biotechnics

This is a catch-all term to include a wide range of techniques which are observed from nature and duplicated in human systems. At this point we often reach conclusions which are not 'provable' in laboratories. It is not proposed in Permaculture that one must believe anything unprovable, but there is strong evidence to suggest that there are many subtle energies in the life of the planet which we do not fully understand. If observation shows any of these energy patterns benefit yields, then we should surely use them.

The first area we should consider is the influence of the moon on our planet. 'The watery star', as Shakespeare called it, has a measurable influence on our seas, causing (through its gravitational pull) the variation of tides. Less well-known is the measured effect on the land, where it has been proved in large land masses (such as North America) that the land also rises and falls with the movements of the Moon relative to the Earth. The menstrual cycle in women (during which the water content of the body rises and falls) often phases with the moon. Scientific proof is now being obtained that the same applies to plants. Crop yields cut at full moon and high tide are higher than otherwise.

It is well known in some cultures that trees cut at the full moon have a higher water content. Many peasant agricultures have long worked on planting and harvesting crops in sequence with lunar effects. Rudolph Steiner, founder of the Anthroposophical movement, was asked to lecture on agriculture and in 1923 proposed a system of growing now known as biodynamics. He implied that yield could be improved by developing consciousness of lunar and cosmic cycles.

Since one knows instinctively when one is in the presence of a powerful personality, or one's neighbour is in a 'prickly mood', we can take it that we still have intact our primaeval ability to sense messages from the Earth and its

Amongst the various areas of geomancy which been proven to work over time is the dowser's art. Dowsers have an ability to sense energy from the earth through their bodies, directly or through dowsing rods. The finding of water for wells is one of the most useful outputs of this technique. The evidence I have seen is that dowsing is learnable, rather than a 'gift'. It is also used by some people in discovering lines of power in the landscape ('ley lines') and for contra-indicating some sites as having 'bad energy'. In Chinese practice the arts of *Feng-shui* relate to the appropriate placing of settlements through this technique.

living structure. In time we may value relearning the skills of listening intuitively to these patterns, and what they tell us.

Going With the Flow

An early pattern to appreciate is to go with the flow. Much energy can be consumed in fighting natural forces, 'taming' the elements, persuading others to our point of view, when in practice there is plenty to be done going with the prevalent direction. We may achieve much more by finding like-minded souls with whom to travel, than in attempting to convert others.

In any circumstance it is possible to find options which, like Judo or Aikido, dissipate the energy of a predator, rather than reducing our own energy by direct conflict. This is why trees bend in the wind, and survive. The best windbreak is the one which lets the wind through, slowing its destructive power, not the one which seeks to stop it dead.

Edge and Ecotones

Ecotones are the meeting of overlapping areas of neighbouring types of ecology. All patterns of occupation or behaviour have edges, and they offer a particularly rich environment. This is because the edge of anything is especially rich in species, supporting plants, animals and activities from both its neighbouring areas, and also the species and activities which only take place in that special zone.

Thus a woodland edge may have canopy trees (e.g. oak, beech) from within the forest, and all the edge species which favour the greater light of the perimeter (e.g. currants, birches, alder buckthorn and so on). There will also be some of the species of neighbouring grassland or wetland. Here, for instance, Brimstone butterflies lay their eggs on the alder buckthorn, and burrow-living animals favour the site for the range of feeding opportunities and protection which it offers.

Maximise Edge

We can maximise productivity by increasing edge. A round pond has the least edge possible for the given area. A square pond has slightly more. A wavy edge can double the edge length, whereas a spiral-shaped pond could have ten times the edge length – and all for the same surface area of water.

We also need to increase edge between our different activities. When different trades, professions and caring skills operate in isolation we lose the opportunity of learning from each other. 'Skills cross-over' can do much to enhance our knowledge by giving new techniques from one discipline to another, and also by giving us a greater

REMAP is a project where engineers and designers offer their skills to work with health care specialists in finding technical solutions for people with disabilities. Equipment is constructed to help with specific difficulties tailored to the individual.

understanding of our indebtedness to the work of others, as well as seeing more of the beneficial consequences of our own output.

Edges operate physically on the horizontal plane, but also vertically through buildings and woodland, as well as through time. Birds singing at dawn and dusk are a beautiful reminder of how the edge between day and night is a special time for feeding and social functions. These temporal boundaries occur many times each day for different reasons, and also in a compelling rhythm through the seasons.

Niches

Nature uses these variations of time, light, space and climate to full advantage by providing species and functions to suit all these various changes in the environment.

There is some woodland in my garden. As I write the trees are all bare, just coming into bud, and the snowdrops have, as usual, been the first life to break the soil. As their flowers fade, wild garlic will emerge, followed by garlic mustard and daffodils. Orange-tip butterflies will feed on the garlic mustard as the bluebells emerge and be gone before the butterbur breaks out with its dinner-plate leaves to shade out the low growing plants till autumn. As the trees come into full leaf, nettles and comfrey will flourish in the shade, and the new shoots of blackberries will twine up the trees to provide fruit in the autumn.

Through all of this is a constant interchange of animal and bird species, not competing, but using the space in a complementary way. Rabbits and pheasants graze the lawn at different times. Rodents come out at night. Some creatures, such as wagtails, are seasonal visitors. In spring the bluetits feed off spiders' webs in the windows. Daily and seasonally there are great variations in space usage enabling bats, cats, rats and the whole range of fauna to find a space, although ostensibly many of the species are mutually exclusive.

Each has its niche, and reminds us that we can design human needs to be accommodated in niches in nature in the same way, without having to eradicate the rest of life's profusion.

Predators

Any system needs predators. Tradition-ally they have a very bad reputation –

just look at the fox! Without them the system would simply grow unhindered to the exclusion of all other life, which would be a true ecological disaster. A more dispassionate definition of predators, and the one we shall use here, is that a predator is anything which reduces yield.

If, in managing a system over a period of time, we take more than the system produces, then we are predators. Other predators may be seen as animals, birds, insects, plants, moulds, fungi, storm, cold, heat, too much or too little moisture, subsidence, other people, or aliens from outer space, if you like, but only when their net effect is to reduce yield. Often our view of something as a predator is a failure to see its complete role in nature. David Stephen (*Highland Animals*) writes, with marvellous per-ception, of the fox's occasional meal of lamb:

Foxes in an area populated by field voles will eat mainly voles – up to a dozen or more a day. We know that a vole weighing an ounce or so will eat two ounces of grass a day, and Jim Lockie has shown that voles in Wester Ross eat twenty-three pounds each in the winter months. Foxes probably eat two thousand voles a year.

The implication is that foxes help sheep on balance by protecting available grazing.

There are patterns of dealing with

predation which can be learned and used where necessary. They keep to the desirable pattern of doing as little as possible, and they can be described in a marvellous term learnt from midwifery:

The Spiral of Intervention

This pattern was described by Dorothy Shipp, a midwife who taught birthing skills when Nancy was having our first child. If a mother gives birth with her trunk in an upright position, gravity will help the baby's head down the birth canal and into the world. If she lies on her back, she can slow down or stop the speed of this movement.

Health Service policy being that all women should first think of having their babies in hospital, that's what mostly happens in Britain. Policy is also to put each woman on a foetal monitor for twenty minutes on admission. At the hospital where Dorothy worked it was standard procedure to ask women to lie down for this. It was also pretty standard that fifty per cent of the equipment was malfunctioning, and that an hour would be more like the time required to check that all was well.

With painful regularity women found that by this time contractions had stopped. This cycle may eventually lead to a consultant trying to induce birth, and if this fails a Caesarean section is performed to alleviate foetal distress.

Whilst it's not suggested that all foetal monitoring leads to Caesarean sections, it's quite clear, and medically understood, that once you intervene you increase the risk that further intervention will be necessary. Thousands of hospital beds are occupied by people with iatrogenic illness – ill-health caused by medical treatment.

This undesirable pattern can occur in all human systems. If you use heavy agricultural machinery, then more heavy agricultural machinery will be needed to relieve the compaction of the soil. If your body is only used to refined sterile food, you will have lower natural resistance to common infections, and will have to intervene in your food supply continually to keep that 'hygienic' diet.

So we can see a desirable scale of intervention. The ideal is to do nothing, but if yield is still impaired beyond acceptable limits, implement interventions on this scale. Do not go to the next step unless the previous one doesn't work, or you know in advance that it won't.

1 Do nothing.
  Example: I lose five lambs a year to foxes. It's normal.
2 Increase output to compensate for the small (acceptable) loss.
  Example: I'll up my flock by ten sheep to compensate for the lost lambs.
3 Make a biological intervention.

71

Example: I'll run a German Shepherd Dog with my sheep. That will scare off or kill any foxes.

4 Make a mechanical intervention.
Example: I'll put out wire traps for the foxes on their runs.

5 Only as a last resort, make a chemical intervention.
Example: I'll put poison in the fox holes.

Biological interventions are absorbed by the living cosmos. So are mechanical interventions, although they may take a little time to break down. Chemical interventions are made so easily, but are the most dangerous, because we can never measure their full consequence.

To develop these patterned ways of thinking we need only observe nature. We can, however, add to these a whole range of patterns which are directly observable from human behaviour. This is done in the next chapter.

6 UNIVERSAL AIMS – THE PATTERNS IN ALL THINGS

Human performance develops patterns just as nature does. They affect our speech and thinking. There are intangible patterns in the way that we and other living things behave.

Theoretical Patterns

In the same way that we can see physical patterns like raindrops on the window pane, we can also find intangible patterns at work. A typical way in which these are embroidered into our folk culture is in the use of aphorisms; 'Many a true word spoken in jest', for one.

Understanding theoretical patterns helps us to see aims in life which are universal, and if we give them aphoristic titles, they become both easy to remember and easy to spot. They provide us with another framework around which to design solutions to unpredictable situations.

Patterns of Thinking

We dissect nature along lines laid down by our native languages.

Benjamin Lee Whorf 1956

. . . The most positive effect of changing our linguistic practice will be to destroy the pernicious belief that we have to be controlled and oppressed by our language.

Deborah Cameron 1985

Thinking is always patterned. It is patterned most strongly by our use of language. If the words and images we use assume that war is an everyday image, then it makes war acceptable. If we degrade women, or we are racist, in our use of language then those concepts travel into our unconscious, and affect our attitudes.

All of us have an inbuilt conservatism resisting change. Switching to a new diet, or giving up habits like smoking (although it poisons our bodies), are incredibly hard changes to make. To change a world-wide pattern of consumption is going to take a concerted effort. The starting point is to recognise that we do have very patterned

73

ways of thinking, and to acknowledge that change is difficult.

There are also creative patterns of thinking, which are the source of all our leaps forward. It's the 'eureka!' syndrome, the blinding flash of inspiration, or at least the educated guess, which sends us onward, remotivated. This ability of humans to suddenly perceive new directions with enthusiasm and commitment is a pattern worth enjoying.

'Timeless Way of Building'

What we would wish to have in a changed world? There is an indefinable quality to certain times and places which we know or have experienced, which seems hard to put a finger on. Christopher Alexander is an American architect who has 'defined' this quality and given us a process for recognising its patterns. He writes:

There is one timeless way of building.
It is a thousand years old, and the same today as it has always been.

He tells us to look for 'the quality with no name' and has devised a 'pattern language' to be able to repeat what makes that quality special. Pattern languages can be made for any particular situation. They are based on observing the notable elements of the desirable model, and checking them against other instances. Thus in California there is a particular type of old barn which is common in the countryside. These barns have 'the quality with no name'. Yet they can be measured. They have predictable numbers of aisles and arches. They have a minimum and maximum width and length. The materials used in their construction are limited.

The original builders of the barns worked from their instinctive knowledge of the pattern. They were not architects, yet their understanding of the building and its proposed function, the characteristics of the people and animals who would use the construct, all interleaved to create a pattern which could be repeated.

Pattern language and the timeless way of building could be applied to any situation, and it is an advance to know we may make aspects of human systems have this special quality. This reminds us that observation and thinking as precursors to action are worth the delay. It is the same principle as underlies the

The Oregon Experiment is based on Christopher Alexander's team work, and used pattern languages to redesign a hostile university campus using the input of all its potential users (some thousands of people), to create a person-friendly environment.

'masterly inactivity' of the Zen Buddhist.

Minimum Intervention

We have already looked at the spiral of intervention. Minimum intervention is the policy we consciously adopt to avoid the unnecessary work of repairing damage caused by unthinking intervention. 'Do nothing', in simple words.

So, it is better not to till the ground if we can grow crops without, it is better not to prune trees if we can get yield without, it is better not to use up energy if we can live without. If we must intervene, then we do so as little as possible.

Do not underestimate, however, the work required to build systems which will work with minimum intervention. If we are repairing a damaged ecology, there may be highly intensive intervention required to make a system sufficiently fertile that it will function with little intervention, and provide the yields we need to live.

This is a pattern to work towards.

Maximum Useful Relationships

In Permaculture we are looking, not for the greatest number of elements, although diversity is a recommended pattern, but for the greatest number of useful relationships.

Many highly sustainable societies function on very few feedstocks, but make great use of the useful interplay between them. How else could the Inuit (Eskimos) of North America survive in the icy deserts of the far North? No product of their hunting is wasted. They have an intimate knowledge of the resource value of every species available to them. They are part of the complex web of life of their very unforgiving environment.

A large number of useful relationships in a system makes for good risk management. If one element fails, there will be several others which supply the same function, and our ability to meet our needs is unimpaired.

Liabilities Into Assets: 'Everything is a Gift'

'Pattern language' recommends that discernible patterns be given poetic names which encapsulate their meaning. If you cannot do this, then no pattern exists, says Christopher Alexander. 'Everything is a gift' is the central pattern of designing sustainable systems.

Whether something is a liability or an asset has less to do with the situation than our perception of it. 'Imperial Caesar dead and turned to clay, would stop a hole to keep the wind away', says the Bard. Everything has an up and a down side. If I make a fortune, then someone else must have paid for it. Conversely, even the worst catastrophes offer some benefit to someone, somewhere. By accepting that 'everything is a gift' we stop looking at situations in a negative way, and look for the positive gain to be made.

Weeds are a great example of this pattern. In prevalent western agriculture weeds are a predator. In fact, the more you study weeds the more you learn about their many uses as food, fibre, and fodder, and also the more you realise that they are vital soil conditioners, and tend to grow where their ability to break up soil and accumulate minerals is actually doing the farmers' work for them.

Diversity of Elements; Duplicity of Function

Systems which support a great variety of species and constructs have many different possibilities for performing each function. We should check when designing our system, however, that each element is really useful. Three uses for each element are a minimum, and five preferable. Remember that 'looks nice' is not a countable use. So a hedge may be a stock barrier, a windbreak, a source of firewood and wild food, fodder for stock and beneficial insects, a boundary marker, and a soil conditioner. If we build a wall instead, we'll want it to have extra uses, such as solar trap for trained fruit trees, a gutter to collect rainwater, and preferably make it part of another structure as well.

If we have different elements performing the same function, we have defence in depth. It matters less if all elm trees die through Dutch elm disease if we have a good standing mix of woodland, oak, ash, limes and so on to take their place. If our only climax tree were elm, then the result would be disastrous.

Minimum Effort for Maximum Effect

The trick is to work with what we've got. If we're always trying to impose elements and structures on systems which already exist we're making work for ourselves. Far better to see how what exists already can work for us.

There are many techniques available to us which obey this pattern. It's amazing how often, with a bit of thought, we can eliminate a heap of work and introduce a different way of achieving an effect for much less effort. Nature doesn't make compost heaps, yet it effortlessly achieves the biodegrading of organic waste matter. In human affairs we find that the single right sentence can achieve what hours of persuasion could not.

Stacking

Many of these helpful patterns have complementary aspects. Stacking helps

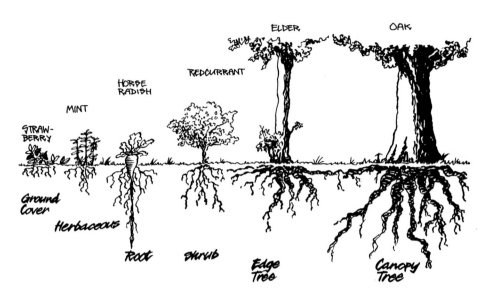

II The layers of forest

us get more out by putting less in, by thinking in multidimensional terms.

Chemically-fed monocultures often appear high yielding because significantly increased tonnages pass the farm gate (or factory gate, or whatever), compared to traditional yields. Look at western agriculture's favourite pastime – wheat growing. What's the first thing you notice about wheat fields? They're flat (or mildly undulating) stretches of land showing a marked lack of variation. This monotony is the hallmark of any monoculture. It's only working in two dimensions.

There's a neglect of vertical space and time as added spaces for yield. A typical mature deciduous tree has an estimated leaf area of two acres. At twelve-foot spacings you get three hundred trees to the acre – so broadleaf plantings at that distance increase the growing area six-hundredfold over bare earth. A combination of tree and wheat crops may give reduced yield of each compared with monoculture forestry or wheat, but the combined yield is vastly superior. Yield must be measured over longer terms than annual cropping. It might include also greater soil health, resistance to plant disease, and improved wildlife opportunities.

Stacking is exemplified in natural forest. There are species which inhabit every niche that's available. Canopy trees make the 'high forest', while others grow

77

less tall and serve as energy traps on the edge of forest – not just the external edge, but in a pioneering role to reclaim natural clearings caused by the death of old trees. A shrub layer takes up light and ground nutrients at animal height. Between this and the ground itself are herbaceous plants (annual and perennial) and creeping plants which follow the surface of the ground. Although nearly all plants have roots in the ground, there are some whose major yield is specifically below ground.

Through all these layers run the climbers, crossing the various boundaries. The last category of plants is the epiphytes – plants which survive above ground level, growing on trees themselves. Though these are more common in the tropics than in temperate climates, we can include mosses and ferns here.

The ancient Norse view of the cosmos was of Valhalla (the Norse equivalent of Heaven) in the upper branches of the World Tree, Yggdrasil, a mighty Ash. Humanity occupied the ground level, and Hell was amongst the roots of this tree. The messenger between Gods and Mortals was a squirrel. This is a nice metaphor for the way in which nature has special places for all her children.

Successions in time make natural systems available through niches to a wide range of species. This is stacking in a temporal or fourth dimensional sense, as well as its three dimensional manifestation.

In human managed ecosystems this is a very useful principle to apply. For instance, schools can become facilities for adults in the evening. The community which invests in expensive libraries and sports facilities can enjoy them as well as the students.

Consequently . . .

. . . There is No Limit to Yield

In any system, natural or managed, it is always possible to introduce more yield. What dimensions aren't covered already?

Examples of plant layers found in woodland

Canopy trees	oak, ash, beech
Small trees	elder, guelder rose, spindle tree
Shrubs	gorse, broom, hazel
Herbaceous plants	comfrey, foxglove, nettles
Ground cover	ground ivy, wood sorrel
Roots	bluebells, iris, cuckoo pint
Climbers	honeysuckle, ivy
Epiphytes	moss, lichens, ferns

There is always some bare space which can be put to good purpose. Even in dense jungle, you can still add in tree houses.

By designing consciously using Permaculture principles we can achieve all the yield we need using less space, and less time. This leaves more of the planet to revert to wilderness, or at very least, the ability of cultures with a high rate of consumption to function without such great dependence on their poorer suppliers. The ability to achieve all our required inputs locally is not some naive pipe dream, but of major importance in achieving a just distribution of the world's wealth. It is the only way to make the planet habitable for human beings on a sustainable basis.

necessary to take away all the business of an immoral or polluting organisation to right its direction. If ten per cent of its consumers object sufficiently strongly by buying their needs in from elsewhere, the manufacturer will be forced to change direction, because they will have lost their profit margin. This principle of consumer pressure has worked very well in the United States where major providers have many times been forced to tidy up their act when radical consumers withdrew their custom.

In a positive sense, it is not necessary to make the ultimate garden in your first season. If the right starting conditions are created it develops its own momentum, and it will evolve in time in the direction you have given it.

The Flywheel Effect

In engineering it is well known that the efficiency of a rotating power source can be increased by adding a flywheel. This is essentially an energy store, a heavy wheel which takes energy to get it going, but has such high momentum that it smooths out peaks and troughs in the engine's performance and gives a more reliable output performance.

All human endeavour can be encouraged to exhibit this tendency. If enough enthusiasm or belief is injected into any change of direction, the new movement will be given a momentum which carries it forward. It is not

Start Near

Avoid scattering your efforts thinly over a large area. It's more effective to start locally, where your efforts are under control, and where results are directly observable. So a neighbourhood recycling scheme is far more likely to succeed than trying to effect a change of national policy. A garden at your back door will be more productive than one the far end of the lawn.

First achieve your objectives on your own doorstep. In time the perimeter of your efforts can be moved out to include a larger area. Don't try and reclaim an acre of wilderness at one go. Start with

.... I JUST PRESUMED YOU'D PLANT IT SOMEWHERE HANDY....

a tenth of the plot, get it under control and then add some more. Learn to work with the neighbours in your street before approaching the whole town. Cleaning up the planet will be the natural conclusion of such a sequence, founded in personal action.

Design Element Template

A template is just an outline which can be fitted to certain different situations to form a helpful mould. The design element template is a useful tool for approaching any aspect of design, as a kind of checklist. Every element in a designed human system can be analysed for the following factors:

What are its uses?
What needs does it have?
Are there any by-products, not covered in its uses?
What would be an integrated design featuring this element?
What predators will it attract?
What species can I list for this element?

You can have great fun applying this to anything. Stock, for instance, might be used for transport, meat, leather, bone meal, company, balancing a grazing regime, and providing organic fertiliser. It will need food, water, shelter, help at birthing times, and containment. Its by-products might include methane, animal noises, and amusement on dull days. An integrated design would be as part of a mixed balanced farm or wilderness. Predators might include foot and mouth disease, cattle rustlers, the collapse of market prices or poor fences. Species could be as varied as you like: alpacas, bison, cattle, donkeys . . . all the way through to yaks and zebras.

How you make such lists will depend on the situation for which you make it, but as a prompter this template will help ask the appropriate questions for any necessary aspect of a design.

PART II

WHAT CAN YOU DO?

7 YOUR HOME – WHERE THE HEART IS

'Think globally, act locally' means that the best place to start any sustainable approach to life is at home.

What Are Homes For?

The word 'ecology' describes the scientific understanding of how living organisms interact with their environment. Literally ecology means the science or theory of home, derived as it is from the Greek word, *oikos*, meaning house. Your home can be seen as many different concentric areas, from the whole planet down to the body in which you live. For now let's set the limits at the building in which you live, and its immediate surroundings.

Your home is the central point in time and space from which all your daily occupations radiate. Designing your home to supply its own needs and consume its own outputs would be a massive contribution to global cleansing.

'The grand necessity, then, for our bodies, is to keep warm, to keep the vital heat in us'. So Thoreau sums up the human needs of 'Shelter, Clothing and Food', as he puts it. His book *Walden* reviews a two-year experiment in simple living, and is a valuable insight into how industrialisation and commerce have driven people into lives of virtual slavery. His suggested remedy is to concentrate on our simple needs, and so to make free time and energy for our spiritual needs. Of course, most of us make many more demands of our environment than Thoreau's simple prescription. I would list love, companionship, security, relaxation, education, and meaningful work as things which are also strong human needs.

What is your home to you? Is it a place in which all these needs are met? Does it have shortcomings – sapping your energy, rather than restoring it? We often talk about somewhere 'feeling homely', as if the qualities of a good home were hard to define and could only be sensed. In *The Natural House Book* David Pearson gives these criteria for a natural house: 'Health for the body, peace for the spirit, harmony with the environment'.

Few are so lucky. Large numbers of people live in flats, rooms, or even cardboard boxes on the streets of our cities. Secondly, we might all appreciate the beauties of an architect-designed natural house, but most of us would be completely without the means to own or even rent one. Many people will have a home already and will simply want to know how to make the best of it. Some will be wanting to find or build a home which suits their personal needs. In addressing such a wide range of situations we must look at an idealised set of criteria for appropriate homes, and leave the individual reader to shape these to their own circumstances.

Where Is The Best Place to Build a Home?

Homes should be sited as near as possible to the source of all their inputs, and should have facilities for collecting (and preferably reusing) their outputs.

The first input is the materials used to build the home. This suggests the obvious solution of respecting historical traditions of building homes from local materials. New techniques in building can also be helpful to increase the range of possible constructions. Britain and Ireland show a huge range of styles using local resources, varying from area to area, depending on availability. Here are some examples:

Limestone walls, slate roofs (Pennines)

Flint walls, tiled roofs (Buckinghamshire)

Lapped wooden board walls, wood shingle roofs (Essex, Kent, Sussex)

Cob walls (rammed earth and stone), thatch roofs (Devon and Cornwall)

Half timbered (frame) with wattle and daub or stone infill, and thatched roofs (Midlands)

Rubble walls with turf roofs (Western Ireland)

There are no universal rules which say you may or may not use a given material (although planning and building regulations in your area will have an opinion). These examples show that from a materials point of view, you can site your house anywhere, and find natural materials which don't consume large quantities of energy to manufacture (as kiln-fired bricks or concrete do).

The second input to your home is you, and your friends and/or family, as appropriate. It is not very sensible to live large distances from your place or places of work and leisure. Your personal energy is wasted in the travelling, as well as consuming large quantities of (usually fossil) fuels getting there and back.

What other inputs does your home have? Water, food, fuel, clothing, furniture – your list may be longer. It makes sense to build homes near water, food and fuel supplies. Every time we don't do this, we increase the energy inputs necessary to provide our needs.

Homes can be much more efficient simply by the way they are positioned, or laid out internally. Choice of building materials also affects the health and comfort of the building.

Neighbours and Extramural Amenity

We need human company and the services which satisfy our unmet needs to be the right distance away. Out of town superstores suit those with big cars and big wallets:

> You enter a supermarket at your peril. The store manager knows better than you do how you will behave – which way you will walk, where you will look. And he exploits his knowledge with a ruthlessness guaranteed to shoot holes in your bank account.
>
> Peter Martin *The Sunday Times Magazine* November 4th 1990

Corner shops and local bus services are more human scale, create more local wealth, and serve the needs of everyone.

No housing estate should be built without the basic facilities needed by its inhabitants. No such development should take place without canvassing and incorporating the views of its future inhabitants.

Water Provision

We all need drinkable water. We also use water for other needs, such as washing ourselves, our clothes, or even the car, and for watering the garden. Clearly the water quality for all of these needs does not have to be the same, yet municipal water supplies can only provide one quality of water. This is governed by health regulations.

It is likely that as economies inflated by cheap fossil fuels crumble, quality of municipal services will continue to fall. Water quality is a crucial element of a healthy home, and we should all consider how our homes might be better supplied through local resources, including rain catchment and recycling, rather than relying on the 'big' systems of today.

Traditionally houses were built just below the 'spring line'. Building here offers the best source of clear clean water, with minimal work to bring the water to the home. We shall look later at ways of cleansing water which falls short on quality.

Sanitation

High quality sanitation was widespread under the Roman Empire in Europe, and has a long history in Japan. By the nineteenth century declining standards caused such appalling health that a major engineering of sanitary arrange-

13 Section through temperate landscape

ments was necessary. It was a system which had the excellent effect of greatly improving people's health. It is one which we very much take for granted in the countries that enjoy such standards.

Unfortunately it requires a scale of engineering which is impossible without massive capital input, and which treats human wastes as a problem, not an asset. It also is a major consumer of energy and water. However, even small terraced houses can be structured to deal adequately with human wastes without external piping and sewage works. At the next level up the benefits of reprocessing

> In China there are twenty million small scale methane digesters which take human and animal wastes from groups of houses or farms, producing compost and usable gas as output.

human wastes increase dramatically.

Systems which waste as little water as possible are advisable. There is no reason, for instance, why toilets cannot be flushed with water that has been used for hand washing. Compost toilets eradicate the need for water in this role. The separation of urine and faeces greatly reduces the problem. Urine, a valuable source of potassium and nitrogen, is easily recycled through garden composting systems, as it works as an activator, helping the heaps heat up and decompose quickly. Faeces needs much longer to digest into usable compost, and is best rotted with sawdust and ashes. Such compost should never be applied directly to human food, but is quite safe to use for trees and green manure crops. Recycling systems which combine the outputs of blocks of households may be more effective than individual ones.

Access

Sun Side and Shade Side

Your home must be accessible. You need to get all your externally derived needs easily inside. Roads are one system of creating access, but are also massive consumers of energy in developed world culture. Part of the problem is that roads are not seen as multi-functional assets. They are often sold as being 'vital to development', whereas good water-borne and rail transport systems made possible the industrial revolution, and so must have worked extremely well, whilst being much more environmentally benign.

Siting the house near its needs is the first solution. But look also at roads as water collectors. Remember that access lines (which may just be footpaths) are frequently used, and are therefore good places to put things which you do often, such as collecting salads.

It should be law that all public buildings be accessible to wheelchair users. The difficulties of building design are equally felt by parents with pushchairs and prams. Heavy and narrow doors, and steps are the chief obstacles. There is little need for any ground floor of a new building to be inaccessible to such essential wheeled transport. It can be harder to adapt old buildings. As in future we're all going to have to learn to do without our cars so much, bicycle access is another important consideration. Space in the home to park all these human powered vehicles is also essential.

To design well it is necessary to observe and become conscious of the solar cycle. This has been covered in Chapter 5, 'Looking at Nature'.

Shaded porches over sun side entrances will help to cool a house in summer. Glasshouses built on to the building are good at trapping solar energy, and creating a buffer to heat loss from the main building.

We tend to think of shade as a disadvantage in temperate climates. It's as much an asset as sunshine, and may become more of one if global warming gets serious. So place things appropriately. Cool larders should be on the shade side of the house, living rooms where the light and warmth comes from the sun. The importance of kitchens as living rooms tends to be underestimated in modern house design, being placed 'at the back', often on the shade side of the house, the 'living room' being treated as a showpiece and placed at the front. In many homes the kitchen is occupied more of the time, and is a central workplace. It deserves more prominence.

Fire

Anything which is an asset can also become a predator. Fire is the most consuming predator of all, capable of creating desert from plenty in seconds.

87

We are far too complacent in temperate zones about fire, seeing it as more of a problem in hot arid lands. In fact large scale fires are frequent and hideously destructive in temperate zones. If, as I hope, people respond to the threat of climatic change by massive reforestation throughout the world, then fire will increase as a risk.

Some forms of building construction are more liable to catch fire – the prejudice against wooden houses amongst insurers is based on this risk. However, in the event of large scale fire the type of building is going to make little difference – even steel burns! The best strategy is understanding what fire does, and acting accordingly. Fire will run with the wind, and will favour going uphill. So houses should be protected against fire on the downhill and windward sides.

Certain foliage is fire resistant, hence the old practice of growing *Sempervivum* on roofs, and their common name of House Leeks. Succulents like these retain high levels of water, so they can live where there is little soil to hold rainwater. Other plants are highly flammable, such as pine trees, with their resinous content. Some broadleaved trees are effective at slowing fires because although they burn, their high moisture content cools the blaze.

A tree-free belt around the house will reduce the risk from burning in nearby woodland. Ponds between the home and the direction of risk are another safety measure. In short, don't dismiss fire as a design consideration!

Winds

In cool climates winds show great variation. In temperate maritime zones the prevailing winds are south-westerly in the northern hemisphere, and north-easterly in the southern. These are the warmer winds which bring rain. The colder winds come from the north and east (northern hemisphere) or south and west (southern hemisphere). These tend to be drier winds and bring snow and extremes of cold. Colder winds occur more frequently in winter than summer.

The individual site must be read as you find it. If we take the northern hemisphere as our example, it means that windbreaks will be needed most often in the south-west quarter, but if north-easterly directions are not protected, we are left open to the coldest (albeit infrequent) winds. The answer is to protect in each direction. This has a major benefit, not just to crops and stock, but also to energy efficiency in buildings. Reduction of wind chill reduces heat loss in human structures as well as living things, and so reduces energy input otherwise needed to compensate.

Be careful in making sun side windbreaks that you are not obscuring the sun in all its glory. Leave sufficient room between structures and wind-

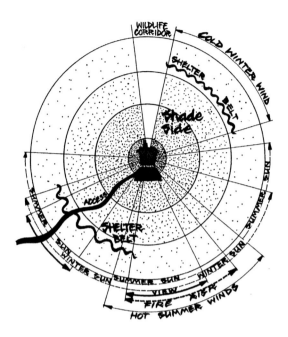

breaks to achieve solar gain, particularly in winter, when it is most needed. In practice this is quite easy as any windbreak will slow the wind for at least three to four times the height of the windbreak in a horizontal direction.

Frost Topography

Frost tends to form hardest on flat hill tops and in valley bottoms. Because it is made by colder air, which is denser, it flows downhill. Frost pockets form where there are dips in the landscape without outlets. Hence the old practice in areas which walled their fields of leaving gaps at the base of the wall in dips

'to let the frost run away'. Frost will also lie longest in places which get little or no sun, so shade side hill slopes are much colder in winter. Housing should be sun facing if possible, and avoid frost pockets.

Micro-climates may break the general rule. Some very northerly parts of Scotland are quite frost-free because of warm ocean currents coming to the North Atlantic from the Gulf of Mexico. Some warm hilly areas in the southern temperate band have notorious frost pockets. It is also good to note the first and last days with frost each year. This is important knowledge for managing the growing season. Plants which are not frost hardy need to be in as early as possible to gain best yield, but not so early that a sudden late frost kills them. Some types of maintenance on the land are best done before the first frost.

Many temperate trees will not function properly without frost, and there's a sense in which unseasonably mild winters feel unhealthy, as if temperate lands need good frosts to 'kill off the bugs', cull insect populations, and generally revitalise the land for the next growing season.

Zones

Work is what we do every time we have a need which is not fulfilled by our immediate surroundings. Picture, if you will, Adam and Eve in the Garden of Eden. Happy days! Why? Because there's no work to do. Everything they want is at hand. However, work can also be a pleasurable creative experience. For instance, my life would be diminished if I never had the pleasure of cooking

again. However, I should not enjoy cooking a meal with poor ingredients, insufficient tools and inadequate notice for unappreciative diners. It's all a question of suitable placement.

The first step to achieving 'suitable placement' is to consider our calendar of actions in relation to our environment. In simpler words that just means measuring time and space. In Permaculture we talk about 'zones.'

Zones are areas having definable time/space relationships. Some of our actions are daily, some occur many times a day, and some are less frequent. Other things may be done weekly, monthly or only at certain times of the year. Consider a smallholding – chickens, an orchard, a vegetable patch, a herb garden, and maybe a few pigs.

The smallholder may visit the herb garden every time they cook a meal. The chickens may be visited once a day, to feed them, and to collect the eggs. The pig may get two visits a day, whilst the orchard really only needs to be seen now

15 Zones

and then, with intensive care at pruning and fruit-picking time.

It makes sense, therefore, to put all these things in appropriate order – that is, to put the things you need to do most often nearest home, and the things you need to do least often, furthest away. For the sake of convenience we number the zones – the lower the number, the nearer in is the zone. So zone zero is home itself, zone one your immediate garden, going out to zone five which is wilderness. The drawing is an idealised situation to show the principle – don't expect anyone's home or land to look exactly like this!

Labour Saving

Homes nowadays have labour saving devices galore. In 1984 in Britain the percentage of each household which had the following appliances is shown against the product concerned:

And this doesn't count all the shavers, electric toothbrushes, cars, telephones, toasters and food processors. It would be a brave author that told the good citizens of the developed world that they could no longer use such devices, when clearly they have saved enormous amounts of drudgery in recent times. Or have they? Have we not just transferred the cost of these appliances to some other wage earning drudgery? Why is it any more noble to sit at a desk pushing papers than rinse nappies by hand?

Domestic appliances may be appropriate, as long as we realise the true cost of all these items in raw materials as well as energy used. The continual growth of 'consumer durables' as they are known in the advertising business, cannot, however, be regarded as sustainable. The health benefits of, for instance, the refrigerator, are provable. The need to iron our clothes seems less so, but that is a personal view.

Limiting our consumption is a good moral. Can we really have these labour saving benefits, and still be taking responsibility for our own needs and outputs? In reasonable amounts, personal physical labour is important for our health and fitness, and is less stress-inducing than office-based jobs.

Meanwhile there *are* other ways of saving labour. Tools can be placed on the way to the job. It's often more efficient to have small stores of useful items close to hand than have to travel to the depths

Percentage of population in the UK owning domestic appliances, 1986
(source: AGB Home Audit)

Washing machine	83%	Clothes drier	42%
Dishwasher	5%	Gas cooker	49%
Electric cooker	40%	Microwave oven	11%
Refrigerator	97%	Separate freezer	35%
Vacuum cleaner	95%	Power lawn mower	53%

of the house somewhere to access the larger store. Kitchens should be designed using plans of the room space, with cutouts for all work surfaces and so on, which can be manoeuvred on the drawing until distances between tasks are minimised.

Houses tend to be designed and built for average-sized men. It is often the case therefore that light switches, work surfaces and so on, are at completely the wrong height for the people that use them most, who are women, children (and sometimes men) of all shapes and sizes. If you're lucky enough to be designing and building for your own needs, a great way of saving labour is to have all these things fixed at the most comfortable height for *your* household.

Energy Efficiency

Energy is used in the home to power appliances, to provide lighting, to heat the space of the house, and to cook with. There are many ways in which we can be *more* efficient in the way we use energy, and this follows the pattern of reducing personal consumption.

The most radical energy saving is to reduce usage to nil. This can be achieved by throwing out all appliances, going to bed when it's dark, not heating the house and wearing more clothes instead, and by eating raw food. Potentially, this is an extremely healthy way to live. Not, however, one I would choose myself,

although tent dwelling has its adherents.

Moderate reduction of consumption is the next option, and might involve things like turning off lights when they're not in use, shutting doors and windows to prevent heat loss through draughts, and turning the central heating down by five degrees.

Energy consumption is often measured by cost rather than by energy units, as different forms of energy saving measures are themselves justifiable by 'pay-back period'. That is, the time it takes in saved energy costs to pay the price of the alteration. The payback time for certain measures may be a couple of months, and for others, twenty-five years. Pay-back times vary according to the cost of the fuel saved, and prices vary considerably for given unit of energy from fuel to fuel.

The sensible level of intervention after 'use less' strategies have been applied is to make an integrated plan for energy conservation measures. The most effective control is to insulate the building 'envelope'. This term describes the external surfaces of the house. Draughts should be reduced, and buildings should be planned to take advantage of maximum solar gain. Finally attention should be paid to 'comfort levels'.

Insulating the whole envelope is much more effective than treating one surface (e.g. loft insulation) in isolation. It is the single most effective energy conservation measure for temperate climates, where solar gain is low in autumn and spring weather. Insulation of external walls and under floors is just as important. Draught exclusion works, not just on increasing comfort levels, but also by reducing the frequency of air change in the building. 'Room air changes per hour' is the usual measure of this factor. A minimum of one air change per hour is needed for healthy living. Many buildings in cool climates run at three to ten times this rate. Draught stripping of doors and windows helps, but the most effective measure is to ensure that all external doors have lobbies.

Solar gain refers to the trapping of the sun's heat in a building. If insulation has taken place this will happen most noticeably through glazed areas. Buildings with equal windows to east and west are slightly more efficient than buildings with equal windows to north and south. The most efficient distribution is to have large sun side facing windows and only small or non-existent shade side lights.

Comfort levels are affected by the 'warmth' or 'coldness' of surfaces internally. Warm surfaces (soft fabrics, warm colours) reduce radiant heat loss, and can give the same comfort level at ambient temperatures up to 30% lower, significantly reducing heating costs. All such energy efficiency measures should be designed to ensure adequate airflow, and no condensation.

Finally, new technology in electric lighting means significant reductions in energy consumption are possible by

The family of Dr Kevin Woodbridge, general practitioner on the island of North Ronaldsay, off the north of Scotland, worked with architects Jacques and Adams of Bath, England to build a passive solar house which meets its low energy needs entirely from a wind generator. He is a keen ornithologist, and his house looks out over exposed windy views. If energy efficient housing can be built in these adverse conditions, it will work anywhere.

using long-life low wattage lamps which generate the same light levels as the old tungsten filament bulb. There are various products on the market, which are all relatively expensive to fit, but are much cheaper in the long run. In average home usage these will pay for themselves within two years. Then there's always making your own candles or oil lamps . . .

Natural Materials

Legionnaire's disease, and the 'sick building syndrome' have highlighted the worries of many people that building products commonly used in the past are not appropriate in a healthy building. Asbestos went some years ago (though there's plenty of it lurking in odd corners still). But all sorts of laminates and chemical products have been shown to degrade and give off undesirable fumes. Others may have very undesirable side products in their manufacture, or become lethal gas generators in the event of a house fire.

We can avoid these risks by using natural materials wherever possible. Wood, stone, natural fabrics, paper, waxes and water-based paints all offer softer technology than polystyrene, petroleum-based varnishes and paints and other chemically manufactured materials. The super insulated house may give good energy efficiency, but may not 'breathe' in a healthy way, so emphasising solar gain and light airy structures is energy efficient in a more pleasant way.

Construction Ideas

Passive energy efficiency is more rewarding than high input systems, encouraging the design of buildings which by their nature work well, rather than needing the additional inputs of further technology. Houses built into the earth are known as 'bermed' structures.

Underground building provides a high degree of temperature stability, built into sun side banks, offering external surfaces in the best direction for solar gain, but burying all shade side surfaces in the ground for insulation. Another

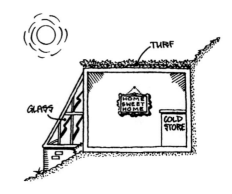

16 A bermed home

attractive and comfortable method is to keep all solid materials (stone or brick) and heat sources at the centre of the structure and to surround this with a light open glazed structure. This gives high solar gain, and the core of the building acts as a heat store.

Building the house over animal sheds is an old tradition for getting free central heating.

Building regulations were introduced for the best possible reasons, and have had very varied effects. In the UK, building innovation has been restricted by conservative public taste and planning officers who have not looked favourably on radical building design. There are many more examples of innovative architecture for the home in Scandinavia and the United States. Germany, with its 'baubiologie' movement, has led in the re-introduction of natural materials.

There is more to the subject for the

serious house builder than can be covered in this space. I hope the possibilities for healthier housing have at least been hinted at, and that the enthusiast will find good sources for further research in the book list.

Retrofit Ideas

Not many people are in a position to throw their home away and start again. How possible is it to fit existing homes in the ways talked about here? Some areas have free energy consulting services, and elsewhere there are consultants who charge. It can be well worth paying someone to conduct an energy audit on a building, or it is something you can do yourself. Various bodies advise on the procedures. Organisations listed at the end of the book can help with further information.

Draughtproofing and insulating lofts, walls, floors and water tanks are the most efficient measures to take. Double

---

Neighbourhood Energy Action is a charity which helps communities establish programmes to increase the energy efficiency of homes. It is particularly motivated by the energy needs of the poor and elderly who are most at risk from hypothermia, and from an in-ability to pay high fuel bills.

---

glazing may save up to ten per cent heat loss, but is so expensive that the pay-back times are very long. It's cheaper to use secondary glazing; panels that fit on the inside of existing windows. Thick curtains closed at night are another help. When redecorating you can choose to remove undesirable materials and refit with natural ones.

Furniture

The same applies to furniture as for buildings – natural materials are better for health and comfort, as well as kinder to the environment. The inventive householder can find furniture from many quarters. Why buy expensive futon bases when they can be made out of recycled pallets? Refuse skips are a wonderful source of other people's cast-offs. (In some parts of the world it is illegal to remove things from skips without permission.) In big city centres wealthy companies refurnish their executive suites and boardrooms, and throw out carpets and furniture that are of higher quality than most people can ever afford to buy. Second-hand furniture shops, old farm sales, house clearance pieces from removers – there are any number of sources of cheap or free furniture, and a growing number of networks for recycling unwanted items.

In the first world we discard so many things which in poorer parts of the world are looked on as primary resources. A lot of this material is good enough to sit and sleep on, or even to eat from.

Stoves

If we are to take personal responsibility for our needs, then the stove becomes a vital tool. How can you keep yourself warm, apart from by cuddling up to someone else?

Electricity is not a fuel, but a secondary energy source derived from fuels elsewhere. Unless we generate our own electricity by wind or water power, it is unlikely that we are in a position to take responsibility for providing our own electrical heating and cooking facilities. Most people who do generate their own electricity do so on a scale large enough to power lighting, or low wattage appliances, but rarely is home generation achieved on the multiple kilowatt level required to run ovens, electric cooking rings and heating appliances. It is not the most appropriate energy source for these.

Gas from mains supplies can be a comparatively cheap fuel, efficient and relatively clean to burn. We can produce gas from our own methane generation plant, but again this is a fairly major step. There is also bottled gas (propane or butane), which is expensive, but easily transported to places without mains supplies. Anyone installing gas boilers should consider the latest condensing boiler technology, which is very efficient.

Few people are likely to be keen to install oil-fired systems today because of expense. It is an efficient fuel in many ways because oil-fired systems easily adjust output to fluctuating demands. However, there is little to recommend it as a fuel in systems where we are trying to take responsibility for inputs and outputs – unless there's an oil well in your back yard.

This brings us to solid fuel. Coal, and more especially, smokeless derivatives of coal, are efficient fuels, but can have filthy outputs. These fuels burn very hot, and some little residue of the fuel remains; the gaseous outputs are, however, contributory to our atmospheric pollution. Anthracite is the highest grade, being nearly pure carbon. In descending order come: semi-bituminous or dry steam coals, bituminous coal, and lignite, or brown coal. The first stage of coal in the making is peat. The best way to convert energy from peat is to grow trees in it. It does make sense to use coal in areas where there are surface deposits, and where sea coal is found on the beaches. New stoves are being developed which burn the residues nearly completely, and have relatively clean output.

The preferred fuel for the Permaculture stove is likely to be wood. Doesn't burning wood release gases which add to the greenhouse effect? True. And isn't wood less efficient as a fuel than coal? In one sense, yes. The answer is that wood is renewable. If we plant and grow trees faster than we use them for fuel, then we are trapping carbon in the biomass faster than we are releasing it. If we use any of the other fuels we are simply releasing damaging gases and making no attempt to control our input/output cycle. The use of solid fuel stoves will give the option of burning coal or coal-derived fuels as an alternative if wood is in short supply, or for short term increased heat output. The important thing is to understand how to run stoves efficiently.

The open fire has had its day. It is only one-third as efficient as an enclosed stove, and causes draughts in rooms where it is used. If you want the occasional cheerful glow of an open fire, install a stove with glass or opening doors. Stoves should always be placed on

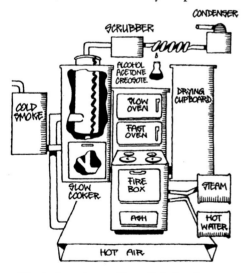

17 A clean stove with multiple functions

an inside wall, so that heat is exchanged as efficiently as possible through the house. Heat passes in three ways, by conduction (through direct contact only), by convection, through the passage of warm air or water, and by radiation, through the transmission of wavelengths of radiation which transmit heat through clear air. Warming radiation is blocked by solid objects.

Radiant heat offers the highest comfort level, and so stoves intended to heat living space should be freely viewed from the widest possible floor area. Convection can be aided by making air ducts from the room with the stove in, through to other parts of the house. Conduction and convection combine in stoves with integral water heaters, either to provide hot water for washing, pumped water for radiator systems, or both. Warm air can be pumped as part of the system, either directly from the stove, or as a heat recovery system, extracting warm air that has risen to the top of the house and returning it to ground floor level. The most efficient systems incorporate heat stores. These may take several forms, from underfloor pits of gravel, through large water tanks, to a massive central core, or under-insulated slab floor.

Whilst it is desirable to extract as much heat as possible from the fire, overcooling of the flue gases will lead to inefficient combustion. This leaves more polluting gases in the chimney vent, and can lead to the build-up of creosote and

97

tar in the chimney. This may later result in chimney fires. Wood stoves should be run extremely hot at least once a day to remove this residue. In theory creosote can be collected as a wood preservative from a tapped flue pipe, but in practice, any build-up indicates the fire is not running hot enough.

Buildings tend either to the massive or the light scale of things. Stone and brick buildings are more massive, heat more slowly, and stay warm for longer. Wooden buildings heat and cool more quickly. In either case it may prove more efficient and comfortable to keep a constant low level of heat input maintaining a desirable ambient temperature than to be putting in high amounts of fuel at peak periods and suffering cold spells whilst the building warms up twice a day.

Waste Usage

Households should look to use their waste products as much as possible. Organic material can be composted. That includes paper, some fabrics, hair and nail clippings as well as vegetable wastes. Given appropriate systems it may include faeces and urine.

It is no good lamenting the failure of local authorities to recycle our waste products if we do not co-operate. Increasingly we see bottle banks, paper and plastic recycling units and can deposit systems. Supermarkets have been shamed into accepting some responsibility for reducing the waste of a consumer society. It is very much a surface change. Far preferable, as in Sweden, to ban the non-returnable bottle, and go back to a system of reusing these artefacts, rather than the high energy cost of continually recycling them. A first stage in planet repair work here is to use these systems enthusiastically when offered. We have to be prepared to sort our rubbish to make it all work.

Some local authorities are getting the message and returning to refuse collection systems which sort garbage as reusable waste, rather than treating everything as junk to be burned and buried. In the United States urban corporations are running out of landfill sites. Since we create the mess, it's up to us to clear it up, and imaginative schemes have appeared all over the world for turning household waste into useful objects once again.

Greenhouses

Greenhouses are an excellent solution to conserving energy, whilst also providing an artificial climate which extends the growing system. By using triple-glazed polycarbonate it has even been shown possible to grow lemons and bananas in an unheated greenhouse at latitude 58 degrees north in Scotland! Greenhouses multiply their uses if positioned against dwellings, offering increased solar gain, and reduction of heat loss by convection. They also create handy gardens in zone zero.

Home as Garden

This use of home as garden can extend within the structure. I have known people grow mushrooms under the bed. Herbs and fresh sprouting for salads on the windowsill are possible in any home. Tenement balconies and city rooftops are capable of producing large quantities of food. Every external wall presents a growing opportunity for climbing plants for food, or for training fruit trees which will benefit from the added heat of the adjacent structure. In return the living plants reduce heat loss from the building by breaking up airflow over the external surface.

Fences and Boundaries

Fences and boundaries offer similar opportunities for high yield. Why just plant an ornamental hedge? A fruiting hedge will be quite as ornamental and offer the added yield of crops each summer and autumn. No fence need be left bare – it is always a marvellous opportunity for climbing squashes, beans, peas, vine fruits and so on.

Security

In an ideal world no-one would worry about security. Every home should be designed with security in mind. Leaving your door unlocked can sometimes deter burglars better than a cheap lock – tentative burglars may think twice about stepping into a house where people might be up and about. Any physical security measure may send an intruder to look for weaker points in the system. They may be safer going round to the back window where they can't be seen, if you've made the front door impregnable. If the worst comes to the worst it's not worth confronting enraged thieves, it's far better to run away. Possessions can be remade, life and limb cannot.

The scale of intervention can be applied and offers some nice biological solutions. There are plenty of ferocious plants which can make boundaries very uninviting. The *ferox* varieties of holly make porcupines look cuddly, and grow quickly into thick hedges. There are many varieties of roses and edible berries with heavy and painful thorns. Blackthorn and hawthorn are quick-growing barriers. Many people are tempted to get watch dogs, but dogs require a lot of care and attention. They can also be a threat to one's own children as well as to other people. Geese and guinea fowl make far more noise and can be much better guards. Geese can be quite vicious; guinea fowl are just noisy, but have the added advantage that they're self-roosting and need very little care. They're both more acceptable to eat in Western society than dogs, offering additional yield.

Viewpoints

People often want to put the house where the view is. They dream of sitting in front of the fire looking out through picture windows at great sweeps of countryside. If there's a fine view you want to preserve then make it a sacred spot, somewhere special to visit, with a bench or pagoda, but a walk away from the house. Let it be appreciated in solitude and reflection. The best views are always from the top of hills, and that's a silly place to put a house. It's a great place to look out from at the land beyond and feel your connections to your community. That's our next port of call.

8 YOUR COMMUNITY

We all live by interaction with our immediate community. Making these ties strong and fruitful is the next priority after looking at how your home is resourced.

What is Community?

Any group of people occupying a physical community are potentially able to *live* as a community, but no-one is going to give away anything to their neighbour unless it is in their self-interest to do so. This is a crucial distinction. Communities which work on the human level do so because people know that they derive individual benefit from the organisation of the community, not because they have an altruistic belief in it being 'better'.

Poverty is the greatest builder of communities. People alive in the Great Depression recall such times: 'we had no choice but to help each other'. If present economic trends continue, and population continues to grow, we can expect to see a lot more poverty. This may be an ideal opportunity to rediscover community.

Many people have attempted to create communities as liberating and self-supporting entities. One of the most fruitful of these was Robert Owen. A radical philanthropist in the 1820s, he attracted support amongst working people in America and Europe, establishing several utopian communities. Owenites called themselves 'socialists'; not in the present sense, but to identify their culture as belonging to the people as a whole rather than the needs of the individual. In 1844 Owenites established the world's first 'co-operative store' at Rochdale in Lancashire.

Historical and International Examples

In many ways the labourist policies which created the welfare state in Britain stemmed from these early philosophies. The main difference is that Owenites saw the community as its own support, not as tied to administrative structures too large for the beneficiaries to control. Present day 'communes' or 'intentional communities', where people live in shared accommodation in small groups, work at building a new and better philosophy of life. Community only has meaning for the future when it extends into and includes all of society.

The concentration of our consumer society on the individual probably seems very strange in Asian or African cultures which have maintained their cohesive strength. Whilst collectivism clearly has drawbacks, it is the only way our burgeoning world population can seriously expect to confront future ecological crises.

Designing for People

People are not all average fit young men. They come in all sizes, shades of opinion, a full range of gender, and have needs which change from the cradle to the grave. Community will only work, therefore, if it is designed *by* all these different people, rather than *for* them. Designing human habitats must invite the participation of the users. Permaculture is a disciplined way of consciously designing human habitats which invites the participation of the users. It is not a method for designers,

aid workers, or other 'experts' to 'solve' the problems of a client group. Such experienced people can facilitate the process of community design, but only where invited.

Co-operation

We are singularly short on the skills of co-operating in modern industrialised society. We have much re-learning to do. To co-operate we need a tolerance of others' failings, and a willingness to learn from our mistakes.

Japan has led the field in how to do this in large-scale industries. The successful outcome is dependent on a highly organised approach to the problem, with groups of people agreeing their targets and working for those

Saul D. Alinsky developed community organising in the US to a fine art. From the 1930s on he developed practical mass organising for poor city dwellers to achieve better living conditions. The Alinsky approach suggests that such change comes from confrontation with institutions across the negotiating table. Alinsky groups use dramatic numbers of people to give poor people power in expressing their needs.

specific goals. It will never come from idealistic exclusion from 'the system', but only from turning large power structures into bodies addressing our real needs through involvement and contact.

Communication

Clearly no such change can work without communication, both spoken and technological. Personal verbal communication is the most effective method of learning and teaching social change. All cycles of intense social development tend to bring with them a rash of publications; the penny pamphleteers of the nineteenth century gave many common people access to ideas for political change. They brought a debate to the people, of which the 'paperback' and the 'periodical' are the modern equivalents.

At the forefront of the information age is the technology which makes global contact as instantaneous as you would like it: telephone, fax, computers, telex, short wave radio (as used by 'hams'), citizen's band radio (CB) have all reached levels of cheapness at which they have fallen into the hands of such subversive agents as you and I. The microcomputer has brought immense power of communication to individuals and organisations of moderate financial means. Despite the precious metals they consume, and the slave labour of their original construction, they may yet be tools of liberation for us all.

Trade

Trade is an essential aspect of global communication, and on a local scale the very thing which pulls communities together. One of the most powerful acts you can make to strengthen your community is to resolve to spend your money locally.

Here is a game for proving this. All trading organisations spend some of their own buying power locally, and some at a distance. Some of the local trade is owned locally, and some at a distance. Thus most supermarkets belong to remote multinationals, and buy most of their inputs on a global market. The shoemakers at the corner shop, who own their own business, may buy all their leather from the local tanner, who in turn buys from local slaughter houses, who in turn buy from local farmers. Everyone has to spend some money on remote inputs (e.g. petrol) and some on local inputs (e.g. labour, local tax etc.).

The significance is the proportion spent with whom. In the supermarket you can reckon that for every £10 you spend, £2 comes back into the community, and £8 leaves on the next banking day. With our shoemaker we keep £8 in the community and £2 leaves. The figures are hypothetical, but realistic. Let's assume the money keeps circulating on the same basis. What happens to it?

Total expended in the left hand

103

| Locally owned/local inputs | | Remotely owned/remote inputs | |
| £ / $ | | £ / $ | |
In	Remaining	In	Remaining
10.00	8.00	10.00	2.00
8.00	5.60	2.00	0.40
5.60	4.48	0.40	0.08
4.48	3.58	0.08	0.02
3.58	2.86	0.02	nil
2.86	2.21		
2.21	1.77		
1.77	1.42		
1.42	1.14		
1.14	0.91		
0.91	0.80		
0.80	0.56		
0.56	0.45		
0.45	0.36		
0.36	0.29		
0.29	0.23		
0.23	0.18		
0.18	0.14		
0.14	0.11		
0.11	0.09		
0.09	0.07		
0.07	0.04		
0.04	0.03		
0.03	0.02		
0.02	0.01		
0.01	nil		
44.35		12.50	

column shows that those who choose to spend their money on locally made produce at locally owned businesses bring four times as much wealth to their community as those who do the opposite *without spending a penny more than they would otherwise.* Local goods can cost twice as much or more and local people are still better off.

Bring wealth to your community – shop locally!

Decision Making

But who runs the community? If the people who constitute the community don't then it's not a community, it's another baronial outpost. However, it is foolish to expect two hundred people to be able to reach accord on anything. So invite your community to engage in trust. The indications are that the maximum number of people who can rationally organise anything is three. If you can ever avoid having more than three people make a decision, then do. Two can get the work of decision-making done quicker, and one is just brilliant. Particularly if it's yourself.

This raises two terrible spectres. The first is that 'someone else is in charge'. The second is 'help! I'm in charge'. The solution is easy. You share out the work of being in charge. Everyone takes responsibility for some aspect of the community, and gets on with being in charge of that bit. You meet in as small a group as possible to discuss progress as infrequently as possible. You're all so busy doing it that you don't need meetings very often. When you have meetings, you report what you've done briefly. If you don't like what's going on you say so in a way which makes it very clear that the person who has that responsibility knows that you are taking responsibility for helping it work better, and is going to get your support. You continually identify other up-and-coming people to take your own role off you soon.

Practise it, it works. It starts and ends with believing that everyone is doing the best they can, and that you are a valuable leader. It all helps develop trust and giving as the main currency of international exchange.

Community Banks

Meanwhile communities can help themselves with the existing currency. Community banking is a tool for local development. Legal structures exist which make it possible for credit unions, trusts and other financial combines to be created by communities for their own benefit. The aim is to attract investment from individuals in the community to be available for reinvestment in their own interests. Why put your savings in the building society for them to invest in someone else's projects over which you have no control? Your investment may actually be harming your health. Start a community bank and help revitalise your own neighbourhood.

Community Transport

Our possessions separate us from each other. This is nowhere truer than in the motor car. Here we sit in another traffic jam on another four-lane highway, thousands of us all alone in our little metal boxes. You have only to enjoy a good chat with your transitory neighbour on a bus in Glasgow, Copenhagen, or any other major conurbation to see how community transport can, not only bring us together, but make travelling a delight.

It would make good economic sense to make public transport free in the centre of major conurbations. This would see off the motor car and the hideous cost to the community of supporting it.

Meanwhile local communities can create this access for themselves by investing in minibuses and so forth for shared beneficial use. Car sharing schemes are another way forward for this policy. Bicycles are a friendly alternative. Then there's always the ultimate community transport – legs. No better way to test your neighbourhood than by regularly walking it. Mind out for dog mess! One hears there are areas of America where the police stop and ask you what you're doing if you cycle or

walk. Hopefully we are in time to prevent these vital limbs atrophying. Skateboarding may be an easy step to achieving withdrawal from the car addiction, and has the added advantage of keeping you out of the dogshit, until you lose your balance.

Opting In

Community, a more caring, sharing society, has achieved some bad publicity through the phrase 'self-sufficiency'. Permaculture design and community living are not about retreat from society, they're about opting in. Community development begins with the conscious decision that what happens in your street is the one thing you can affect in the world. Anyone can join in, starting today.

Benefits

The benefits are having your neighbour understand your needs in life, and agree to co-operate in getting them. This is only going to happen because they get the same benefit in return. It means we create a safer future society, where we all look out for each other. It means that when the hard times come, we're not alone. It means the next generation grow up with these attitudes as part of their culture.

Permanent Culture

Essentially the word culture simply implies a sense of history. Without culture we are individuals, hell-bent on our personal needs to the exclusion of all others. Without history we have no clan loyalty. Without that there is no society, and all dissolves into fear, disorder and violence. We can no longer afford to be individuals scrabbling over one bone. There are too many of us, and we have stretched the resources of our planet too far, and our weapons are too potent to risk this level of conflict in future.

We must relearn a respect for culture.

A society with a strong sense of history has many group and individual rituals which punctuate the cyclical nature of life. Rites of passage are celebrated with dignity and honour. Birth, adolescence, pairing and death are seen not so much as endings and beginnings, but as points of renewal. The seasons demand special repeated actions, words, meals, dances, songs, poems, drawings or even just silences.

To an outsider the rituals may seem absurd, over-intricate or ridiculously naive, irrelevant or foolishly compliant. To the society itself, to its members who perform the time-honoured ceremonies, the importance lies in the sense of place, trust and honour that is given to the individual and the tribe, rather than the form of the ritual itself.

Unfortunately, watching the television does not do much to strengthen the clan structure, or we would have little need of any other ritual, given how much time it consumes in people's lives. We need in the 'Green World' of tomorrow to be aware and conscious of our culture. Perhaps we need new myths, new legends, new songs, and perhaps they are still to be written.

The cornerstone of all strong cultures is the oral tradition. Try making up a song in your head, remembering it, and then teach it to someone else, *without ever writing it down*. It needn't be clever or complicated or even have a good tune. A hymn of praise to something important in your life, perhaps – your favourite pudding, your partner, or the cat. In the age of mass communications and 'literacy' we have lost the art of the most literate, to know and tell their own culture. Practise storytelling. Practise giving instructions on some detailed task, verbally, with no notes. Practice makes perfect.

A culture transferable by voice cannot be changed other than by the speaker. With writing, editing and selection change the context, and messages are not received in their imperfect totality. Impressions are changed, and views are homogenised. The individual's importance is reduced, without strengthening the bonds of society, which can only be strong when each individual is a person of importance. Learning to love using your voice is the best way to make a permanent culture.

I include sign language as the 'voice' of

107

those who have no spoken language, and remind myself and the reader of how important it is for speakers to learn this means of communicating with those who have difficulty with the spoken word.

People with Special Needs

Who are they, these people with special needs? People who use wheelchairs, maybe. You mean disabled people? No. We are all 'able' at some things and 'disabled' at others. At some times in our lives we all have special needs, because we are infants, because we are elderly and infirm, because we are sick, because we are pregnant, because we are injured, because we have learning difficulties, because we are chronically depressed, or whatever. The ability to see this whole area of special needs as an essential provision is what distinguishes a humanitarian society. In a sense it is the definition of community.

Security

All these aspects of community are designed to offer security to the

The Breakthrough Trust works for the integration of deaf and hearing people, running workshops to teach signing, always as a direct communication between those who can hear and those who can't. By talking with deaf people, rather than about them, hearers overcome prejudice and enjoy the learning experience.

individual, by offering them a place in a tribal structure. As much as physical structures cannot imprison the liberated soul, nor can they exclude threat and fear.

Stone walls do not a prison make
Nor iron bars a cage;
Minds innocent and quiet take
That for an hermitage;
If I have freedom in my love,
And in my soul am free;
Angels alone that soar above,
Enjoy such liberty.

Richard Lovelace 1618-1658

9 ABOUT TOWNS

It often seems as if you have to return to the countryside to find the 'green' lifestyle. Yet most people live in urban areas. Can Permaculture offer a way forward for the majority?

Urban Gardening

Visions of Ecotopia are usually rich in images of peaceful living in rich productive land – happy families working and playing together in low energy accommodation, living off the fruits of their own labour.

Our cities today are the opposite of that. There is little public right to use the land. Municipal authorities and private landlords control the land quite jealously. Some town dwellers own a garden or rent one as part of their tenancy of a flat or house. Clearly, town gardens are smaller than you might expect in the country – land is at a premium. Despite this, many allotments have plots standing empty, and very few gardens are used for intensive food production in our towns today. The biggest town crop is the front lawn.

We have to eat to live. Diet is increasingly being understood as central to many more of our health problems than was previously thought. Good diet consists of having enough of the right mix of the right kinds of foods easily available, and that means available locally at the prices you can afford.

Most of the food consumed in our towns has not only been grown using chemical methods, but has additionally then been processed. The preparation of canned or frozen foods, bread or meat, has not only been handled by machine; it has probably seen a string of chemical additives ending with colouring, flavouring and vitamins to add the finishing touches that will make the processed product palatable once more. You can also buy fresh produce in cities, often much more readily available than that to be found in the agricultural countryside, because of wholesaling being based in urban centres.

The methods of modern farming ensure that high levels of additives reach our tables in nearly all our food. Food imported from abroad may contain traces of pesticides and so forth that even our broad-minded chemical censors have seen fit to ban. Organic wholefood, free of such impurities, is scarce, and usually more expensive. It's easy to say that it's worth paying more for – but that isn't an option open to many people whose family commitments, unemployment or age ensure they must make every penny count in the weekly shopping basket. For other busy urbanites, there just isn't the time to travel the extra distance to find such food.

An additional problem with buying fresh produce away from the growing areas is that food loses nutritional value from the moment it's picked. Think how much pollution gathers on the average lettuce after a hot summer's day on the fruit and veg. stall on your local high street. 'Fresh' can clearly mean a wide variety of things.

Cities can, however, provide a much more inviting food supply. Shanghai, in China, grows all its own green food. Even the densely populated trading city of Hong Kong is 40 per cent self-sufficient in vegetables.

Waste land is all around us in our towns, of both short term and long term availability. In the UK we are fortunate in having an Allotments Act which requires local authorities to provide land for allotment associations (minimum: five people), so the legal framework is already there to allow people to reclaim the land. During the Second World War the population was largely fed from these small plots. The many gardens of our towns provide a much richer resource than is apparently used now. Even window boxes can bring forth abundance. The reasons why people should be interested in growing their own food are simple:

i) It's the only way of ensuring that your diet is free from harmful additives;

ii) The exercise and fresh air of gardening is good for you;

iii) Home-grown fresh vegetables reach your table within hours of picking, which means they keep more of their nutritional value than bought vegetables.

The same reasons apply in favour of the commercial cultivation of food within towns. In addition, there is employment to be created in the restoration of waste land to productive usage. State and local assistance to the creation of new businesses can be harnessed to support such schemes. Community-based land schemes can also be started to ensure that unused gardens are let out (with protection of tenure for the producer, and ownership for the freeholder) where age or disability (or lack of interest) prevents cultivation taking place.

Eating may be one of life's most simple pursuits. In a Permaculture City it will also be recognised as amongst the most important, and better attention to its simple delights is a fitting balance for life in cities as the world's pace becomes faster and more technological. If concerned about quality of produce from polluted city environments, soil tests will indicate the availability of necessary nutrients and the presence of harmful toxins. Root crops are more likely to accumulate toxins than leaf vegetables. If your concern stretches to this level, just ask yourself when you had food analysed for purity that was from an unknown source. Cities are stressful places to live.

There are many other fertile aspects of urban dwelling. Concentrated populations make possible many community facilities, such as arts centres, printing workshops, meeting spaces and other human scale installations. They can do this because the density of population makes economically possible facilities which are hard to provide for a more disparate population.

City Farms

Around sixty City Farms operate in cities throughout Britain, but on the present scale their purpose is primarily educational and social. Though they are also productive in a food sense, they can hardly be said to feed the population they serve.

City Farms are an important focus for urban populations, giving substance to understanding about food sources and

China is one outstanding example of urban culture which strives to meet its own needs (see above). In New York an organisation called the Green Guerrillas has been so successful in colonising and making fertile waste areas in the city that they now grow 40 per cent of the city's herb consumption. At Davis in California, the Village Homes area of town has been designed more as a garden with homes in than otherwise. People are welcome to pick fruit from trees that line the pedestrian ways. One area of fruit trees is reserved as a crop, the income from which is used to pay maintenance staff for the town's green areas.

Examples of greenness in the city are a strong symbol for the hope that human communities can be places of creativity and pleasure, rather than greed and conflict. It is delightful to find in central Helsinki a wilderness park stretching over hundreds of acres, reaching to the heart of town.

quality. They also have strong potential as points for bringing together local communities, in rescuing waste land and in providing a central point for community development. The ideal future for our cities would be for the gradual greening of these open spaces to

Ashram Acres is a City Farm in Birmingham, England, started because small-scale growing was the common strand in the native cultures of a community of very mixed races. In turn it has founded a business growing Asian vegetables, a credit union, and runs an advice centre. The gardens are open on certain days to women only, so that women have the opportunity to make contact and learn growing skills in a supportive way. Saturday is open day, and small groups of local people come to help work the farm.

fragment conurbations back into strings of villages, each serving the needs of the immediate population. Food production can be brought back and taken over by the consumers themselves. As computer technology reduces the need for massive centralised administrations, and as town dwellers become increasingly dissatisfied with their polluted and traffic-choked environment, the reclamation of our cities will become more evident. Meanwhile the change has started, and is nowhere more visible than in city farms.

City-Country Fingers

'City-country fingers' is a pattern that lays down a quality in towns achieved by having every part of the city within short distance of green space.

This is the planning policy on Tyneside, in North-East England. As you drive two miles into the conurbation you are confronted with the rare sight of cattle grazing on the large expanse of the Town Moor. Great areas of allotments lie just opposite the TV studios. In many other towns and cities planners are learning that near access to green space is important to people's ability to de-stress urban life.

Increasingly we will see this green space become productive forest or small scale farmland. Town dwellers can gain access to vacant lots to plant trees or grow food. They can insist that their parks authorities stop planting ornamental cherries, and start putting in fruiting varieties. 'But people will take the fruit!' say the municipal authorities. 'Yes, that's the idea', you reply.

Farm Link-ups

Another avenue for increased understanding is for consumers and growers to make a direct contract. Farm link-ups have been hugely successful in Japan, where as many as two hundred thousand customers buy this way. In Germany, Switzerland and the United States they are under way, and they are just starting in Britain too.

Farmers the world over are hard pushed to earn a margin which keeps pace with other sources of income. One of the main difficulties is that when you are competing with industry for labour, the wage rate becomes prohibitive, particularly as industrialised nations all have policies of looking for cheap food. They would rather import food from poorer nations than look after their own farmers better.

Consumers are becoming more aware that they want quality food of known provenance and purity. The solution is for collectives of town consumers to contract with farmers near cities to meet their needs. Consumers specify the crops they wish to purchase, and may be available to provide labour at peak times. Customers can pre-order their crops for the year, or buy-in appropriate sized shareholdings for the year. An annual statement will show the food supplied and might give a comparative breakdown of savings against supermarket prices. Farmers get a known market, and may be funded by their customers, as well as the possibility of overcoming labour problems, and therefore being able to grow more intensively. The consumers get the product they want and the chance of a bit of healthy country exercise.

City Culture

It is evident that in cities the concept of zoning is very difficult to unravel. Every home can have a zone one, sure enough, but zone two may be at the allotment some distance away, or if you buy in all this level of produce, it can be on the other side of the globe. Clearly the energy cost of transporting your daily needs over long distances makes nonsense of our present urban structures. Far from wealthy commerce and industry supporting poor peasant economies it is the latter who carry the financial and physical burden of supporting the city dwellers' high rate of consumption.

The Lee Valley in North East London stretches from the heart of industrial land on the River Thames, miles back into Epping Forest. It supports a string of reservoirs and water works (its recycled sewage water is the largest tributary of the Thames) and is an excellent example of how zone 5 (wilderness) can be brought right into the heart of our cities. When city effluents are treated through biological systems by consciously designing marsh lagoon and reed bed water cleansing on a vast scale, all our cities can have their effluents naturally cleansed and benefit from the wetland wildlife and crops.

Cities are in their autumn, all over the world. Choked to death by their own burgeoning, they are withering into the next stage of their evolution. Just as, amidst decay, autumn offers the promise of renewal, the buds of newly-regenerated human scale townships lurk beneath the grimy exterior. They need nurturing.

113

Cosmopolitan communities offer the widest range of cultural mix and as such are extremely good places to learn from people from the human melting pot. In practice these cultures are often separated, if not into ghettos, at least by barriers of ignorance and prejudice. The 'first world' has much to learn from the rest of the planet. When there is environmental disaster and social collapse in the future it is the citizens of the poor South who have the experience and the skills to deal with it. We would do well to build the cultural links now which make possible an open sharing global future. Our cities provide the ideal place to plant that seed.

10 WILDERNESS

Furthest out from our home zone is the area of wilderness, potentially the most important and fragile resource we need to preserve.

Why Wilderness?

Wilderness might be defined as environments which are self-controlled, unchanged by human activity. Writing in Southern Scotland I am conscious that the nearest untouched wilderness forest is in Czechoslovakia, half a continent away. It comes as a shock to people in a crowded small island like Britain to be told there is no wilderness left. Even the tiny island of Rockall, eighty kilometres off the Hebridean coasts, has had every plant counted by naturalists. North America is less densely populated than Europe, and has active wilderness conservation organisations. Nevertheless, very little of our planet is left in a truly wild state. The hand of human intervention is far-reaching.

Wilderness is crucial to a balanced lifecycle on the planet's surface. It gives mammal species the only opportunity they have to complete their lifecycles according to their own way, by allowing them free range, mating and feeding as nature intended. It is a chance for the natural regeneration of woodlands, plants and animals, birds and insects to take place. Wilderness is the only complete system on the planet, a self designing storehouse of species. Destroying wilderness removes a magnificent tool for learning.

Many of the areas we see as 'wilderness' are human-created deserts. Not just the Sahara, but also the acid heathlands of Europe, the treeless Highlands of Scotland, the dry massifs of France and Spain and the steppes of Asia are degraded wastelands derived from burning out game, slash-and-burn agricultures and overgrazing. This degradation has taken centuries, but this is a tiny timescale compared to the thousands of years over which the former forest cover evolved.

On a geological timescale we need have little concern for the planet's ability to survive. Life in all temperate areas is

> Bounded on two sides by the sea, and protected by its inhospitable terrain and distance from centres of population, Olympic National Park on the Olympic Peninsula, in Washington State, is one of America's best-preserved natural wildernesses. No roads and few footpaths breach the wilderness, a treasure intact for the future.

expendable in the cycles of ice-ages. Six thousand years ago (four thousand years after the building of the Great Pyramid in Egypt) Northern Europe and Canada were largely bare of trees and people, as the ice receded. Our own longevity as a species is threatened by the next ice-age.

Lastly, as anyone can testify who has experienced true wilderness, these areas of the planet are sacred for their beauty and abundance alone. How could anyone who had destroyed a rainforest, or a wild oak wood, a penguin colony or a dolphin habitat sleep easy at night? Yet unless we protect existing wilderness, and set aside space for the regeneration of new ones, then we are all party to this kind of destruction.

Regeneration Techniques

As there is precious little wilderness remaining, then we need to make more. We may never know the full reasons why, precisely because they are an investment for the future. Once we have killed the last living thing, how then will we live? This principle insists that we help regenerate what we have over-culled.

The best and most effective technique for regenerating wilderness is to do nothing. If we plant or plan a wilderness, then it is not wild, it is a plantation. We do, however, need to protect the space. This means fencing, either physically, or metaphorically. In Britain and North Africa the great destroyers of forest, the people, brought in sheep and goats in vast numbers to achieve the destruction. The wealth of Britain is so founded on this cycle of destruction that the Speaker of the House of Commons still sits, ceremonially, on The Woolsack. The wonder-beast of the Middle Ages, with its yield of meat, milk and fibre, has denuded many a landscape of trees.

Other predators to exclude are rabbits, deer, people, and pollution. The natural cycle of any environment is always one of succession. If unhindered nature will colonise even the most marginal area, and in time build fertile systems. For instance, into the bare moorland comes bracken, which draws potassium from the subsoil, and in dying, automatically mulches the ground to protect against erosion. Depleted bare soils are its niche, and there it thrives.

By simply protecting moorland which has gone to bracken, gorse and broom will appear, or on very wet ground bog

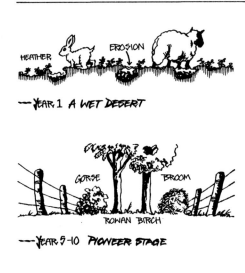

— YEAR 1 *A WET DESERT*

— YEAR 9-10 *PIONEER STAGE*

— YEAR 20-100 *REGENERATED FOREST*

fruit of Eden and cast the seeds in their droppings, spreading the edge of paradise a little each year. With each stage of regeneration the richness of plant and animal species increases as microclimates and niches are brought into being.

We can speed up the process by introducing pioneers (gorse, broom, alder and so on). That, definitely, is all we need do. We have examined one particular succession here for one particular type of wilderness. In fact it is possible to create very small areas of wild land and water within human systems. Every community should plan to reserve some of its land for wilderness. Even a town garden can have its unweeded corner for wildlife to breed, butterflies, birds and mammals alike.

Wild Harvests

myrtle. These are nitrogen-fixing plants, and need potassium before they can establish. They succeed bracken, flourishing to leave a richer soil. Gorse will spread outwards, dying at its heart, and into this space in the enriched soil, rowan and birch will seed. They are edge trees and will gradually build scrub woodland. In time they will give way to climax trees, oak, pine and ash in particular.

The seeds are brought by wind, by stream and by living creatures. Birds are the outriders of the forest who eat of the

Wilderness is abundant without human planning. At one time, when populations were a fraction of today, we lived as hunter-gatherers, living entirely off the yield of this wild harvest. We took only the surplus the wild had to offer. Until very recently the Indians of the Amazon rainforest lived by this same skilled management of their environment. It is no small tragedy that we put commercial exploitation before preserving this treasure. Yet it is not surprising when we look at the wanton destruction of our landscape and at the damage done

Advice: freely obtainable in most pubs

Blackberries: edible, vertical hedging

Comfrey: edible, green manure, vitamin E source

Driftwood: firewood, timber, ornaments

Elder: edible flowers and fruit, prolific compostable fibre

Fireweed: edible (asparagus substitute), animal fodder

Ground Elder: edible salad

Horseradish: edible root and leaves, green manure

Ivy: *(Hedera helix)* winter fodder for bees, fodder for some livestock

Jew's Ears: edible fungi

Kingfishers: magical moments of reverie

Lime trees: flowers make a relaxing tea

Mallow: edible flowers rich in vitamin C, edible leaves

Nuts: hazels for winter food

Oyster Mushrooms: edible

Pigeons: edible, feathers, bones for manure

Quercus **species:** acorns, from the oak, sweet enough to eat, timber

Rose Hips: edible, rich source of vitamin C

Sycamore: firewood, timber, insect fodder

Tweed: a river bubbling with messages and life from all quarters of a vibrant planet

Umbelliferae: a marvellous family of useful plants including: fennel, ground elder, hogweed, chervil, wild carrot, wild parsnip, giant hogweed, some of which are edible, some poisonous, some green manure, and all pioneers

Violet: one of the edible flowers

Willow: natural aspirin, basketry materials, firewood

Xyloliths: (things made of sawdust) there are masses of wasps' nests, beautiful constructions which aid pollination of trees, and for which (one day) I shall find a human usage

Yarrow: edible salad, medicinal herb

Zzzzzzz: and there are still plenty of places in this tiny radius with the space and attraction to be meditative spaces in which we may breathe and rest.

to native peoples in Europe and North America. We are allowing a process of destruction of a resource which has already been completed in our own environments.

The power of nature to occupy even the smallest niches with productive regenerative systems is such that we can see harvestable yield in even the smallest wilderness. Wild species offer many economically valuable crops. A five minutes walk from my house offers the free yields shown opposite.

There are hundreds more yielding species within the five minutes' walk of my home in one fairly insignificant part of one small island. Knowing the uses of wild species greatly increases available foods. You can eat salad 365 days a year in any temperate zone, if you know which plants are edible – and it's all free.

This is an invitation to extend the range of species you regard as edible. It also implies that the intensive work we put into gardens and farming might well be reduced, with no reduction in standard of living, if we simply learnt to recognise as beneficial the many crops which (largely ignored) stare us in the face.

Two warnings:

1 Eat nothing about which you are not sure. If in doubt, leave it out. Some wild plants are deadly poisonous, and it isn't worth the risk.
2 It is an offence in Britain, and other countries, to pick wild plants from

other people's land, without permission. This law has the interest of wilderness very much in mind. In learning about what is edible and useful in other ways, it is also very easy to learn what is rare and should be preserved. No-one is going to get excited about you taking dandelion leaves. They may well feel differently if you dig up orchid roots. Take care to respect the countryside if you take to foraging for food.

The extent to which it is within our power to create wilderness is greater than we think. Huge areas of the developed world have disappeared beneath lawns. Yet greensward can be highly productive, whilst still being green. Here's a list of ten species to turn your lawn into an edible space:

Chickweed, dandelion, fat hen, ground elder, hairy bittercress, land cress, marigold, sorrel, spinach, wild garlic.

These will make your lawn a vibrant green wilderness, without grass or chemical additives, and they are all edible in part or whole.

See the Plants section in the booklist for wild plant references.

11 LANDSCAPE

Understanding the form and content of landscape enables us to place and design human needs in context.

Maps

Maps let us to look at large spaces in two dimensions, giving us a language whereby we can understand landshape even from a book. They also reduce scale, so that we can sit at home and look intelligently at a river valley system, or fifty acres, without moving. They take the large and complex and make it manageable.

Maps are offered in a number of scales. This is slightly complicated by the incomplete changeover in the UK from Imperial to Metric systems. Metric are listed to the left, and Imperial to the right below.

1:50 000 Scale was 1:63 360 (1″ to the mile)
1:25 000 Scale was (2½″ to the mile)
1:10 000 Scale was 1:10 550 (6″ to the mile)
1:2500 Scale was (25″ to the mile)
and for urban areas only:
1:1250 Scale (50″ to the mile, or 500sq m per map)

Smaller scale maps than these serve little purpose in landscape or community design, although they are useful to view long distance communications, or the shape of a large watershed. The larger the scale the more expensive the map. 1:50 000 Scale shows roads and footpaths. 1:25 000 includes field boundaries. These are small scale maps and are useful to gain a broad view. From 1:10 000 Scale upwards the drawings are technically 'plans', not maps. This scale is the definitive map for footpaths. At 1:2500 we have field sizes and reference numbers marked. They also show water courses in detail, and are the base maps from which all other maps are taken, except that they do not show contours. For large scale, detailed planning you really need to work at this scale and draw in the contours.

There are also geological and soil maps. Geological maps (usually only at 1:50 000 scale) show the underlying rock structure which has great influence on the landscape. Soil maps show soil types and, if accompanied by the detailed guides which are also available, are invaluable for determining what land usage is possible on a site. There are also maps showing the grading of land for agricultural purposes on the following scale:

Grade 1: Land capable of producing a very wide range of crops

Grade 2: Land capable of producing a wide range of crops

Grade 3: Land capable of producing a moderate range of crops

Grade 4: Land capable of producing a narrow range of crops

Grade 5: Land suited only to improved grassland and rough grazings

Grade 6: Land capable of use only as rough grazings

Grade 7: Land of very limited agricultural usage

ungraded: Built up areas

Some private companies offer satellite or infrared aerial photographs which give useful graphic information about climate, building efficiency, water forms or landshape.

Maps help us understand orientation of a site and review the consequences of detailed placements of buildings, structures and trees or other crops on a site.

Symbols

Symbols vary from map scale to map scale and from publisher to publisher. Every map should have a 'key' which explains what all the symbols mean. The use of symbols means that many more pieces of information can be fitted into a given space than if accurate miniature drawings were made of each detail, or if long-winded verbal explanations were required.

The Map is Not the Land

Maps are not the land itself, only a tool. Microclimates don't show up, and the contours shown are always a generalisation. You will find the land has a lot more variation than is apparent from the map. For detailed knowledge, you must walk the land. The map cannot show climate and seasonal variation either. Nor will it record all the detailed little changes since the map was last reviewed. Notwithstanding these comments, maps are invaluable aids.

Contours

Contours are imaginary lines which join every point in the landscape at a given height above 'datum', which is usually sea-level. The distance they are apart will be specified on the map. Contours give a language which can be 'read' to understand landshape.

121

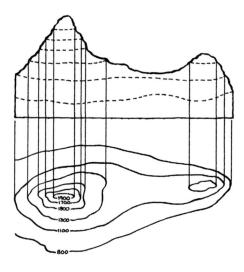

First distinguish valleys, which offer shelter, from ridges, which are exposed. Valleys tend to collect water, ridges to drain it. Secondly, become aware of when a slope is convex or concave. Can you tell how steep a slope is from the map? Is flat land obvious? Remember that flat land occurs on ridge tops as well as on hillsides, and in valley bottoms, and not just on the great plains. If you can understand from a map these variations in shape, then you are well placed to see the effects on the energy flows in the landscape.

Water Tables, Water Flow

No-one has access to all the landscape, or time or strength to deal with it. This matters, because we are always only looking at a section of energy flow. It appears that water leaves and enters our environment at certain points, although water moves across whole continents and oceans. Understanding these larger flows is helpful.

Water operates across three dimensions and time, usually flowing downwards. It is not just running over the ground, but also under the ground and in all living matter. The water table is the level to which water has saturated the ground below us. Rocks and soils will affect differently how the water penetrates and is stored in the ground. Some make impervious layers (that is – impassable to water), others absorb and hold water.

The height of the water table is crucial from the point of view of the viability of springs and wells. Springs tend to appear in hillsides near the top level of the water table. In exceptionally dry weather the water table may sink so far that the springs dry up, or the well no longer reaches down to a usable supply.

When water collects in sufficient quantity it creates a flow, always seeking (as all energy does) to balance forces by coming to rest. This it can only do at the 'lowest point'. Water naturally flows in curved lines giving it high 'turbidity', or a good ability to carry particles. Water forced into straight channels loses turbidity, and deposits any matter it is carrying. The effect of this is silting-up and much labour is required to dredge straight channels clean. If the available channel is narrowed, the speed of the water will increase, or if broadened, slow down.

Prevailing and Other Winds

The effect of prevailing winds on the local scale depends on the shape of the land and the available shelter. Other winds, although less frequent than the prevailing one, may be more damaging. Three days of icy polar gales in the early spring can ruin a fruit crop which cheerfully withstands two hundred days of cool moist winds up from the tropics.

If you have no local experience, ask your neighbours. Detailed records can be obtained from the Meteorological Office in Britain. In the United States there are TV and newspaper records, local airports, local fire stations or the Forestry Department. Schools and colleges often keep records. There are plenty of sources. The most invaluable document you can obtain is a windrose. This shows in printed form the duration of winds from each point of the compass, and the proportion of that time for which they blew at different stated velocities. This information can be expensive to buy, but will soon pay for itself in saving mistakes through bad planning. You can set up your own weather station, or monitor daily forecasts and records in the papers and on the airwaves.

Climate (Cold/Warm?)

Taking long slow walks on frosty mornings, and watching where thaw sets in, can tell you a lot about where it is very cold in winter. Frost pockets are not the place to put dwellings or crops that need the benefit of the ends of the growing season to make their cycle complete. Some slopes will be warmer, others particularly cold. This may be because of exposure to the sun and wind, shade from trees or buildings, or due to wetness or dryness of the ground.

These are all important considerations in making appropriate placements on the landscape.

Rock and Soil Structure

Rocks are a historical record of other life on the planet, and they are inescapably a daily influence on our lives. Some were formed as the planet was made. The outer crust has rocks which are largely solid, although the inner core of the planet is composed of magma – hot rocks which are liquid. Along fault lines in the Earth's crust we get volcanic activity, as magma forces its way into the sea or the atmosphere, cooling to form volcanic rocks. Volcanoes also throw up ash in the form of pumice. Adjacent rocks may be melted by the heat of the volcanic eruption, making metamorphic rocks. Other rocks are formed as layers of sediment build up under water, or in deserts. Wind, temperature changes and water erode existing rocks which break into smaller fragments. The eroding forces move these sediments across the surface of the Earth and into the seas.

Some of the rock particles form soils, often with organic matter. There are many kinds of soils, from those in fertile alluvial plains, which have been left by river flows as they moved their courses, to boulder clays, remnants of previous ice ages. Some soils, like peat, are almost pure organic matter, built up from rotted mosses and trees, others, like sand, are pure rock particles. Sedimentary rocks remind us of their interaction with living matter by carrying a record of plants and animals in fossil form. Chalk is entirely composed of the remains of tiny sea creatures.

Some rocks display a preordained symmetry, their chemical composition reflecting regular shapes, such as the famous hexagonal columns of basalt in the Giant's Causeway in Northern Ireland. The characteristics of individual rocks are affected by rate of cooling when they formed, relative temperature and pressure of their situation, and oxidation and weathering which has taken place since.

Soils are usually classified as running from sand through loam to clay. The main differences between the extremes of soil are in size and shape of particle. Sand particles may be six thousand times larger than clay, and are round or sharp in shape. Clay particles are mostly plate-shaped, giving clay its slippery feel.

Sand absorbs water and dries quickly. Its fertility is greatly improved by large additions of humus (rotted vegetable matter). It is most likely to be deficient in available minerals.

Loam is an admixture of the two extremes and is very workable, whilst relatively retentive of water.

Clay is mineral-rich, relatively impervious to water, and when wet it becomes as unworkable as cold porridge, being a good substitute for concrete when dry. It needs breaking up to improve drainage and will also benefit from increased humic content. It will improve with the addition of lime, 'flocculating' to form larger particles.

There is little you can do to manage rocks in a landscape on the broad scale. Sedimentary rocks, being layered, will split easily and make good building materials; granitic rocks are less desirable as building blocks because of their high background radiation levels. At the end of the day you only have the rocks there are to work with.

Soil is different. It will have some strong characteristics, which are hard to change, but it can more easily be improved. The ideal soils for growing are high in humic content and slightly acid with good mineral content. These will support the widest range of crops. There are, however, crops which will adapt to a wide range of conditions from salt marsh to freezing deserts.

Dam Sites

Certain land features suggest good points to place dams. Dams are a worthwhile investment, even in wet climates, because they offer storage of energy high in the landscape. If small scale dams become more common, then we reduce the necessity for large centralised structures which are more ecologically damaging, and more prone to failure than a web of small resources. They enable quite small scale farmers or townships to take responsibility for their own water supply. If recent weather vagaries are anything to go by, they will also offer greatly increased security against extremes of drought. An additional aspect is that strategies for soil management which encourage the collection and retention of rainwater will reduce run-off. Increased water storage will be needed to compensate for the lower throughflow.

Valley dams are the easiest to construct, and can be placed in series down descending valleys. Other sites are possible between rounded hilltops ('saddle dams'), on any sloping hillside, and even on flat ground, be that a ridge or a plain. The higher in the landscape the water storage is created, the more potential energy is stored.

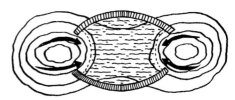

Saddle Dam

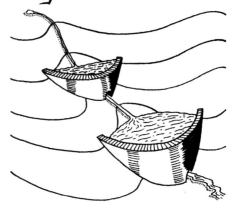

Valley Dams

Complete Ring Dam

In reading the landscape it is well to note such potential sites early, as they are best created before other structures. Also look for ways of channelling water into the dams. Long collection drains can be run down-contour to gather water into comparatively concentrated areas. They can also be used to make water run back up valleys for irrigation, and for gathering water from ridges, and bringing it in to valley storages. Understanding slope and contour is important for making such systems work.

Dams are potentially extremely destructive intrusions on the landscape, and should only be built with expert knowledge. Knowing where to put them is easier to learn. If seriously contemplating large dam construction, take professional advice.

Wind Sites

Where relatively small output is required, there is less concern about site suitability. However, on any site, winds which are too strong will damage the equipment. Sites with constant moderate winds are better.

Where larger constructions are envisaged, landshape is very important. Trees, fences, buildings, cliffs, and irregularly shaped landscapes all create high turbulence in their wind shadow. The ideal shape for stability of performance and safety from stress damage in windmills is a smooth flow shape. In general this means that the best sites for large windmills are round-shaped hills of regular cross section. These appropriate sites are easy to tell apart on maps from the regularity of their contour shape. There is an added advantage on such sites. Windflow over such shapes causes

increased velocity above the hill and raised pressure at ground level. There is therefore stronger and faster wind available for collection.

Wind velocity increases with altitude. This is not so marked at coastal sites, where there are already higher winds than inland. Ground level inspection is needed to establish that sites are usable, as boggy ground or poor access will make construction impossible.

Proximity to point of usage is an important consideration. Windmills for motive power need to work on site, and if using the site for electricity generation, much power will be lost through voltage drop on long runs of cable.

Slope Management and Erosion Resistance

In managing landscape a consciousness of slope means also being aware of the dangers of erosion. Slopes over 30 degrees are unsuitable for cultivation, and should be kept in permanent pasture, or preferably woodland. Even the continual grazing of sheep and cattle can lead to down-slope soil movement and damage to the hillside. Erosion can be extremely damaging over very small areas, causing soil losses in thousands of tonnes in individual storm incidents.

Once the protective cover of biomass is breached on steep hill slopes the degradation of the landscape can be very quick. When ploughing hillslopes, damage can be minimised by ploughing at right angles to the slope, either on or slightly off the contour. Few tractor drivers will enjoy the discomfort of spending their day perched at an angle on one buttock to do this, and there is always the danger of turning over the vehicle. There are (expensive) tractors which can tilt their cabs, or adjust their wheel angles to compensate. Horse-drawn ploughs are an easier method of ploughing slopes. Better still, don't till at all.

Erosion can be stemmed by the intro-duction of pioneer plants (biological intervention). Seeding quick growing species into the bare soil will help. Cross contour barriers can be constructed of inorganic materials (mechanical intervention).

In recent years expertise has grown in the area of geotextiles. These are meshes and woven materials designed to give reinforcement, separation or filtration where needed in the landscape. A steep

---

Roman roads, mediaeval cath-edrals and early railway viaducts were often built on bundles of sticks which gave spreading of load to enable heavier structures to 'float' on soft ground. The use of natural fibres is clearly more sustainable than using petro-chemical products. Either way geotextiles are not a new idea.

---

newly cut bank, such as a dam, may be seeded and overlaid with a mesh. The mesh gives interim protection from rain splash, and provides a supporting structure for retentive root systems as they establish. In this case the likely seed would be grasses. In more severely exposed situations successive layers might be used, with a surface scattering of rock to dissipate water energy. Overflow areas might be lined with porous material which allows flood water to seep into the ground without causing erosion.

Changing Landscape: Earthworks, Water Storage and Forest

Engineers have shown many times over the last few thousand years that we can indeed move mountains. We have a great ally in such work in the form of road engineers who are experienced in shifting and stabilising large volumes of earth and rock. They also have appropriate equipment for doing this work – bulldozers and scrapers. Do not assume that because these people work with heavy machinery, they are insensitive to the environment. The digger driver who spends his life dredging waterways is probably the best person to ask where the water fowl nest!

Earthworking on the large scale is appropriate for constructing roads, drains, dams, diversion channels, and flood meadows, and earth bermed buildings, where needed. You can do these jobs with a bucket and spade, but this is just as destructive in the long run, and a lot slower and more tiring. It's much better to get stuck in with heavy equipment, and repair the damage quickly by reseeding and planting appropriately. The scars quickly heal.

Diversion drains and swales running round hillsides are an essential part of increasing water storage in the landscape. Swales are a method of designing ditches which are absorbent to run-off water. With sensitive planning there is no reason why roads and swales cannot be the same structures on large parts of the landscape. Our present practice of draining and getting rid of water at every opportunity hastens the cycle by which water returns to the sea instead of maximising its potential as it passes through our system. Swales present great possibilities for keeping water on the contour, and increasing crop yields in strip cultivations.

Forests are great retainers of water. The biological structure of the trees is largely water, and the root systems increase the capacity of the soil to build humus and to hold water in the tiny spaces between particles. Planting forests along contours will tend to trap down-slope runoff and erosion, creating terracing effects. If these are slightly off contour, then gently sloping access is left for future harvesting efforts.

Creating a forest is a major adjustment to the landscape. The ambient temperature where I live has probably increased ten degrees Fahrenheit in the sixty years since Kielder forest was planted thirty miles to our south-west. Forests are great interceptors of moisture in the atmosphere, increasing precipitation through condensation on their massive surface areas. They expire water vapour in large volumes, making more humid air available for precipitation downwind. Forest, or at very least permanent pasture, is essential cover for the watersheds high in the landscape. Degradation of this natural cover invites dropping of the water table and erosion.

12 ENERGY

If we divide our living area into zones then energy is the dimension which crosses the boundaries and transports all our inputs and outputs from our home out into the community or back. Careful management of this energy expenditure is the key to creating sustainable human settlements.

If you are puzzled how to select a starting point for designing . . . try working out from the energy interfaces

Gordon L Clegg

towards cool air masses. High pressure will move towards low pressure. Things with greater gravitational force attract things with lesser gravitational force. In lay terms, 'nature abhors a vacuum'.

Entropy Versus Availability of Energy

Energy is called kinetic energy if it is doing work, such as a rotating wheel bearing a vehicle going downhill. Potential energy is energy available to do work. Thus a stationary vehicle at the top of a hill has high potential energy. Entropy is the state of energy when it is chaotic. Entropy is not an absolute; it is a relative measure. Living beings have low entropy. As things decay or become inert they gain entropy. The laws of physics tell us that the tendency of all energy is to seek forms of high entropy.

Thus heated air masses will seek to equalise their temperature by moving

Conservation

Fasting is an act of homage to the majesty of appetite.

Laurie Lee 1975

The fastest way to reduce wastage is not to use energy in the first place, eating raw food being one example. The principle can be extended to more complex situations. For instance, eating lentils may seem like a low energy input source of protein. All well and good. But lentils are grown in hot climates using cheap labour and high transport costs to bring them to your door. Why not grow and dry your own cool climate field beans, instead?

Is this a hair-shirt philosophy? Appetite is dulled by overstimulation, so if we enjoy luxuries frequently and in large quantities then they cease to have the same pleasurable effect. Far better to party less often, and enjoy it more.

Primary Versus Secondary Uses

An interface is the time at which two different energies meet. Whether they remain separate, power each other or intermingle is part of the management of energy. If we are conscious of the natural characteristics of each form of energy we can make these interfaces work for our benefit.

A front to rear drive shaft on a car can be turned into the rotation of axles, allowing the car also to turn corners (when each wheel is travelling at a different speed) by the use of a differential gear. The gear is the device which manages the energy interface. Without it, even the most efficient internal combustion engine cannot propel the vehicle. The carburettor, which mixes air and fuel to make a combustible mixture, is another crucial interface in this machine.

Biological systems have such energy interfaces also. This is why soil management is crucial. Many of the organisms which co-operate to make plants healthy flourish around the permeable cell walls of root structures. Here minerals, water, growing cells and nutrients are each distinct, but each interfaced to provide an efficient functioning system with mutual benefits to all living components.

To manage a system well we must become aware of where relations are direct (primary energy sources) and where indirect (secondary energy sources). Thus wood in our stove is a fuel, but electricity in a heater element is a secondary energy source derived from a remote consumption of fuel. These distinctions are important because at each interface some energy is lost to the system. Nothing is 100% efficient, and so the more energy interfaces, the less efficient the system overall. Electricity arriving at the house from a coal-fired power station is never more than 30 per cent of the original energy input to the system. 70 per cent was 'wasted'.

Yet we can increase yield by harnessing the 'leakage' at the energy interfaces. Thus combined heat and power systems are far more efficient. Here the waste heat from electricity generation is used for space heating homes, factories or greenhouses. Observation and understanding of the energy cycle helps us make effective usage.

Food as Energy

Without food energy people cannot live. Energy debates often describe all manner of engineering devices and forget the biological flow of energy. Food is stored solar energy, produced by living organisms accumulating nutrients. There is an energy interface when the inputs of sunlight, rain and soil are converted into vegetable matter. There is another when our bodies convert the food into cell matter or energy in our bodily functions.

Making the food cycle as efficient as possible is necessary to limit our destruction of the planetary environment. Food growing should be the ultimate passive solar system.

Sun Power

The sun is our senior primary energy source. Ultimately all power is solar power. Wood is solar energy stored by growing trees, and becomes coal and oil over millions of years of compaction underground. When we burn coal we are releasing trapped solar energy from countless generations ago.

The whole cycle of water evaporation and precipitation is made possible by sunlight, either directly or through the force of the winds, which are the result of uneven solar heating. We could not get energy from wind or water, but for the sun.

We could not see to work but for its light, and the moon lights the night by reflecting solar energy. The planets rotate under the gravitational influence of the sun, and the other stars visible at night are distant suns performing similar cycles.

Energy Cycles

Energy implies continual movement. All matter is composed of particles (atoms, molecules and so on) which are not themselves definable as 'solid' substances, but may rather be energy operating in wave forms. The faster these particles move, the higher the energy levels. Thus hot objects have their atoms moving faster than the same objects when cool.

Energy does not begin or end, it occurs in cycles, and the frequency and wavelength of each cycle determines the form of the energy. In any process, energy is continually changing form. When a train moves at speed it displaces air, and creates wind as the air is pushed aside. Heat is generated by the combustion of fuel. The chemical composition of the fuel changes as it is burnt. Friction between the wheels and the rails generate heat. The noise of the train is waves of energy travelling out from the centre of all this activity. The flows of heat, noise, light, wind, vibration and so on are all absorbed into the overall environment where they too are converted to other energies, in a web too complex to measure.

This ability of energy to move out from the incident is why we can never fully comprehend the consequence of any action. This is also why we should be careful how we use energy.

Maximised Flow from Source to Sink

'Energy efficiency' involves understanding the relationships of energy flow in all directions, temporal as well as physical, not just using a source of energy once thoroughly.

An example will help. I have a garden and I return to the soil compost made from waste vegetable matter. I have completed a cycle, but have I maximised it? No, there are always more possible loops which can be designed into the cycle. Firstly, I could have fed the scraps to hens, storing energy in the living matter of the birds, and gaining the additional yields they provide. The waste matter would still return to the garden

through their droppings. Then I could increase the energy yield of the hens by running them in a 'chicken tractor'. This would be a small movable pen in which the hens were confined. The natural characteristics of the hen being to feed and scratch on the ground, they gradually clear small plots for gardening. I move them on at frequent intervals to new pastures. Meanwhile I am saved the energy of digging the plots myself.

Nothing is ever 'wasted' in the sense of becoming useless. 'Waste' just means we haven't imagined a yield for that part of the flow. We should always try and return used energy to a point 'higher' in the system, leaving it with high potential.

Water and Wind as Energy

Water and wind are attractive sources of energy to emerging industrial cultures, because it is easy to sense the *power* behind their natural flows. There is an inexorable strength about gentle tides and small streams which is shown in their continual ability to grind rock, and erode much harder substances than water itself. The power of wind and water at storm strength is awesome.

Wind and water also have disadvantages as power sources. They are hard to control, and they are site specific, being by nature of variable force. Light breezes provide little usable

23 Maximising energy storage in a water course

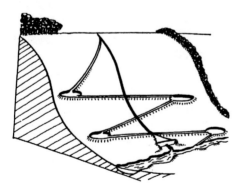

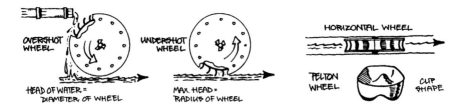

24 Some examples of watermills

power, storm force winds too much to use safely, so that windmills have to cut out above design-acceptable strengths of gusting. Water is hard to capture at its most energetic (e.g. stormy seas) and very gentle flows will not drive much machinery. Water has the advantage over wind in that it can be stored, by creating dams or tanks to hold a flow which can be released at a later time. Both water and wind power are often most available away from where the greatest users of energy are concentrated.

One way round this last problem is to use water and wind to drive turbines or sails which will in turn drive generators, so creating electricity. This is energy in a form which can be transmitted across great distances, and converted to other useful forms of power (light, mechanical force, heat) at remote sites. It is also a form of energy which can be stored, either in batteries, or by propelling other mechanical storages, such as pumping water or winching weights to higher levels.

Harnessing Water

The most successful way of harnessing water power through history has been the water wheel – this can be arranged in three main ways: overshot, undershot and horizontal. The first two assume the axis of the wheel is horizontal (with the wheel rotating in the vertical plane), and the last that the axis is vertical (with the wheel rotating in the horizontal plane). This is also the descending priority of power.

Overshot wheels will only work if there is enough 'head' of water. The 'head' is the distance through which the water must fall vertically to drive the wheel. Undershot wheels can operate on half the 'head' for the same size of wheel, whilst horizontal wheels require only enough throughflow to turn them.

The efficiency of the whole arrangement can be increased by minimising the losses in the wheel. A Pelton Wheel has buttock-shaped cups which are particularly efficient at

133

absorbing the force of the water. Narrowing the inlet pipes can increase the speed of the water on the wheel. Dams creating water storage are another method of increasing available power. Corn mills (grinding flour) tended not to run for more than a few hours a day, so millponds could be built to run them which filled for the balance of the day. Another way of extracting maximum benefit from the wheel was common in Victorian water mills. This is the 'longshaft' – a system for propelling a drive shaft from the wheel which could operate other machinery, such as metal grinding wheels, timber saws and so.

Another device which runs with no other human powered input than that needed to make it in the first place is the ram pump. This ingenious device pumps a small proportion of water flow by harnessing the power of the balance. The maximum throughput is probably 10% of the available supply, but ram pumps can hold a sizable head of water (20-30 metres being common).

Harnessing Wind

There are two basic types of windmill. Those which collect wind energy by moving in the direction of the wind, and those which do so by moving at an angle (usually perpendicular) to the wind. In general vertical axis windmills follow the wind direction and horizontal axis mills rotate at right angles to the wind. The last kind are known as 'panemones'.

The advantage of vertical axis mills is that they are not dependent on wind direction. Their disadvantage is that because their vanes rotate into the wind for half of any rotation, they need a system reducing resistance on the return half of the rotation to achieve any effective power. This is achieved by sheltering half the rotor or by 'feathering' the vanes. Feathering is the process of reducing the resistance of the vanes to the wind. This is usually done by turning them round so that they present a narrow profile when coming into the wind, and a broad one when travelling with it. Thus resistance to the wind is high when drawing power from the wind and low when opposing it.

Modern technology has made great advances with wave and tidal power. Japan uses wave powered generators to light shipping buoys, in a design developed at Queen's University, Belfast. Norway has been very successful at producing turbines which are driven by the compressive action of incoming waves on rocky shorelines. Big tidal barrages have been used for years in Holland, and are projected for various sites in Britain. The drawback is their environmental impact on sensitive estuarine ecologies.

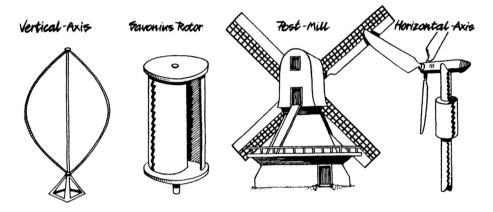

25 Some examples of windmills

Two cleverly designed static shapes achieve the same characteristics. They are the cup shape seen on anemometers (instruments for measuring wind speed), and the Savonius rotor. Both are only useful for small scale wind turbines.

Aerofoil shaped vertical axis windmills are used for large scale electrical power generation. Historically, however, most successful large windmills have used horizontal axis designs. The problem with this arrangement is that to be effective they have to be able to turn to point into the wind. The most common type of windmills were for grinding corn and for pumping water for drainage. These had two principal forms: the post mill, which has the whole building housing the mill able to rotate, and the tower mill, which has a rotating cap. There are still examples working after four hundred years' usage.

The post mill has a strong central timber core on which the upper part rotates. Steps go nearly to the ground, built over a tailpole, which the miller pushes manually to align the mill with the wind direction. Tower mills use a small wheel, called a 'fantail' on the opposite side of the rotating cap to the main sail, and perpendicular to it. The fantail has the effect of driving the cap round until it is becalmed, thus turning the sails to the wind automatically. Modern systems tend to use aircraft-style propellers to drive them for electricity generation, notably in Denmark and California.

Before investing in any significant wind power system it is sensible to monitor the wind's behaviour. There are portable systems which can measure wind speed and direction and record it over periods of time. The ideal would be

135

a year-round measurement. With prevailing winds we are talking about 'higher than average' proportion of wind from one direction. If we had constant wind (which we don't because every site is calm on occasions) the average amount of wind from one of sixteen points of the compass would be 6.25 per cent. 10 per cent wind from this direction would be all that we needed to make it the 'prevailing wind', yet this is a tiny fraction of the time for which we need to harvest energy. At most sites in western Britain the wind is in the South-West quarter for 40 per cent of the time, but this is any direction from due South to due West. In designing wind harvesting we need to be clear about these specific details.

Another consideration is that in practice, wind can only really be harvested between 15 and 75 kph. Below this speed the effect is rather feeble, and above it too violent to risk the equipment being damaged. Wind monitoring needs to show the viable *harvestable* wind, not the overall windflow, which is less useful.

Other considerations of wind sites are covered in Chapter 11, Landscape.

Passive Versus Active Systems

Many of the above technologies derive from essentially industrial requirements. Concentrations of power are needed to do big jobs quickly. There is, however, a subtler approach. This might be characterised as a passive, rather than an active approach to harnessing energy, and as such fits with an important pattern of priorities:

1 First do the things which create energy
2 Then do the things which conserve it
3 Only finally do that which consumes energy.

The power of the natural elements exists whether we use it or not. All our suggested devices are simply ways of concentrating it in time and space so that we can convert it into useful processes. Yet there are many passive systems which do the same work for less effort. For instance: why build wind-powered generators to produce electricity for space heating, if we can simply design our buildings to have high solar gain?

Here are some ways in which water can be made to work for us by passively using its qualities.

Ponds as reflectors House is built at low angle above shade side of pond and low winter sun increases solar gain as it bounces off the water surface.

Saline solar ponds Salt water has a different refractive index from fresh water. It's also denser, so fresh water floats on top. Sunlight penetrates the pond, and is bounced around inside the water causing a build-up of heat. This can be collected by a throughflow of water in salt-resistant piping. A circulatory system will work like any central heating circuit.

Solar panels Water will rise when hotter, and fall when cooler. This natural flow enables the removal and circulation of heat captured by solar panels.

Waste water leaving houses has high heat content, both from our bodily wastes, and from the energy we put in it to cook, wash etc. By running the outflow through grey water ponds, or gravel beds inside adjacent greenhouses, we can extract the heat passively. This heats the greenhouse and reduces heat loss from the building 'envelope'.

Heat stores Water is a poor conductor of heat. This means that water also loses heat slowly, keeping its heat, once gained, for long periods. Large water storages can be built under houses, or centrally within them, to store heat, releasing it slowly. This can be used to even temperatures between winter and summer.

Mulching This technique of gardening builds high humic content in the
soil, and greatly increases the capacity of the soil to store water. It reduces damage from heavy rain, and reduces need to water in the event of drought.

Roof water Roofs are massive areas of water collection. All you have to supply is the storage and guttering, and gravity does the rest, reducing reliance on centralised energy consuming supplies.

Plant/Animal Cycles

We looked at food as an energy cycle, but in its full performance the food chain is more complex. This is sometimes expressed as 'trophic' levels, because the food chain concentrates nutrients through different stages. A guideline is that each stage of the chain works on a factor of ten, so a chicken eats ten pounds of grain protein to make one pound of chicken protein. A fox will eat ten pounds of chicken to make one pound of fox, or indirectly, one hundred pounds of grain.

The logic of this argument says that if you eat vegetable protein it is better for the environment because it can be grown on one tenth the land needed to make the same amount of animal protein. In fact the system is far more diffuse than this calculation implies. What of the products the chicken or the fox return to the biosphere, other than the food involved? Their urine and faeces are important sources of nitrogen and phosphates. They dig and drain the land by their scratching and burrowing. In their natural ecosystems they maintain the balance of nature, as does every other element in the web of life.

Everywhere we take from the system we are depleting the inputs to another part, which we must replace or see an overall diminution of yield. Every input to the food chain which we cannot supply leads us to bringing in inputs and the lessening of our resources in doing that. Growing tree fodder for our stock may only provide ten per cent of their food needs, but this might cover the lean time of the year when other site grown fodder is not available. By eradicating the need to buy in feed we reduce an expensive input with all the suppliers' profit margins on it thus increasing the net yield on our crop by maybe thirty per cent.

The management of these energies *within the system* can often have benefits out of all proportion to their apparent input value.

Biomass

Biomass is the total planetary living store of energy, including all the plant life, marine creatures, birds, animals and microbial activity. It is a tremendous accumulation of energy. In designing durable societies, our first priority must be to increase biological energy stores. If we apply all that we have learned about making machines to building complex biological 'machines', we will have gone a long way to solving the seeming shortages of our present approach.

By setting out to design increased biomass as the basis of our culture we create homes in which farm, garden, dwelling, school and community space become imperceptibly merged. Distinctions in function become blurred precisely because we manage energy interfaces to be mutually productive of many processes. Because biomass can be created quickly it is possible to turn our cool climate lands entirely into such highly productive webs of activity within one generation. The restoration of some of the more damaged deserts might take a little longer, but become more possible if we had thus succeeded in meeting our own needs and using our own outputs at home.

Transport

One of the greatest consumers of energy is transport. Every stroke of every internal combustion engine devours fossil fuels which will take millions of years to recreate. In two hundred years of usage we shall have exhausted fuel sources which took thousands of millions of years to become available. Each breath of these hungry engines takes oxygen which the planetary biomass is struggling to replace. Whilst this happens we are destroying the green carpet of forests and polluting the seas with their delicate planktonic lungs, and thus reducing the Earth's capacity to repair the damage. The exhalations of the vehicles are so poisonous that they make the air unbreathable, so corrosive that the rain kills forests and our historic buildings dissolve before our eyes.

And what does this marvellous engine do for us? It takes us to the supermarket in town to buy food and drink which has been shipped half way round the globe to satisfy our taste for novelty. It drives huge trucks up the highways of the world to deliver commodities which are at the same instant being shipped in the opposite direction from another source to another destination, simply because we don't have an overall system for managing supply and demand, other than eventual extinction – the logic of a supply and demand economy. It has also done some constructive work in the world, so before we dismiss the internal combustion engine entirely, here are some suggested priorities:

1   Don't travel unless you have to.
2   Walking is better than horse riding is better than cycling is better than the bus is better than the train is better than the private car is better than aircraft. Narrow boats on canals and sailing boats are pretty good ways to get about. Fossil fuelled ships are slightly more environmentally damaging, but still a lot better than jet aircraft. Balloons and hang-gliders have potential.

The priorities are not absolute, but the general picture remains that biological transport is ideal if you can't stay still. Mechanical systems are better than chemical ones.

Necessary?

Transport is not just about where you go personally. It's also about the whole system of moving commodities around the globe. This is where local production can help to cut the energy bill.

We need to ask of each energy expenditure whether it's really necessary. I am moved by a letter from my brother in India: 'It's sad that Goa has been so destroyed by tourism. Although it's obviously aided the development and increased the wealth of local people, the damage done to their lifestyle and culture is immense. It does raise questions about the morality of all this travelling business.'

Cultural Interchange

Transport does also have an up side in that it enables cultural exchange. His letter continues: 'If you travel with respect and care you can also do a lot of good and help increase our and their understandings of our respective cultures.' 'Treading lightly on the planet' is a precise image for this ethic of care. We may learn from the pilgrims of the Middle Ages in Europe who were constrained to walk to the holy places, with all outward aspects of poverty. This way we come to our destination receptive to what we find rather than as missionaries of change.

Another possibility for creative action in the field of travel is to see international trade as 'fairs'. We come together to buy and exchange commodities, not just for economic benefit, but as a kind of holiday in which we look forward to and expect to receive an expansion of our cultural perception.

National/Personal Versus Local/Communal

Western energy consumption is vastly greater per capita than that in developing countries. It is the most marked contrast between the rich and poor parts of the world. Americans consume fifty times as much primary fuel energy per head each year as Indians do. Britons use half as much energy as Americans, or twenty-five times as much as people in India.

One of the major differences is between cultures which are based on personal ownership and usage, and those which see communal ownership and usage as part of a local community as normal. Do Americans have fifty times the quality of life that people in India do, for all their comparative wealth and poverty?

A society which insists on private separate dwellings for each individual or small family, private cars for each person, and so on, is bound to use more energy than societies which thrive on extended families living cheek by jowl, and the familiarity of public transport. If we wish to reduce our energy budget we need to find ways in which we can be comfortable with a more communal sharing of energy resources, and a more direct fuelling of those resources from within our local community.

We also need, as communities, to take responsibility for cleaning up our own outputs. In Britain government after government has ignored the representations of the Swedish administration that our uncleaned gaseous industrial output crosses the seas and kills their lakes and forests with acid rain. Germany and Poland have equally bad habits.

It's time to accept responsibility and clean up.

Water/Land/Air

Because a piece of land is shown a different colour on the map it doesn't mean the energy flows stop at the border. Finding residual DDT in the fat of Antarctic penguins is a solemn reminder that pollution becomes global.

The same linked energies are available for us to manage beneficially. Transport by water may be slower than air or land, but it is much easier to move large loads like coal in this way. We simply need to adjust our demands to the pace of life of the most appropriate energy system. A society based on watching videos of war movies probably needs nuclear power stations. One which centres on beautiful productive gardens can make do with wood stoves.

Public Transport

Public transport is only going to work as a system if it has the support of the

In Sweden the government dropped rail fares by thirty per cent. A massive increase in usage resulted, making the rail network far more profitable, and increasing the capital available to reinvest in the process.

prevalent political will and of the consumers. Taking the bus rather than driving the car is a political act of affirmation in sharing energy resources communally. It becomes hard or impossible to do this if the public transport system is not adequate to the demands of our travelling patterns. If public services decay beyond a certain point, then their ultimate demise is hastened. People will wait for a reasonably regular reliable service. They will not wait for an infrequent and erratic one.

One secret of making public transport work is that it must address the needs of all the people. Designing rail networks to be high speed and super-comfortable may compete with airlines for profitable business class travellers. Does it get the chickens to market, or grandma to hospital? We must reintroduce a healthy

peasant element into our public transport systems. Perhaps a campaign of people taking pigs on trains would make the point. Where I grew up in the Yorkshire Dales the buses delivered milk and parcels, and stopped for anyone who waved an arm, as well as at regular signed points. This is what I call public transport.

Draught Animals

The age of the motor-car has largely diverted Western imagination from the potential of draught animals. In the past they were so successful that by the late nineteenth century cities like London and New York were coming to a grinding halt (much as they are today, courtesy of the automobile) with the volume of horse traffic.

We are due for a renaissance of this biological solution. Heavy horses are better at logging steep slopes than tractors. They have potential allies in draught work from donkeys, sheep, goats, pigs, alpacas, llamas, camels and dogs. We might even include humans. The one advantage that all these flesh and blood vehicles have over metal ones, is that they are self-reproducing.

Pedal Power

The human body is one source of energy we should not overlook. At one time the treadmill had a certain currency, but being relatively inefficient and associated with forced labour it's not so popular nowadays. Fortunately it's also not necessary.

Studies of relative energy output in travelling for energy input show that a fit person on a bicycle is the most efficient moving animal on the planet, going more metres per calorie than even the fleetest leopard. Cycles are therefore the most energy efficient way to travel. The limitation is only one of stamina and distance. There are appropriate tricycles for parents to go downtown with a couple of children on the back, to get the shopping, or visit school. There are cycles for carrying heavy loads. There are machines for touring over long distances in great comfort, and others designed for maximum speed over shorter distances, such as between towns or villages. You can ride a cycle if you're a child, a grandparent, or disabled. They are safe and environmentally friendly, and because they run off your body power, they help keep you fit.

In recent years the mountain bike has reintroduced the idea that cycling can be a fashionable activity. Because cycles are 'low technology' they didn't attract this sort of support when, post-World War II, we were all trying to raise our standard of living. Now there is a growing awareness that the real measure of living standard is spiritual and physical health, not material possessions, there is hope that the technology of the cycle will become a leading symbol of appropriate development.

Pedal power can also be harnessed to drive machinery. Cycling systems have been used to power generators, grinding wheels, water pumps, lawnmowers, and musical instruments. It is also something that anyone can learn to build or maintain, and as such is a great asset in enabling people to take control of their own lives.

Alternative Fuels

There are many other sources of appropriate energy. I do not count nuclear power as appropriate in any circumstances because the end products are deadly poisonous and of incredible longevity. We have no safe means of controlling them. How can anyone pretend to be 'in charge' of residual plutonium with a half life of ten thousand years? It's absurd.

Methane is a better option. This is produced in copious quantities by living organisms as they decay. The human gut is one point of production. By containing chambers in which organic matter is rotted it is possible to capture the gas for usage. Farms with housed stock in winter can gather the gas from the slurry pits to warm or light the dwellings or animal sheds.

Fuels can be distilled from biomass. In Brazil most cars run on alcohol produced from sugar cane. The advisability of using vast masses of biomass to sustain anything as destructive as the motor car is debatable; nevertheless it is possible to do so. One source of energy for heating or electricity generation is to burn refuse. This is one step better than shoving it in holes in the ground, and one step worse than recycling the material.

We need to work towards recognising all the energy resources available to us, and harnessing what we have intelligently. As with all stages of establishing a Permaculture approach to planet management, improvement is a good step on the path to perfection. Healing the Earth of the scars of a wasteful energy policy will be a natural outcome of adopting this approach.

PART III

HELPFUL TECHNIQUES

13 GARDENING

Creating a home garden is the best first step you can take to care for the land. Apart from the increased production of your own plot, there is the benefit of reducing your demands for produce from land elsewhere. It is also a great learning experience.

Minimum Tillage

Why do we dig? To break up the soil, make a good seed bed, remove weeds, improve aeration, improve water penetration and retention, but probably mostly because it's a compulsive habit. Every winter and spring millions of gardeners repair to their bare plots and dig millions of tons of soil between them. Is it any wonder that bad backs are the next most common cause of lost work days after the common cold?

Stop digging! The garden can have within it all it needs to care for itself. If it has not, we will still find it easy to create conditions which will soon establish self-managing cycles.

Why soil must not be inverted becomes clear on the microscopic scale. Soil is not merely a collection of old leaves and ground-up rocks. It is an amazing universe of myriad species of fungi, microbes, worms, and other tiny flora and fauna – teeming with life.

There are literally tonnes of these creatures per hectare, with an energy output equivalent to that of 15 000 human beings. They serve several vital functions.

1 They corrode and break down dead organic matter in the soil.
2 In burrowing and moving under the land they naturally aerate the soil for us.
3 In dying themselves they are a valuable source of nutrients to other life forms.
4 They make a web of water-retentive tissues in the soil which constitute the humic matter, so obvious when you crumble a handful of rich black soil between your fingers.

If you follow the techniques listed below, you will get valuable evidence of these benefits as the soil visibly improves. Another point to deter you from unnecessary spadework is that each of these organisms flourishes in its own niche. If you bury surface bacteria, they die of suffocation and cold; if you expose to the surface the microbes which do well a spade-depth down, they will oxidise and die. The short-term feed of their dead forms adds to the fertility of the soil, but the long-term life of the soil is reduced.

I do use a spade, for instance, to dig out unwanted tree roots, or to harvest potatoes. I dig edges of beds back into the centre to improve water infiltration and reduce grass invasion. I would dig to trench rubble into impervious clay, or to break up iron pan below the soil. But I would no longer dig as a matter of course. Tillage is limited as much as possible to establishing a self-managing system. With time, the intervention becomes unnecessary.

Mulching

No-dig garden methods go hand in hand with mulching. Watering the garden is time-consuming and usually uses up water from the tap, which is highly wasteful as such treated water is neither good for the garden, nor necessary for it. Mulching is the process of covering the bare soil with other matter. This protects the living creatures in the soil from dehydration and oxidation. If the mulch is organic it also feeds them. Rather than dig humic matter into the soil it allows the earthworms to rise up and carry the

organic substances down into their burrows, which is what they like to do. It makes the soil surface resistant to erosion by heavy rain as it breaks the impact of the rainfall, and retaining moisture, slows run-off. In time a colloidal mass develops near the surface which is very good at protecting the crops from drought. Colloids are tiny fibrous organic remains which swell to the jelly-like consistency of wallpaper paste, trapping water which comes their way.

Above all, mulching is something that you can see is clearly emulating nature. When a wood drops its leaves in winter it doesn't rake them into a pile and burn them because they're untidy. It scatters them on the surface in a thin layer. When uncut grasses and other herbage die back in the winter they make a thick but airy mat across the surface. In the next growing season they stay there, decaying, and new shoots grow up through them.

By mulching we make the least intervention we can to simulate the natural cycle for feeding the soil. The mulch itself can be made from kitchen waste, leaves, grass clippings, green manures, old straw, hair and nail clippings, wood ash, chipped wood and bark, paper and cardboard or compost. It is not always appropriate to compost everything. Kitchen waste spread thinly will rot down where you put it. If you find any of these mulching materials unsightly, you can always cover them up with more acceptable stuff.

Avoid using paper with colours in – yellow or red dyes in particular contain heavy metals. If you use straw or other materials from off site they may be contaminated with chemical sprays. Most of these will have broken down within a year, so composting first can help make usable organic matter in one season. Bracken also has drawbacks in that it exudes a natural chemical growth inhibitor.

There is a side benefit of mulching for those who don't eat weeds, in that the mulch tends to suppress the growth of annual weed seeds in the soil, reducing competition with the intended crop. Black polythene mulch is an alternative which, because of its colour, absorbs heat into the soil. It is also the most effective weed suppressant. Unfortunately it uses fossil fuel reserves in its production, and adds no humic matter. Whilst beneficial in reducing oxidation of peaty soils, and preventing evaporative loss, it does not have the long-term future of organic mulches.

Rotations

In classic organic gardening, rotations are always advised. The suggestion is that crops of one type should not be repeated continually on the same plot, as this invites trouble by presenting an easy target for species-specific diseases and pests. Carrot fly, eelworm and club root will destroy your crop if they get a hold.

The usual pattern is to recommend four-course rotations. This means dividing your plot into four, and in each quarter at a time growing in rotation, potatoes, legumes (bean family), brassicas (cabbage family), and root crops. Rotations also have the effect of improving soil fertility, as these different families all add and subtract different things in their growing cycle. Beans add nitrogen which they 'fix' from the air through beneficial association with certain fungi on their roots. Potatoes break up the soil, and leave their fibrous roots behind, opening up the soil structure.

If you are going to grow single crops on any scale it is certainly the system to use. Twelve people live in my house and we eat our own potatoes all year round. We grow them in plots around five metres square, and the plots are in different spots of the garden each year.

However, other crops are generally grown in smaller blocks. We are conscious not to follow any crop with another of the same, but if you mix all your plants up together more, the risk reduces. If you think about it, nature does not operate a system of rotations. Rather it practises succession. Bare soil is colonised by pioneer species, like chickweed. Then deep-rooted plants appear, like docks. Brambles may come next. After a while shrubs make their way in, and in perhaps five or ten years, trees start to appear. Wild successions are usually staged advances where specific plants rehabilitate the soil to be followed by a gradual return to forest.

Perhaps this kind of change over time can be seen as complementary to crop rotations, which are maintaining the development of the system at an artificially fixed point. Avoid planting brassicas, potatoes, onions and carrots in the same spot two seasons running, as they are the major attractants for disease and pests.

Bed Types

The use of no-dig and mulching techniques favour certain types of bed design. If I move into a house with a garden which is a complete wilderness, how can I produce crops by not digging? The answer is to make a base for the beds on top of whatever is growing there now. If it's scrub or brambles, a goat could be brought in to eat the lot out first. If there's no goat you may want to make a drastic intervention like cutting the lot down and digging out the roots of bushes, although pigs are good at this! Assuming it is just long grass and annual weeds, define your area by spreading thick cardboard on the ground. Old boxes which shops throw away are just fine. Old clothes with buttons and zips cut off are good too, and carpets are splendid for the job. Just make sure that all this material is organic – no foam-backed carpets or plastic materials.

You can aid the arrival of worms by spreading a little blood and bone meal, but this is not essential. Next, having laid out all your matting, make sure it overlaps well so weeds can't grow up through it. If a few persistent ones do, don't worry about it, they won't be a problem. Next layer the upper surface 150mm thick in organic matter. Horse manure is ideal, kitchen scraps, compost, rotted leaves, green manures – there are many possibilities. The best choice is those things which are rich in nitrogen. When this layer is in place, cover the whole surface with 150-200mm of straw, sawdust, small twigs, bark chippings, or other carbon-rich material. It's best to carry out this bed making in the autumn, and leave it to rot down over winter. In practice it can be done any time of year.

Assuming you start in autumn, your bed will be ready for planting in the spring. The rather rough surface will not readily accept fine seed, so the first crops to use are potatoes, beans, or greens which have been grown as seedlings in trays elsewhere. You can also scatter green manures like mustard, spinach, and buckwheat. Potatoes and broad beans make a good first crop and leave the soil well broken up. Although the process sounds messy and haphazard when you've never tried it before, you get marvellous rich crumbly soil, on any type of subsoil, within one growing season, without back-breaking digging.

You will find variations on this no-dig

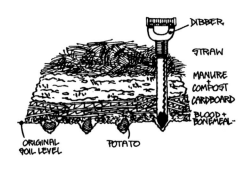

ORIGINAL
SOIL LEVEL
POTATO

27 Section through sheet mulched raised bed

method, which is also sometimes called sheet mulching. Be careful that, in adding fresh manures as mulch, you do not place them next to plants which will be burnt by their strong acidity. Be warned also that brassicas will become more disease-prone on very nitrogen-rich soils. This can be compensated by liming. Soil tests can be made to check on acidity/alkalinity of soil. In general, however, a balanced programme of soil maintenance will achieve a deep rich loam very quickly. You should soon get healthy populations of earthworms, and if clover grows on your plots, then it's a pretty good indication that all is well.

Raised beds are another variation on the no-dig theme, which do require digging to get them going. Using a line, peg out rectangular beds which can be as long as you need them, but narrow enough so that the middle can be reached comfortably from either side. The idea is to make a heaped bed which

you are never going to walk on. Double digging is the next step. This means going down two spade depths. Into the bottom of the trench you put the upturned turf from the top layer, and cover this with the soil from below. The first section is put on one side to fill the other end of the oblong. You can add in other organic material as you go, but the end product should be a heaped bed, curved in cross section, which is higher than the surrounding ground. The turf below rots slowly, providing nitrogen. The sloped surfaces drain well into 'gutters' at the edge of the bed which give very good infiltration of water to the root layer. These beds are very drought and flood resistant. They also offer more growing area than a flat bed of the same dimensions.

Crops can be rotated through these beds as with any other. Their great advantage is that they are easily worked without walking on them. This means there is no soil compaction, and no interference with the lifecycles of all our living allies in the soil. The deep topsoil created is highly desirable for earthworms and so forth.

The next aspect of bed design open to improvement is shape. We rather habitually make garden beds round or rectangular. These offer very little edge. Variations on the raised bed theme can be much more productive in providing microclimates and edges, and also in offering greater possibilities for useful plant associations. The first of these is

151

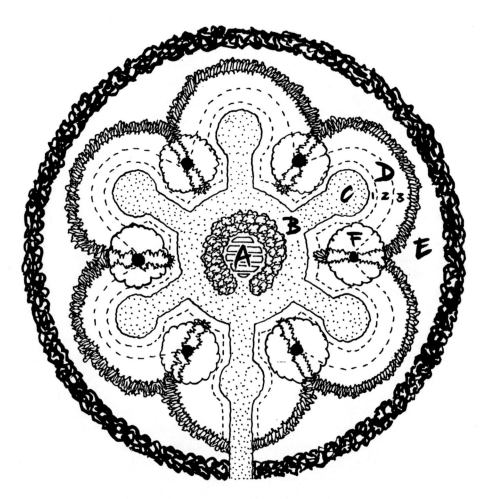

A: Shrub circle with shower grill centre (e.g. bamboos, astilbe, *Philadelphus*)

B: Mulched paths: woodchip or gravel over cardboard

C: Keyhole path as B

D: Keyhole beds

    1) low creeping and herbaceous plants (e.g. salads)

    2) taller plants (e.g. broad beans)

    3) one visit plants (e.g. raspberries, standard gooseberries)

E: Protection from wind, weeds and animal predators (e.g. hazel, escalonia, blackberry, roses, blackthorn, holly, hawthorn)

F: Trees between keyholes to give vertical yield (e.g. semi-dwarfing apple, alder) the 'keyhole bed'. Here, a small access path and round centre can give accessibility to a whole rectangular bed, but removing the necessity for walking on the bed. An extension of this principle is the 'mandala garden', which is basically an assembly of keyhole beds. Shapes can be as intricate as your imagination allows.

Companion Planting

Various plants have beneficial relationships. Planting carrots and onions together helps deter both carrot and onion fly. Both pests locate their favourite food by smell, and the scent of each plant tends to mask that of the other. 'Companion planting' is the study of such beneficial associations on a one-to-one basis. Marigolds are deterrent to nematodes, tiny worm-like creatures which damage underground roots and stems. Feverfew helps heal sick plants, and so on. There are many sources of information about companion planting, some detailed in the booklist.

It is possible to take the process a stage further, by building communities of plants and animals, called 'guilds'. A guild will consist of plants and animals which are good companions in all senses. They will occupy all the possible layers of ground and air, as well as having healthy exchanges of nutrients and disease resistance. They will maintain permanent ground cover and offer maximum economic yield. A well-designed guild will eliminate much stock care by offering feed and bedding to the animals which they can harvest themselves.

Perennial Versus Annual

Temperate horticulture is very biased to the use of annual crops. This is work-inducing: annuals need planting and disposal each year. Seed has to be saved or purchased. In building permanent agricultures we need to use more perennial crops.

Given two crops with the same function, choose the perennial one. Many of the crops described as annuals on seed packets are actually perennial. Lettuces are a good example. However, if you leave lettuces they tend to become more bitter with time. One option is to develop a taste for more bitter vegetables and salads. Another way of saving work is to keep the annuals, but to try and grow them in ways which allow them to self-seed. Spinach does this well. Leave free areas round the plants where the seeds can germinate after falling naturally. Many of our vegetables are quite attractive in flowering and seeding; for example, parsnips send up metre-high sprays of yellow flowers which last a month or two, and chicory flowers are a breath-taking blue. There are also many benefits to plant and soil health.

153

The extra plant growth makes green manure. The flowers attract beneficial insects, such as hoverfly.

Trees are the greatest example of perennial crops, and the use of trees as centre of garden guilds takes us on the path to turning our gardens into productive city forests.

Fruit/Vegetable/Fibre Crops

Understanding the uses of individual species helps us serve our own needs. The world in general is terribly dependent on a few crops for food, and a tiny minority of people take responsibility for growing other plant products for their own usage. Fibre crops are a point in case. At one time nearly every village in Britain had its own flax fields for cropping fibre. Nettles were also used.

There is a huge range of plants which can be grown successfully in cool climates, and I hope you find some new ones in the species lists. It's great fun to add to this knowledge and experiment with more unusual crops. It also greatly increases our ability to see to our own needs, and also to understand all plants as having important functions in the web of life.

Crops as Fertiliser

Every crop is a fertiliser, providing decaying vegetable matter to the soil, as well as the indirect residues of animal wastes which result from their use as food. There are a few ways in which we can increase this usefulness.

One way is to avoid pulling up roots wherever possible. We shouldn't leave carrots or any other root crop or brassica in the ground if we're afraid of attracting pests, or if the plant is an invasive weed which we're trying to remove. However, when the bean crop is finished, try cutting off the plant at ground level. The root will gradually rot in the soil, and the life below will remain undisturbed. A following crop will find the root path of the old bean an easy nutritive way for sinking quick deep roots itself, and a ready source of nitrogen.

Many plants have high values as green manures. Their leaf matter can simply be cut and scattered as mulch to rot on the ground. These are covered more fully in Chapter 17, on fertility.

Maximum Ground Cover

Avoiding bare soil is important in getting most benefit from the land. The length of the growing cycle for each crop is determined by how long it takes for the plant to receive the necessary amount of warmth. Bare soils cool more quickly in winter and at night. They warm more quickly in the spring, but on balance it is more beneficial to keep the soil covered.

Mulch is one tactic here, but mulch

itself is not a crop. There are many plants which can be used to overgrow the soil or mulch, both to give yield themselves, and also to protect and feed the soil. Creeping members of the clover family feed the earth with nitrogen, whilst strawberries or nasturtiums are edible crops. Poached egg plant attracts hoverflies which are prodigious devourers of aphids, whilst yarrow and bugle have medicinal uses. Succulents, such as stonecrop, hold water and are drought resistant. Maximum ground cover is a simple rule to remember, and one that is enhanced by each new discovery you make of useful ground cover plants.

Use of All Layers and Seasons

A garden which is bare in winter, or has only one layer of growth, has missed the opportunities for yield. We remember the seven layers of plants in the forest and remind ourselves that a garden which has climax trees, edge trees, shrubs, herbaceous plants, ground cover, root crops and climbers might forgive us if we still haven't thought of many epiphytes.

Our plans should include a good mixture of successions, and reserves of mulch to get in quick and cover any soil bared by a lifted crop when we have no replacement to hand. One way to help build the soil and to ensure the activity of the ground over winter is to sow quick-growing cover crops in the autumn such as mustard and field beans.

Particularly as Japanese and Chinese varieties arrive in Europe and America we find there are now crops to grow all year round. There are plenty of plants which flower or have attractive bare winter branches if we want beautiful things in the winter months as well.

'Weeds'

A weed is a plant where you don't want it. They may also be the true native residents. Past weeders might one day gather at groups of 'Weeders Anonymous' (myself amongst them) and confess to the pathological stresses which drove them to rip unwanted plants from the garden. I suspect that the biggest cause is ignorance.

Weeds are extremely useful. They tend to be pioneer plants, that is they are plants whose natural role is to reclaim damaged environments. Many of them are edible. Nearly all of them have the ability to extract valuable minerals from the subsoil, or even rock, and cast it into the growing fertility of their chosen plot. These are called 'dynamic accumulators'.

We shall never know the full usefulness of weeds, so learning to recognise them and appreciate their value makes us rather more wary of destroying them at first sight. You can learn to 'read' weeds, and appreciate that there are common guilds of them which are very reliable indicators of the soil's condition. You can also replace weeds with more acceptable crops which carry out similar functions to the weed in question. Thus a patch of thistles can be replaced by globe artichokes; heavy infestations of buttercup (which is poisonous) make good ground for strawberries.

Salads and Herbs

Raw food, salads and herbs in particular, are highly nutritious, and remove the need for the energy input of cooking. They keep their vitamin content intact, particularly if eaten straight from the garden. They are good for the digestion, and invigorating to the body. Although I still dream more of steak and kidney pudding than I do of lettuce, I am convinced that we would all be better off for eating more salads.

Most herbs used in present day cooking have their origins in the Mediterranean, although most are hardy. Herbs are best used in small quantities with other salads, and some are actually quite poisonous if eaten too much. This includes sage and parsley, which, with the green salads, spinach and sorrel, are high in oxalic acid.

Salads may be eaten as green leaves, grated roots, seedlings (like cress), or are especially attractive as flowers. Comprehensive lists are given in the species section. Many wild plants make excellent salads. A good way of growing salads is to sow them broadcast in mixed beds. These are best managed as 'cut and come again' plots, picking leaves to make up the crop, and leaving the stem to regenerate, which most salad plants will do in a few weeks. Salads are also ideal for 'edible landscaping', making attractive beds of coloured leaves and shapes. Some of the Italian chicories and lettuces are particularly noticeable, with blushing red leaves, and ornamental kales are as handsome as roses in your borders. Edible flowers add to the vibrant energy of the well-designed salad garden.

Indigenous Versus Exotic Species

If it is better to work with what you have than to strive for what you don't, then it is more desirable to use indigenous species than exotic ones. 'Exotic' in this case simply means 'not local', as some exotics are pretty plain to look at.

What is indigenous and what is local? For instance, some trees in Britain are generally agreed to be native, such as the Scots pine. Others are usually considered exotic, like the sycamore. Six thousand years ago there were no pines in Scotland, only ice. Sycamores are known to have grown here since at least 1250 AD, or over seven hundred years ago.

Some plants are allowed to be 'naturalised', thus an attractive resident of the Spey Valley in north-west Scotland is the alpine lupin, a native of the North American Rocky Mountains.

Clearly there is no neat dividing line, and all distinctions are to some extent arbitrary. In any event we can never know the whole historical truth. It is arguable that a person travelling by jet plane with a pocket full of seed is just as much a part of nature as turtle doves migrating two thousand miles north-westwards from Africa, spreading seeds as they go.

If we have species in our environment that provide our needs, then we should use them. If there are exotics which can prevent us plundering some other part of the globe to sustain our fancy, then use them too. But do not introduce species, as Europeans did to Australia and New Zealand, which can have a catastrophic effect on the environment. In other words, intervene as little as possible, and with great care.

Seed Conservation

Another little survival tactic is to become a seed saver. Throughout the world major companies have been buying up the rights to seed varieties, and legislation has been introduced to prevent the unauthorised sale of seeds. You may not grow plants in your garden, harvest the seed, and sell it to your neighbour without a licence. This can be justified on the grounds of limiting the spread of disease, and ensuring quality of product.

However, many of the companies which buy up seed rights are the same companies which manufacture chemical sprays and fertilisers. They are developing strains of plants which are vigorous and high cropping, but which are also disease-prone and cannot do well without the applications made by the agricultural chemical divisions. These same companies have no interest in preserving old varieties of seeds which are better for small-scale usage, having greater flavour or known keeping qualities.

The only way these will be preserved is by small organisations and individuals saving and sharing the seed amongst themselves. This may one day prove vital for the health of our genetic reserves in the event of failure of the mainstream crops.

The Henry Doubleday Research Association in the UK, and Seed Savers Exchange in the United States are two groups carrying on this work who invite your participation. 'Seed Banks Serving People', based in Arizona, promotes the work on a global basis.

Growing Under Glass

We saw that growing under glass offers the opportunity of extending the growing season. It also means we can produce crops which come from warmer climates. There is some warming of the environment inside any greenhouse. This can be increased by installing heating systems, which in a well-linked system might be chickens, or by using products like triple glazed polycarbonate, which trap solar energy so well that sub-tropical fruit can be grown in unheated conditions as far north as Sweden and Norway.

Integrating Trees and Stock

The next chapter, Orchards, looks at the potential for trees in the garden. The fully-developed garden is not exclusive of animal life. Birds and mammals have their own place in nature, and also offer us many significant yields. The most popular animal crops for gardens are hens. Realistically we might extend the list to include the following: pigs, sheep, goats, rabbits, ducks, geese, pigeons, turkeys and quail. Those with more exotic tastes might consider peacocks and guinea pigs. In fact, there is a huge range of garden-scale stock which are edible and which will survive in cool climates.

Remember that animals and birds have many roles in a fully-developed system other than bolting down bought feed so they can be devoured in turn. Moles, for instance, in tunnelling underground, are natural field drain builders. Pigeons bring phosphates to usable form in their droppings. Rabbits provide useful pelts, or mow the lawn for free. Chickens and pigs can dig the ground for us.

In the burgeoning fertility of a forest garden foxes and beetles, rodents and wild bees, robins and other wildlife might all find their place, passing through at one time or another, without reducing available yield, and even, perhaps, adding to the fruits of our labours.

14 ORCHARDS

Trees are important as perennial crops. The art of husbanding orchards has been perfected over two thousand years and more to increase yield from the garden.

Tree Techniques

The development of our present range of cultivars appears to have begun with the Romans, who understood about the nature of different varieties, knowing how to graft as extensively as we do today. Pliny, for instance, lists twenty-seven distinct varieties of apple.

Trees can be propagated by sexual and by vegetative means. Sexual reproduction takes place when a fruit is formed by (male) pollen reaching the (female) part of the flower. Often, to be successful, the pollen must have come from a different variety of the same tree. The resulting fruit contains seed which, if germinated, produces a new tree. This tree will have very different characteristics from its parents, although it will be based on a combination of their qualities with its own individual development. Not unlike breeding people, really.

In orchard trees, however, vegetative propagation is a process of human management. A 'stock' is selected for its particular virtues, such as hardiness and vigour of growth and disease resistance. This is a young tree with a good single stem and healthy rooting system. On to this stock is grafted a living branch from a tree which has some particularly desirable fruiting characteristic. After one year the remains of the top of the stock are cut away, and the choice variety takes over.

Sexual reproduction offers random variation, whilst vegetative propagation offers reliability. Trees which have random variations, that is new characteristics, are known as 'sports'. If planting a seed, we do not know what the new 'sport' will be like. The offspring of two excellent fruiting trees may not itself do so well, or it may be a great improvement. Good varieties are multiplied 'true to form' by grafting on to stocks. So Cox's Orange Pippin was originally a tree grown from the pips of a much-enjoyed apple. Every Cox's Orange

Pippin since then has been propagated by grafting living matter from that tree, or its grafted descendants, on to fresh wood.

The same process is used with favoured varieties of nuts and other fruits. Curiously, the stock need not always be of the same tree as the fruit. So peaches are commonly grafted onto quince stocks. A great source of stocks for the whole world is East Malling Research Station in Kent, England. Stocks often have coded names, and East Malling types start with 'M'. Thus M26 is an apple stock which is dwarfing, making mature trees about three metres across, and two and a half metres high. Varieties of fruit and nuts are known as 'cultivars' indicating that they are the product of human management rather than varieties collected in the wild. Most cultivars are sold on stocks selected to limit the size of the tree to increase its fruit yield and to make it easier for picking. There are a small number of cultivars which are genetic dwarf trees, that is, they naturally grow very small.

Trees develop a root system underground equally large to the size of the tree above ground. It's therefore a good idea to prepare the ground well, as once the tree is in you cannot get underneath it to improve matters. Trees are best bought bare rooted from recognised nurseries. Bare rooted means they are dug in late autumn or winter, and shipped to you without soil on their roots. This can be done when the tree is dormant without undue damage, although the tree will lose roots in the process. With proper care these will regenerate. Trees sold in pots with their root ball intact will be less successful in sending down new roots, as they will tend to feed off the existing root ball. If using container grown trees tease apart the root ends, and be sure to plant into similar soil to that in the container, importing it to your orchard if necessary.

Plant the tree into a prepared pit, being careful not to cover the graft. If possible it is better to avoid stakes so that the tree grows with a natural resistance to wind stress. Tree guards should be used if there is a risk of damage by rabbits, hare and deer. They can be bought, or fabricated by tying plastic bags round the lower part of the tree.

Detailed planting requirements are

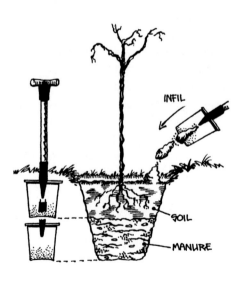

INFIL

SOIL

MANURE

only for high value trees, such as bought fruiting cultivars. If planting 'wild' fruit or forest trees it is quite adequate to make a slit a spade's depth in the soil, or to cut through the back of an upturned turf to bury the roots. The labour required is much less, and the success rate extremely high.

Make sure the tree is watered well in its first year of establishment. A bucket of water a week is advisable. Don't pay lots of money to buy large trees. Smaller ones will establish quicker, and soon catch up on the older plantings.

Deciduous fruiting trees need frost to keep their cycles regular. Unseasonably mild winters lead to stress induced budding, which can be damaged by late frosts. Without proper cold seasons the tree's biological clock goes wrong. In warmer zones these trees can be planted in frost hollows. In cooler climates, it is important to plant trees running down slope to let the frost run away. Trees planted in lines across the slope will tend to trap frost and this can lead to bud and flower damage.

The first technique to baffle the new orchard owner is pruning. This is the art of cutting back the tree to make it more productive. You may choose not to do this, but most purchased fruit trees have already been pruned, and if you do not continue to prune them they can develop a very stressed shape, with too many branches causing bark wounds and poor reception of light. There are plenty of fruit guides which will show you how

to do this, but best of all is a friendly and experienced neighbour. Pruning is a good way of removing small areas of diseased wood from a tree, and keeping the plant healthy.

Certain shapes of tree offer opportunities for increased yield: pruning the tree to a pyramid shape means trees can be planted closer together. An open 'bowl' shape admits maximum sunlight, encouraging high yield per tree, whilst keeping the tree short and easy to pick from. Other shapes offer the opportunity of growing trees two-dimensionally, either against walls and fences, or as barriers in their own right. The most common shapes for this are cordons, espaliers and fans.

Cordon means growing the tree as a single stem with fruiting spurs on it, planted at an angle, pruning out any side branches.

Espaliers have a central vertical trunk with three or four horizontal branches on each side.

Fans have a short central trunk with many radiating branches growing straight from the crown.

Some species prefer different shapes, cherries and peaches making good fans, whilst apples and pears can be espaliered. Cordons take less space and fruit earlier in their lives than the other two shapes, and mean that you can get more varieties into a smaller space. They have smaller yield per tree. A neat variation on the theme is the step-over espalier, which has a single horizontal branch usually

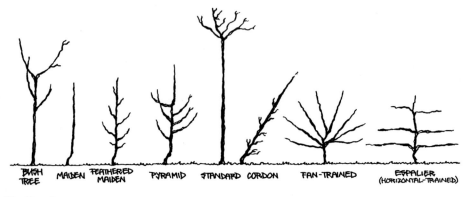

BUSH TREE · MAIDEN · FEATHERED MAIDEN · PYRAMID · STANDARD · CORDON · FAN-TRAINED · ESPALIER (HORIZONTAL-TRAINED)

30 Tree forms

less than a foot from the ground, which makes a fruiting border to a vegetable plot.

All of these shapes require 'training', tying the branches of the tree to bamboo poles attached to wires fixed on the wall through vine-eyes. Trees tied directly to the wires would bruise in the wind. Pruning keeps the shape of the tree required. It is usually carried out in the autumn (for major cutting back) and late summer (for light trimming). Autumn pruning is reckoned to encourage growth of wood, and summer pruning to encourage fruiting. Another way to encourage fruiting is to bend branches down. The tension in the wood's upper surface encourages buds to make flowers and therefore fruit, rather than woody growth. This can be done with string and pegs or weights. Care should be taken not to damage the branches when training.

The choice of tree crops for your plot will be difficult (and often expensive) to reverse, so it is well to plan any plantings thoroughly. It is essential that you know the local climate before deciding on cultivars. The next section is designed to help you do this.

Fruit and Nut Varieties

The most studied, and the most popular, temperate fruit tree is the apple. We shall take this as an example.

Apple trees flower in the Spring and set fruit when their flowers are cross-pollinated by insects (bees particularly). One or two apples are fairly self-fertile, that is, the female part of the flower can be fertilised by (male) pollen from the same tree. Most apples, however, require a pollinating partner. If the cultivar is *triploid* it requires *two* pollinating

Key:

Po = Pollination period

D/C = Dessert or cooker

FR = Frost resistant

B = Tending to biennialism

GFG = *Good Fruit Guide*

Rec/R = Recommended for flavour

T = Triploid

N = Hardy in the north

(south if New Zealand)

CFB = *Cultivated Fruits in Britain*

Apples

Po	Rec	Name	D/C	T	FR	N	B	Comments
2	R	Egremont Russet	D		FR	N		Cordons well
2		Golden Spire	D&C			N		
2	R	Irish Peach	D			N		Tip fruiting
2	R	Ribston Pippin	D	T		N		Highest Vitamin C
								Espaliers well
2		Warner's King	C	T		N		

Notes:
This is a natural grouping. Both *Ribston Pippin* & *Warner's King* are Triploid and therefore require two other pollinating partners. *Egremont Russet* & *Adam's Pearmain* are recommended partners for *Ribston Pippin*, although *Adam's Pearmain* is not specifically North suited. Perhaps planting on a slope with the triploids between two duploids for satisfactory pollination, and the *Egremont Russet* lowest on the slope for its frost resistance.

Po	Rec	Name	D/C	T	FR	N	B	Comments
3	R	Greensleeves	D		FR	N		Self fertile
3		Ontario	C		FR			High Vitamin C
								Good keeper
3		Suntan	D	T	FR			
3	R	Tydeman's Late Or.	D		FR			
3		Worcester Pearmain	D		FR			Universal Po.
								Tip fruiting
3	R	Epicure	D		FR			
3	R	James Grieve	D			N		Scottish bred
								Espaliers well
								Universal Po.
3		Grenadier	C			N		
3		Howgate Wonder	C			N		
3	R	Margil	D			N		'Delicious'
3		Tower of Glamis	D			N		Scotland's
								oldest apple

Notes:
Suntan likes *Greensleeves* and *James Grieve* as pollinating partners. *Fortune, Wagener* & *Laxton's Superb* are also frost resistant, but are subject to biennialism. This applies also to *Allington Pippin* & *Early Victoria* which are recommended for the North.

| 4 | | Ellison's Orange | D | FR | N | B | |
| 4 | | Lady Sudeley | D | | N | | |

Notes:
Ellison's Orange is both frost resistant and hardy in the North. Lady Sudeley is the only other period 4 apple cited as hardy.

5		Lord Derby	C		N		
5		Newton Wonder	C		N	B	Doesn't Po.
5	R	American Mother	D		N		

Notes:
These are the only period 5 apples thought hardy, and therefore all three would be needed to achieve pollination.

6		Court Pendu Plat	D		N		
6		Edward VII	C		N		Espaliers well
6	R	Laxton's Royalty	D		N		
6		Royal Jubilee	D		N		

Notes:
GFG calls Court Pendu Plat England's oldest apple. CFB suggests otherwise (e.g. Decio). However, it may be the oldest commonly available, and therefore of great interest.

| 7 | | Crawley Beauty | C | | N | | |

Notes:
This is the only period 7 apple that exists, but it is very self fertile, and so plants well alone.

partners. Apples flower through seven different periods, from terribly early (1) to rather late (7). To get cross-pollination, the two (or three) apple trees have to be in flower at the same time.

Apple trees are of limited hardiness. Some are particularly frost resistant, whilst others will drop their flowering material at the very mention of Jack Frost. Some thrive in the shorter growing season of the north (northern hemisphere), while others like to bask in semi-Mediterranean conditions.

Some are good dessert apples (eaten raw) whilst others are best cooked. A few are good both ways. Some are at their best only when eaten straight off the tree, whilst others keep well and can be enjoyed months after cropping if stored properly. Some apples are subject to biennialism – they crop heavily one year and then disappoint the next. This is more crucial if they're also expected to cross-pollinate another tree. Your whole crop may disappear!

To illustrate the complex requirements of matching trees I include a list made for my own garden. At 56 degrees North we're on the same latitude as Copenhagen, Moscow and Labrador, Canada. Average annual rainfall is 27 inches. Wetter climates are more stressful for trees than drier climates with the same temperature.

This gives you an idea of why the cultivars selected as suitable for this site emphasise hardiness and there are no early flowering varieties. Each site will be different, the important point here is the *considerations* needed to make the design work.

You can find all the details you need to make a similar plan for your own site in the booklist. If you've only time for one, read Lawrence Hills' *Good Fruit Guide*. To design for pears, plums and cherries is similar, if a little less complicated, there being fewer varieties to choose from.

An Alternative Selection for North America

The main problem here is that climatic variations are enormous, and that certain varieties will only do well in certain local conditions.

Other Points

An additional consideration is timing crops and storage qualities to give a balanced harvest, which is useful. It's no good growing tonnes of James Grieve or Worcester Pearmain apples, because they don't keep well. It is possible, with a good cool store, to be eating the last of the previous year's apples when the first ones come ripe. Judicious planning will also give you a good balance of dessert and cooking fruit. If you want to make cider then there is a whole other range of adapted cultivars to look at.

Group I Apples for everyone, graded from compact to vigorous

Variety	Comments
Gala	Thin to prevent small fruit
Jonathon	Tendency to bitter pit in storage
Red Delicious	Eat young. Poor pollinator
Golden Delicious	Russets in humid areas
Fuji	Sweet, stores well
Jonalicious	Flavoursome, disease prone
Jonagold	Delicious, poor keeper
Mutsu (Crispin)	Later Golden Delicious type
Blushing Golden	Tarter, stores well
Braeburn	Early blossom, quite tart
Empire	Crisp, needs thinning
Melrose	Large, dull red
Idared	Better for storage
Stayman Winesap	Excellent keeper

165

Variety	Comments
Granny Smith	Late, excellent keeper
Mantet	Cold hardy
Mollies Delicious	Early red, good pollinator
Chieftain	Good keeper, nice sharp taste
Splendor	Pinkish, juicy

Group 2 Disease resistant apples

Liberty	Dessert quality, medium keeper
Redfree	Big red summer apple
Dayton	Bright red, tart
Prima	Long harvesting season
Sir Prize	Log yellow, easy bruiser

Group 3 Gourmet varieties

Ashmead's Kernel
Tydeman's Late Orange
St Edmund's Pippin
Pitmaston Pineapple
Cox's Orange Pippin Will only succeed in Pacific NW

Group 4 Exceptionally hardy apples, surviving −35 degrees F in winter.

Mantet	Canadian
Haralson	Quick to come into bearing
Empire	(See above)
Honeygold	Like Golden Delicious
Keepsake	Hard, crisp, good keeper
Yellow Transparent	Cooker, very early, doesn't keep
State Fair	Late summer ripening
Wealthy	Long ripening period, eat from tree
Fireside	Large, productive
Sweet Sixteen	Crisp, good flavour

In the Southern US there will be insufficient chill to allow apples to break dormancy. Yellow apples do better here. These varieties are suggested as good 'beginner's' apples.

Small Fruit

There is a large range of fruit known as 'small fruit' rather than orchard varieties. This includes blackberries, currants, gooseberries, strawberries and so on. Small fruit are either climbers (like blackberries) or grow on small bushes. However, harvesting can be made easier by using trained bush shapes, as with trees. Gooseberries, for instance, are available as standard bushes, about a metre high. This makes it much easier to reach the fruit, and to prune the bush in such a way that you can pick without being savaged by the plant's thorns. Other varieties of thorny small fruits have been bred thornless. This means blackberries, in particular, can now be enjoyed by the bucketful without bleeding knuckles.

Some small fruits are especially hardy, such as redcurrants, most raspberries, the *Vaccinium* family (that is blueberries, cranberries, bilberries and so forth), and can be produced on poor soils with short growing seasons. Others are shade tolerant, such as the Whinham's Industry, a red variety of gooseberry, and strawberries, which are naturally a woodland edge plant.

There is also a large range of wild small fruits. Indeed, most wild fruits are smaller than the cultivated varieties. Autumn berrying is to my mind the most satisfying harvest of the year. The golden and red colours of autumnal foliage with the rich juicy baskets of gathered fruits make winter a bearable prospect. The rush to eat the hedgerow jelly gives away its quality. Wild fruits are naturally high in pectin and vitamins. By using them in jams, pies, jellies and wines their sharper taste can be disguised. Rose hips, haws, sloes, bullaces, crab apples, and from North America the *Amelanchiers* are all desirable crops.

Rhubarb is the fruit that never was, being in fact a stem. It is commonly used to fill the gap in spring where the fruit runs out. Rhubarb is extremely hardy, but does like to be well fed with manure. It is a good cleanser of the digestive system, and many people find it too tart for their taste. This can be cured by cooking it with cheese or angelica, both of which neutralise its acidity without adding sugar.

Refined sugar is a common additive to fruit recipes, and a hard one to replace. However, sugar in this concentrated form is very bad for the body. Fruits are naturally high in sugar themselves, and so recipes which reduce or cut out sugar are to be preferred.

Nuts

With the availability of cheap imports from hotter countries, nuts declined in importance in temperate climates. Many trees protect themselves by accumulating unpalatable chemicals in their living matter, so that acorns, for instance, although widely available in cool latitudes, are made bitter by high levels of tannin. For centuries people had carefully selected the sweetest and most prolific fruits of nut trees, and grown them on to establish edible nut groves.

Nuts present a yield with very high protein content, beneficial oils, and good storing qualities. Some, such as beech mast, may only crop well periodically. The very high density of growing area created by the vertical scale of mature woodland means that with good management nut crops are an additional yield to a standing timber crop. This is a fine example of the principle of 'stacking'.

Last autumn I located two rows of sweet oaks planted on old established estates some two hundred years ago. I found the acorns from these palatable raw. Some acorns will need 'leaching' in cold water to remove bitterness before using.

Walnuts are high yielding if good varieties are chosen. The 'English' walnut *Juglans regia* is in fact derived from Persia. Selected trees will fruit quite far north in maritime climates, and in Germany grafted varieties have been developed which fruit within five years. Continental climates will do better with trees derived from China, which suit more extreme conditions, and the black walnut of America, *Juglans nigra*. The productivity of the hazel family *Avellana* spp. has been increased by breeding in Mediterranean strains to give filberts and cobs with larger nuts. Sweet chestnuts are also a possibility in many areas.

In general, nut trees should be planted as grafted named varieties, unless you really are planting for crops in sixty years' time, which is how long some oaks and beeches take before they produce seed. Grafted varieties fruit better, and usually within five to ten years of planting.

All fruit and nut crops will benefit from wind protection, and unless conditions are marginal there is a possibility of crops on quite exotic trees in occasional good years. The trees themselves, such as kumquats and some varieties of orange and lemon, may be hardy to ten degrees of frost. It is the buds and blossom which will not survive these conditions. All trees become hardier when established.

Stock Integration

There are a number of traditional ways of integrating stock into orchards and nut groves. Hens, geese and ducks can run quite happily amongst young orchards, keeping down insect populations and grass, and feeding the soil with their manures. With mature half standard or standard trees sheep can be grazed below the orchard. This was common practice in traditional apple growing areas like Kent, England, but has declined as smaller trees are being used, leaving lower branches prone to damage by stock. The practice still continues in cider orchards in the Somerset levels.

Particularly prized as meat is 'apple-fed pork'. This comes from pigs fattened in orchards at windfall time. The pigs simply clear up all the apples lying on the ground in a labour-free exercise which also gives the orchard a quick manuring. There are no fallen apples left to attract disease or pests. In North America, pigs fed on mulberries are a similar beneficial relationship, and other pig fodder includes honey locust, hickory nuts and sand cherries. Ranging the animals in the orchard may secure as much as two months of feed without additions.

The practice of ranging stock in woodland to gather nuts is known as pannage. There are still people with registered pannage rights in the New Forest in Hampshire, England. At Rothiemurchus in Scotland, forest rangers are considering using pigs to aid regeneration in the natural pine forest. Overpopulations of stock become predatory in forests. Yet their absence is counterproductive. Because of their nuzzling and scuffing actions forest floor litter is cleared, allowing fallen seed to germinate. Without this input the seed cannot get a hold and perishes.

Deer and cattle will also flourish in woodlands, both needing the open grassy glades of natural woodland for grazing. There are many beneficial leaf fodders for stock, which we shall look at in the next chapter.

Forest Gardens

The natural climax of succession for your orchard or nut grove is a forest garden. Such a development can be actively designed. The trees should be planted far enough apart so that they do not touch at full size. When the trees are young this leaves a considerable space between, which presents many growing possibilities.

Young trees do not like competition from grass, and so ground for a metre around each tree should be kept free of grass. Whether this is because grasses exude chemicals not liked by young roots, or whether it is just competition for nutrients, is not known. However, the tree needs protection until it is established. Mulching will be a good way of doing this with some added advantages. Mulching around the drip line of the tree will help capture nutrients running off the branch ends. It also tends to be the point at which the root tips are growing and so is a way of protecting the roots from drought, and of increasing damp and nutrient infiltration into the soil by all the usual advantages offered by mulching. Care should be taken with mulching in especially cold dry climates. The mulch encourages root growth near the surface, and these roots can dehydrate in frozen conditions. Here other techniques will be needed to keep down competition until the tree is established.

Now, another thing has happened – a

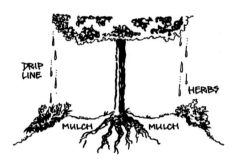

Robert Hart lives in Shropshire, England and has created around his home a magnificent Forest Garden, a temperate wilderness rich in fruit, vegetables and herbs, as productive as any garden, for far less work. His example has inspired many others to experiment with creating edible woodlands.

small round garden has appeared round each tree. This can be planted with herbs, onions, green salads, peas and beans, in fact any crop which is not too nitrogen-hungry (like cabbages) and which offers good associations for the tree in repelling pests or attracting beneficial insects.

The fruit and nut trees may be interplanted with species like rowan and birch which are fast-growing and which can be cut for firewood when the orchard crops are larger. Now our trees are making more connections with their neighbours and an orchard starts to become the developed system of a forest garden. We see the seven layers of growth from roots to climax trees develop, and each has its own place. Mistletoe is a common crop in orchards in south-west Britain, grown on apple trees for the Christmas market. So your forest garden can even aid the progress of love in the season of goodwill.

15 AGRICULTURE

The development of sustainable agriculture will not happen overnight and it will not be easy, for consumers, farmers or bankers. It is, however, our most urgent priority. The techniques discussed in this chapter are examples of ways of achieving it. They are not the whole story.

How many a poor immortal soul have I met well-nigh crushed and smothered under its load, creeping down the road of life, pushing before it a barn seventy-five foot by forty, its Augean stables never cleansed, and one hundred acres of land, tillage, mowing, pasture, and woodlot! The portionless, who struggle with no such inherited encumbrances, find it labour enough to subdue and cultivate a few cubic feet of flesh.

Henry David Thoreau, *Walden*

Minimum Tillage

Each environment has plants and animals fitted to profit by its particular characteristics. Pestilential weeds, such as docks, tell us something. In the field below my house, as I write, my neighbouring farmer has a fine crop of docks; they have resisted three chemical sprayings and five cultivations. The particular place of this plant in the ecology is to break up compacted ground. The solution to docks as a weed is to recognise why they appear.

In this case frequent passage of heavy farm vehicles only contributes to the conditions in which the dock flourishes. We talked in the section on gardening about reasons not to till the soil, and the same explanation applies here. How can farmers work without tilling?

Firstly, there are two methods of growing seeded crops which do not require the plough – direct drilling, and surface seeding. In a natural system of crop management we build a mulched soil as crop residues are returned to the soil surface. Seeds are designed by nature to germinate well in just such a humic layer, sending off their exploratory roots into this moist seedbed, and later finding their way into the topsoil.

To the average farmer, with a large overdraft indicating a heavy financial commitment to big equipment, this will

171

not be good news. Nor is the increasing burden of bank debt with which farmers are saddled. If we are to make farming a profitable *and sustainable* enterprise, then we need to support farmers in radical strategies. One of the main difficulties with growing on a 'trash' based system of seeding into mulch is that harvesting equipment is all built to deal with 'clean' soil and minimal stalk lengths.

In working with no-tillage methods there is a period of establishment where crop volume is depressed, but net yield is still worthwhile because of the reduced inputs in expensive fertilisers and pesticides. The additional yield of improved crop, soil and human health is one which is not accounted for in conventional systems.

Other ways of avoiding tillage are to grow crops which do not require plough culture to achieve yield. This may mean a smaller scale and more labour intensive agriculture, with great accent on horticultural crops. But who then will grow our grain? Grain growing in Europe has two expendable outputs. One is the massive amount of overproduction which sits rotting in warehouses, eating up government subsidies, and the other is the large amounts of grain which are grown as animal fodder. Free ranging stock fodder systems can eliminate much of the need for this production. The farmer can also accentuate perennial crops, such as fruit and woodland.

Whenever the River Tweed floods past the end of our road, thousands of tonnes of topsoil wash down in the brown waters to the sea. This is a massive waste of fertility and it ultimately leads to desertification. It is a pattern to be seen in every watershed in the agricultural areas of the developed world. Use of the plough is to blame.

Natural Soil Feeders

If we are not to plough the soil, we must still feed it. As with gardening techniques, we must look to build conditions which favour the natural residents of the soil. Earthworms can build topsoil at the rate of fifteen tonnes per hectare per year, or 30mm all over, every five years. Plentiful humic matter at the surface, and slightly acid soils are two encouraging factors for our wriggly friends.

32 The layers of soil

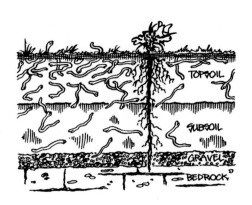

172

It is only recently that the full significance of mycorrhizal associations has been discovered. Mycorrhizae are minute fungi which establish in beneficial relationships with plant roots. Their presence stimulates and aids plant growth and yields. Soil which has been chemically sprayed will be deficient in these organisms, as they are poisoned by as slight an intervention as an overdose of soluble nitrogen fertiliser. Re-colonisation can be hastened by spraying mycorrhizae on the soil. There are also crops, such as field beans, which will stimulate new colonies of these undersoil workers.

Many crops have good effects on the soil if their roots are left in the ground, and other residues returned to the field. This may be by means of composting, but in fact could be dealt with more efficiently by simply leaving the trash to lie.

Grazing regimes where stock run over arable ground, for even short periods, increase the natural fertility by manure, and by degradation of the plant wastes through feeding and trampling.

Erosion Avoidance

Continuous soil cover aids erosion resistance. Never plough land steeper than thirty degrees. Frequent belts of trees, running along or just off the contour, break downslope water flows and slow up erosion if it has started.

These in time have a terracing effect. Similarly, swales and other diversion drains cut into hillsides arrest flooding and divert nutrients and water back into the managed system.

Trees protect banks of streams and drains. There are often policies of cutting back tree growth on river banks to give free drainage and so prevent flooding. In practice the increased incidence of flooding is because of greater run-off as a consequence of present policies, one of which is cutting down upstream woodland. Belts of mixed balanced woodland, continuous groundcover, and land management policies which encourage the creation of a deep open soil structure will all help stem run-off.

Foggage

Foggage is a system of managing pasture by leaving it stand. 'Fog' means the grass which comes after a haymaking, or the long dry grasses which result if hay is not cut. It presents an opportunity of keeping stock overwintered outdoors on a rough kind of pasture. Its advantages for the farmer are that no hay need be cut, and that beasts do not suffer the great stress which is caused to their digestion by a radical change of diet twice yearly, through overwintering indoors.

Permanent pastures are sown with a very wide range of grasses and herbs, to give continual growth of green matter throughout the season, and a high resistance to 'poaching' (the damaging of pasture by the continual treading of the stock). Consequently it needs the incorporation of very vigorous grasses, such as cocksfoots, not much favoured by farmers on short term leys (pastures). The stock must be kept on the foggage all winter to ensure that it is eaten back to the roots, and for this reason works best where mixed stock are available, although cattle will graze it alone. Sheep, however, will not eat coarse grass and need new growth to keep them going. They will find the young shoots coming up under the standing hay of the rough grasses, much earlier than in a cropped open sward.

The herbal content of the sward gives good mineral balance to the whole. The pastures need reseeding no more than every three years, and this is best done by scraping up the trashy layer with any dead grasses, and returning the whole to the surface, chopped and mixed with fresh seed. There is machinery to do this job.

The effect of this system of low intervention is to create a deep topsoil, and year-round feed of high value. Come springtime, the cattle in particular will look pretty thin, but as the new growth comes in they put on weight fast and soon overtake stock which have been overwintered in sheds, which suffer loss of condition on being readmitted to pasture.

Field-based feed can be supplemented

Arthur Hollins has pioneered foggage as a system for the modern farmer from his holding in Shropshire, England. The above observations are based on his work. His vigour and commitment in sixty years as a farmer in the face of official hostility has left him cheerful and inspiring. His life story is amongst the booklist.

by the planting of edible hedgerows. Alder provides feed rich in nitrogen, good for the protein requirements of young calves, hazel is rich in lactic acids for milking mothers, and many other hedgerow trees such as willow and gorse are edible. The classic English park landscape with its trees grazed up to head height of the cattle remind us that stock actually like to have this mixture in their diet. Horses sick with colic will seek out and eat apples to cure themselves. We might reduce work on the farm and increase stock health by simply planting a wide range of feed and letting them choose what they need. Surplus can be cut for mulch.

Stock Versus Arable

Economic pressures have driven many farmers in the EEC away from stock, and restricted their arable crops to a very narrow range. If farming by natural methods, the broadest possible range of stock and arable is the best way to ensure soil and crop health.

This means returning farming to the practice of land stewardship and food growing for the community in which the farm is situated. It means freeing our farmers from their present burden of farm debt.

Health regulations can make it impossible to produce genuinely organic meat on the farm, as injections, dips and sprays against certain diseases are compulsory. This is for the very good purpose of eliminating illnesses of plague proportions such as foot and mouth disease and swine vesicular disease. Those who want to see a wholly organic farming system find the compromise difficult, and may prefer to move to a vegetarian food economy.

Ranging on foggage systems offers a more healthy solution. Taking less is one option – we certainly do not need the amount of meat protein which we eat in Western developed countries. Yet livestock are part of a balanced natural system, and we do not have the right to exclude them. I would prefer meat products to be derived only from wild animals. However humane the farmer, there are always perceivable injustices in farming stock if you come from an 'animal rights' point of view. They cannot ultimately be eliminated. Nor do we yet have sufficient restored wilderness to which we can return livestock and give them any expectation of survival.

Balanced farming in the Permaculture mould means stock and arable.

Thinking Again About Stock

We have some very conservative attitudes as to what comprises stock. Beef, pork, lamb, and chicken between them form a large part of the consumed meat products. In some parts of Europe, horse meat is cheerfully eaten. In the world as a whole there is a much larger range, and products such as venison are becoming increasingly popular in the home market. How many farmers seriously contemplate growing fish? Yet one of the most valuable crops to the few farmers in southern England who have tried it has been crayfish. In America the tradition of the farm pond has perhaps lingered longer. Why is it that the average Briton eats as much chicken in two weeks as s/he eats duck in a year?

In mediaeval times every village had a fishpond as one of its resources. Unfortunately at the same time wild game became the preserve of the powerful and the concept of 'poaching' appeared. Wild game remains a considerable part of the 'stock' of any land.

Apart from the genetic stock of wild animals there is a need to preserve old breeds, many of which, particularly those which had a strong local significance, such as Belted Galloway cattle, are threatened with extinction as new breeds come in. Rather as with new prolific vegetables and grains, these new breeds have a tendency to vast size and 'high productivity'. This often means that they receive growth-promoting injections, and that their growth rates are such that they can only be sustained by the application of large amounts of concentrated high-protein feed. Re-enter the chemical combines with two sales portfolios in hand, one for stock and the other for all the chemicals needed to keep them going.

This does not help the small producer. Nor does it help the future strength of our stock to be eliminating valuable genetic material. The Rare Breeds Trust keeps information on such animals, and helps maintain breeds through its networks. Using traditional breeds is another way of ensuring that stock have the capacity to do well on the natural resources of the environment in which you have to work. We are not looking for the highest yield from any one element of the farm, but the highest sustainable yield which can be derived from all its elements. The most delightful example of a systematic approach to stock is the recent discovery of a farmer who trained pigs to round up his sheep!

Biogas and Other Energy Cycles

The farm offers many ways to evolve larger energy cycles. Stock offer the yield of muck they produce. If this matter is returned to the land a cycle is complete, but it is not the fullest possible usage. The methane gas will be lost into the atmosphere, when it is a useful product. By storing the sludge in enclosed chambers, the gas can be captured and used as a fuel. Gas production can be enhanced by the rotting of green manures.

Other on-farm energy cycles suggest the use of farm-grown timber for firewood, heating derived from straw bales, the use of stock to heat buildings, and the use of draught animals for transport, milling and lifting gear. Farms which are also orchards will welcome the presence of bees to pollinate their fruit crop, and will benefit from the additional yield of honey.

The underlying principle is to close the energy cycles on the farm into complete systems, and then extend those systems to have more beneficial usage of the available energies.

Rotations

Rotations are as important to crop health on the farm as in the garden. With broadscale cropping they are essential. The general move towards monocropping which we have seen in recent years leads to poor soil fertility and higher incidence of plant diseases. New strains are continually being developed but each is eclipsed by the next outbreak of smut or virus yellows. Wouldn't healthier management policies be the real cure?

Trees in Broadscale Farming

Permanent agriculture calls for perennial crops, and trees are the perennial crop with the greatest number of uses. The return of farming systems to forms of agro-forestry offers many outlets for employment and manufacturing to enrich the rural economy. The work of the new generation of green-wood turners has shown that attractive and saleable products fitting to present tastes can be made from coppice timber. Farm woodlands offer on-site sources of timber for building and fencing.

Agro-forestry can also develop from the 'let's stick some trees in that difficult corner' approach to integrated designs as practised in successful intensive economies like China. Bands of

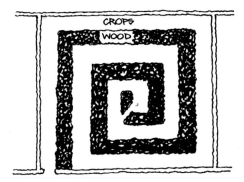

woodland, say thirty metres broad, are interplanted amongst fields used for arable and pastoral rotations. The reduction of windchill is beneficial to plants and animals alike.

Designing for Climate

Farm layouts must be designed around the micro- and macroclimates determined by position and variations in the landscape. A steady scheme of management could take us away from the square field philosophy of the past. Trees planted as bays can become suntraps, creating a web of linked fields with high solar trapping capability, and reduced wind speeds.

Working with the contours of the land increases our sense of understanding of climatic variation. We have, at present, a tendency to design crops around market prices, and not the land. So we have the sight of farmers struggling to make seedbeds for wheat or barley on land that would be much better as permanent pasture. The long-term consideration in sustainable farming must be the fertility of the soils, and the overall capacity of the farm to provide food and a living. This means directing Western agriculture back to working with the land rather than against it.

Diversity and Stacking

Farmers have been saying to each other for some time now that they must diversify for the inherent safety in building systems which have many possible yields. Failure of any one element then has a minor effect on the whole.

Stacking means looking to use all dimensions, all seasons and times as possibilities for yield. Farms which see this have opened up by selling 'pick your own' fruit, by setting up garden centres, turning old houses into holiday lets, or putting aside part of the farm as a 'rare breeds park'. The benefits are not just in the money which changes hands as the consumer pays for their small purchase. They are also in the whole uplift of interest and understanding which is given to the lay person who so encounters the farm. Before 1945 farming was a busy and a mixed business. It was also labour intensive. The whole progression of farming since then has been towards monoculture and machine intensive production. We have lost in our communities the common understanding of farming as a way of life.

Diversity and stacking as principles are no more than common sense. Unfortunately they are not common enough.

Fukuoka/Bonfils

In some respects the cropping is like traditional organic wheat growing. A seed bed is sown with clover. At around midsummer, winter wheat is sown into the bed of clover. The next crop is sown

Masanobu Fukuoka is a Japanese agricultural chemist turned natural farmer. What he has proved over forty years (and the evidence is clearly given in his books) is that intercropping and returning all residues to the soil enable us to build systems for growing grain which are high-yielding, disease free, and entirely without chemical inputs. His system uses an intercropped rotation of rice, clover and barley. Marc Bonfils, in France, has adapted this idea for temperate climate grain rotations, and the following observations are based on his work.

into the standing wheat before cropping after the following midsummer. There should be regeneration of clover between the harvest and the rising of the following crop. Organic waste from the harvest should be returned to the soil surface.

One difference in this system is that wheat grains are sown singly on a widely spaced grid, as much as a metre spacing apart, dependent on vigour of breed and time of sowing. This allows the plant to develop its natural shape and full number of tillers, or side shoots. As many as fifty seed heads per plant may result. Contrast this with the very close spacings of machine-sown wheat. Ideally the wheat should be of old, long-strawed varieties.

It will need to be harvested by hand, as existing machinery cannot cope with the long straw. As with other crops we have discussed, there is a high net yield, as there are very few external inputs. There aren't going to be many thousand acre wheat farmers rushing to take up this one, but then it's a technique for half-acre plots. And there was a time when every cottager grew their own grain. If we're talking about a return to meeting our own needs, then small scale grain production has to be part of the picture. Broadscale farmers who want to tackle some of these issues, but are frightened by the prospect of massively rising labour bills, might like to free the odd plot to enable people to smallhold, whilst gaining the benefit of their labour part time as payment.

The Independent Seed Merchant

Natural farmers will, of course, rush to support their local independent seed merchant rather than fattening the coffers of the all-devouring multinationals. This will be for the same reason as gardeners, but also on the principle of buying locally wherever possible if you want your local economy to flourish.

Added Value Products

One aspect of diversity and a recommended way forward for farmers (and for all small businesses) is to think added value. Most farm produce disappears down the lane leaving a wholesale merchant's cheque in its wake. The satisfaction of selling the crop all at once may be enjoyable, but the margins are small, and the minimum of labour element has been earned on the farm. How can the farmer hold on to a larger margin, and bring their market nearer the consumer? The answer is to add value on-farm.

The added value farmer sells cheese and yogurt, not just milk. Fruit growers sell jam and chutneys. Stock producers move from livestock sales to butchery, meat products and leatherworking. The whole cycle of adding value is essential to revitalising rural areas. The depopulation of the countryside and the booming of cities is happening the world over and ultimately spells a terribly degraded planet. Adding value to the raw materials of the countryside at point of production is the secret to reversing this tide.

Stock/Aquaculture System

Water offers us fishponds in our dammed lakes, preferably not as monocultures. Farm-based aquacultures need to be balanced and diverse, with all the elements of stacking seen on *terra firma*. Examples are: ducks feeding on pond-edge species, with carp bottom-feeding on the detritus and trout

179

dancing in the faster streams. Crayfish get fat in the calcareous streams, and we coppice the willow at the water's edge for basketry materials. Reeds are cropped for thatching, fodder and green manure. All water on the farm is cycled through biological cleansing systems. There might even be a few snipe down in the edge of that wetland for the pot one day. And to think, we used to spend all our time draining this land!

16 AQUACULTURE

Water conjures up the essence of life. In temperate climates with their abundant rainfall and their over-fished seas we have a great opportunity to make our coastal and inland water resources abundant in crops.

Fresh and Salt Water Environments

There are a small number of species which move through both environments. This is either because their lifecycle involves migration, as with eels and salmon, or because they have learned to feed in both, as with cormorants. River estuaries are of variable salinity, dependent on the state of the tide, and so they support edge species which are tolerant of the range.

In general the management of these two environments requires completely different species, and overall design is dealing with quite different climatic conditions.

Food Chains

As in any ecosystem, the survival of the inhabitants depends on a complex web of movement so that nutrients reach each member of the community. Most economic species thrive in water with high oxygen content, so that adequate throughflow is needed to aerate the water. Oxygen is absorbed by water at turbulent surfaces, and carbon dioxide is expelled there to the atmosphere. This means that wind, waves and solid surfaces (such as cause waterfalls) all interact beneficially with the body of water. Green plants need adequate carbon dioxide to survive, and excrete oxygen, and living creatures consume oxygen, exhaling carbon dioxide.

There is also a nitrogen cycle at work. Algae, bacteria, plants and insects provide nitrogen for fish. Fish faeces degrades giving ammonia, which in the presence of oxygenating bacteria eventually forms nitrate ions in solution. This either returns to the atmosphere as nitrogen, or recombines to form nitrate based foods for plant matter, continuing the cycle.

If an artificial water environment is

181

created, the design will need to be balanced to ensure that all these cycles function correctly.

Plant/Animal/Fish/Crustacean/Insect/Bird Species

In the species lists it is mostly the 'economic' species that are listed. These cannot function without a full complement of species which make a working environment, many of which will have little human usage. It is, of course, possible to build fish farms with nothing but fish in appropriate-sized tanks, eating concentrated feeds. But this is just another form of monoculture, and the output will be as tasteless and disease-prone as any other monoculture.

In a well-designed water system the stock and plants are balanced to meet each other's food needs, the water imperceptibly merges with the wetland edge environment, and each level of the water has been planned to support appropriate species. Trees have an important function in that they support insect populations whose larvae will go to bank and surface feeders. The surface fish and bird life will contribute to a rich humic mass on the bed which will help sustain bottom feeders. Some of the species (such as fresh water mussels and reeds) will have a critical role to play in maintaining water quality.

Zones Around and In Water

1 Fresh Water Environments

Here we find bank or cliff sides, beaches, shallow water, mid-water platforms and deep water bottoms, those species which live on the surface, which may or may not be anchored to the bed, and those which swim in the body of the water. So water boatmen are a surface-skimming insect, unlikely to be eaten by carp which are bottom feeders. There are also degrees of association on the land. Thus Chinese water deer are so called because they like to browse on swamp fringes, and alder and willow favour waterside conditions.

2 Maritime Environments

Marine fringes are best considered in cross section. The deep water is the

home of the fishes. Beaches tend to shelve, and just below low water mark, we find the red sea weeds. As the water becomes shallower, and the bed lighter, towards the high water mark we find more green weeds. Above this we find the intertidal area where eelgrass and shellfish live. Here we might find eider ducks grazing. Above the shore line, salt marsh has important functions. It is a source of fibre crops for paper making or thatching. It is important summer grazing for stock and wildlife. But it is also the natural method of land reclamation, trapping silt and nutrients, building a succession to scrub woodland.

The dry shore line may take its place, or may lie above the marsh, and is a special niche for many plants, a surprising number of which are edible.

Feeding

Edges of water environments should allow access. Ducks need shallow beaches to slide in and out of the water. Many fast-water fish like quiet bank-side pools for feeding in the shade. There are artificial devices which can aid self-management of the system, usually in the form of traps.

A floating cage with a one-way valve and some bait to attract flies will trap the insects and hold them at the water surface for fish that feed there. Filter units can be made to trap larvae and freshwater lice in such a way that they become fish food. Beds of plants at shelves in the mid water level make green matter and insects available to the fish that feed there. Bottom feeders can be used as scavengers of the detritus from human systems, and so form the last stage in biological water cleansing systems. It's all a matter of directing outputs and inputs into useful cycles.

Manures

If an aquaculture system is constructed, rather than found, it will need building up or digging down and then waterproofing. If this work is done by puddling with clay, or by lining with artificial impervious material such as butyl or concrete, then the final surface on which the water is stored will be largely sterile. It will need to be made fertile in the same way that any other growing system does. Rotted manure or compost can be layered on the surface.

Ponds accumulate detritus, and plants may have largely exhausted the original humus. Closed aquacultures will need maintaining by draining and clearing out surplus mud, with some refertilisation to follow. The detritus so removed can be used as land fertiliser, although it will be deficient in soluble nutrients.

Watery environments can supply green manure for dry-land cropping systems. This makes invasive water weeds, like water hyacinth, an asset.

Where natural water courses and drainage are eutrophied through excessive nitrogen run-off higher up in the water table, such green manures are a valuable way of trapping the wasted resource whilst cleansing the water supply.

Minerals

Loamy soils of alluvial origin offer the richest water soils as a starting point. Clays will be high in available mineral content, but lacking in nitrogenous matter. Sands and gravels will have the least nutritive effect.

Minerals can be added to the water. So if we want to grow crayfish in a fast-flowing gravelly stream, but the water is too acid, crushed calcareous rock could make the crop possible. In general, however, unless the aquaculture is an enclosed one, in which the water output is returned to the head of the system, we are better to choose species which suit the water quality we have.

Erosion Control

In small ponded systems erosion is not going to present much of a problem, unless it is through the action of large stock coming to drink at the water's edge. Construction of the shoreline in erosion resistant materials, or by diversion of drinking water to self-contained troughs is a solution.

Erosion happens where stream banks or hillslopes have become denuded of their protective covering of plants and trees, and the answer is to replant the natural flora of those areas. Reeds and rushes bind river edges with their root systems. Willows take easily from cuttings, and the cuttings can in turn be woven with thin prunings to make a living hurdle in the river bank. Alders will spread resistant root structures through the mass, and feed the neighbouring plants through their nitrogen fixing ability. Brambles (*Rubus* spp.) are quick at colonising eroded ground.

Anything which reduces the velocity of water over the banks will reduce erosion. If biological solutions do not work, or need some protection to get established, gabions offer a solution. These are wire or basket-work cages filled with rocks. In practice, as bank protectors they tend to cause erosion as their perimeters are undercut. They are most effective at trapping throughflowing sediments if laid across stream, so building up flood plain on their 'up' side. This is a valuable technique in creating growing areas by trapping eroded topsoil, and to stop gullying.

Flotsam

Floating rubbish can become valuable salvage. Firewood, or even constructional timber, floats on water and can be harvested. The possibilities of what you may find are as endless as the variety of things that are thrown or lost to the sea. Watch out you don't pick up any unexploded munitions or canisters of dangerous chemicals – people can be quite unfussy about what they lob in the water!

Design Features

Lagoons and spits at seashore or river and lakesides may be built using mechanical diggers at low tide or in a dry season. This will offer increased edge opportunities for shellfish and shallow-water fish culture. Floating cages can be used for the farming of sea food. This is a vast industry on the Chinese coastline, making the British and Canadian salmon farming industry a small affair.

Used car tyres can make happy environments for mussels and suchlike, whilst also providing erosion resistance at bank sides. In time habitats can be developed which disguise their nature.

Traps for water harvest have been used since time immemorial. There are special traps for lobsters and eels, and nets for salmon. Some 'traps' are there to attract a species without necessarily harvesting it, as when bird and bat boxes are placed to help species establish in a vicinity.

Some constructs are designed to attract by helping species move through the system, so fish weirs and jumps are

an important part of maintaining salmon and trout rivers. Where such waters are interrupted by hydro-electric schemes or dams for other reasons, they become essential.

Water management practices are starting to show that not only is the ecology better maintained by letting rivers take their natural shape, but that in the long run the maintenance costs against flooding are greatly reduced also.

Water Power

Storage of water for aquaculture purposes offers additional yield through harnessing outflows for active water power systems. It will be necessary to use mesh to prevent the loss of livestock from the system, and to protect the water power equipment from damage from floating debris. The size of the filtering mesh will depend on the size of plants, stock or particulate matter which is to be contained.

> Graham Swift's novel *Waterland* is woven around a history of the Fenlands in East Anglia before and during drainage. It is a marvellous insight into how the wet wilderness was sustainable before the eroding practices of farming took over the land. Wilderness makes the most productive aquaculture.

PART IV

UNDERSTANDING RESOURCES

17 FERTILITY

Permaculture is based on the understanding that we can meet our needs and still make the environment more fertile. The most important increase we can make is to our biological resources.

Patterns of Enrichment

There is no better soil analyst than the lowly earthworm.

Sir Albert Howard 1945

Knowing how to create fertile conditions is essential for making self-managing high yielding systems. Enrichment is meant in the sense of increasing the community's potential for sustainable, long-term yield.

From mountain to river valley, from fenland to desert, all can have their capacity for yield increased. History tells us that societies which chose to ignore this perished. The Tigris/Euphrates crescent, the fertile womb of western civilisation, lost political power and population when its soils were exhausted. I have stood on the Libyan coast at the ruins of Leptis Magna, as the dust blew around the remains of a once-magnificent Roman culture, and I have stood in hedgeless, treeless mono-cropped East Anglia, with a single field of oil seed rape stretching to the horizon, and I have seen the fate of the former lying just below the surface of the latter. Our future is wholly dependent on the fertility of our soils.

Chemical farmers would not continue to have their present results if they ceased their fertiliser interventions. These highly soluble artificial applications are subject to leaching. Leaching is the action by which soil water dissolves nutrients from the soil structure into watercourses. Seeking to enrich the capital value of all our assets, we want to make the seed bed (both physical and metaphorical) fertile. Farmers who use chemical methods may have profit which can then be applied to enriching purchases, but the process itself is barren.

Fertility concerns living processes. As soon as the process is interrupted and examined, we are looking at dead components. The key here is to *observe*

189

the living process, not to hope that by dissection and analysis we will find scientific solutions. The more personal your observations, the more relevant they are to your circumstances. So accurate scientific observation can never be completely objective.

If soils are deficient in nutrients, then food will be too and our health will suffer. Analysis can give us answers, but the easiest method of ensuring fertility, and the one you should learn to trust, is your own observation. A skilled gardener can tell a fertile soil by its smell, its texture and by the look of what grows in it.

Maintaining the fertility of soils is no longer enough, as we also need to repair past damage. It is just as much an objective for this year's crops to improve the fertility of the soil, as it is for them to give us this year's food. Media culture brings us images from around the world of starvation and disaster. It's as if this is remote – 'couldn't happen here'. It *is* happening here. An incredibly productive season might build 6mm of fresh topsoil. In recent storms in Southern England, ten times that amount was washed from fields in a single wet day. Similarly, Americans experienced the dust-bowl of the depression years. It's now commonplace to see agricultural topsoils eroding, and they're not being replaced, because the fertility that is relied upon comes in chemical bags, not humus. Farmers are planting into subsoil and chemical

solutions. It can't carry on indefinitely.

This pattern can be applied to all human activity. 'There is no finer investment for any community than putting milk into babies', said Winston Churchill. What he implied, at a time when the intentions of the country were completely and destructively devoted to war, was that if a community in stress ceased building the future, winning the conflict would be futile.

If you do not believe that desertification can happen in a temperate climate, look at a Scottish grouse moor. Where are the people? Where are the trees? Where are the crops? A few game birds and the odd sheep do not make much more of an ecology than the subsistence farming of the Saharan fringes. This land was once natural oak and pine forest, a rich and intimately interconnected environment capable of self-regenerating for centuries, and supporting a human population on its surpluses. It is only the financial income from tourism and bloodsports that support any viable communities at all in such 'wet deserts' now. Present farming practice will continue to reduce the capital worth of all our soils unless there is radical change soon.

Definition of True Yield

Yield is not a fixed sum in any design system. It is the measure of the comprehension, understanding, and ability of the designers and managers of that design.

Bill Mollison: *Permaculture, A Designer's Manual*

Conventional agricultural economics will accept the market price of a single commodity when cropped as the yield figure. We need to look in all directions, physically and in time, to understand the true nature of yield. This is as much so of manufacturing as it is of land usage.

Firstly, the true yield of the crop is *not* the derived income (or weight) of the harvest. It is the difference between what you end up with, and what you put in. If you plant a thousand acres of Sitka spruce, and harvest it over a period spanning some years, the true calculation of yield will involve subtracting the energy cost of creating and maintaining the plantation. This should include machinery and fossil fuel usage, and costs of the tree nursery. It will deduct the environmental impact of acidification and soil poverty caused by the monocropping. It will want to know what consequences the plantation had on local industry, wildlife and amenity. The pollution caused by artificial fertilisers, pesticides and end product generation, including transport, will need to be considered. You might even want to know the cost to the community of not having that land for other purposes.

If accounting was carried out in this holistic way there would be little incentive for manufacturing industries to use polluting processes. Edward de Bono has a graphic solution for this problem – all factories must take their water intake from downstream of their site, and send their waste upstream!

Yield is meaningless if it has no-one to take advantage of it. It is the web of life which gives the product a purpose, and it needs to be able to harvest the yield in a productive way. It's no good knitting sweaters if no-one wants them. It's no good creating corn, milk, butter or wine if they sit in 'mountains' or 'lakes', accumulating storage charges, and ultimately becoming unusable.

Yield also includes intangible needs: health, social harmony, a sense of purpose and being needed, mental stimulation, and time to play, to name a few.

All systems have yield without our intervention. Wilderness is incredibly rich in resources, and even apparently barren landscapes, such as the Arctic tundra, are full of riches for those whose history and observation makes them able to see them, in this case the indigenous people, Inuit (Eskimos) or Sami (Lapps).

A better way of measuring is to think in terms of energy. A good question to ask of any given situation is: 'Does this product increase available energy or does it reduce it?'

It is possible, for instance, to measure the amount of energy consumed to produce a given quantity of a specific

191

food, and the amount of energy which that food makes available when harvested. The unit usually used for this sum is the calorie. Larger quantities can be measured as Kilowatt/Hours (kWh). Peter Segger in *The Organic Food Guide* estimates that the 100 per cent increase in farm food production between 1945 and 1985 in the UK has been achieved at the expense of a 1500 per cent increase in energy input. If we audit the energy side of this business growth we're talking about a trade that has got eight times *less* efficient in forty years! In his book *Ecologistics* Patrick Howden derives figures for a 'reasonable human diet' showing a daily food consumption measured in energy terms at 2.78 kWh (or 2.39×10^6 calories).

If, for example, we rely upon frozen vegetables for this diet, the production efficiency is only 21 per cent, i.e. 100 units of energy input produce 21 units of food energy output. To get 2.78 kWh of food energy its production and its processing, before we cook it, has already consumed 13.23 kWh, or five times the energy it provides. The more the artificial inputs to the farming process (fossil fuels, fertiliser etc.) and to the processing of the product (additives, plant and machinery, packaging) then the worse this equation becomes. To be kind to the environment we must produce all our food for the minimum energy expenditure possible.

There are strategies for achieving energy-efficient food production, which have the desirable by-products of giving tastier, more nutritious food and a more attractive landscape.

Cycles of Growth

. . . All of us are doomed to die. Yet it is often ignored or deliberately forgotten that the unending death-roll of all creatures, including ourselves, is the essential complement to the renewal of life.

James Lovelock, 1979

Life is a self-replenishing cycle within a web of unintelligible complexity. We cannot hope to 'know' the whole of this process, but we can learn from observation at two levels – the scientist equipped with expensive equipment and technical know-how, and the lay practitioner with their basic human senses, and practical experience. Both are helpful in different ways.

The closest science has come to analysing the secret of 'life' is the discovery of deoxyribonucleic acid, or DNA for short. Living matter is composed of structures largely made from cells. Each living organism commences life as a single cell which divides and increases until the mature form of the organism is achieved. Eventually the organism dies. It is also usual for parts of the organism to die during its life, and be replaced by new cells. In dying, the nutrients which

192

created the organism will become available to other life forms.

The direction and pattern of this whole cycle of life is dictated by the DNA within each cell. It is a genetic blueprint carried in each part of the whole which tells it what to do next. The overall picture is one of continual variety and change. Cross-fertilisations and mutations of genes ensure differentiation, aided by adaptation to different environmental conditions, or extinction because of failure to adapt.

Each species requires (in greater and lesser degrees from none to plenty) chemical nutrients, light, water, space and neighbours. For example, fungi may require an absence of light, whereas herbs require strong sunlight, and lots of it. You can't have fish out of water (for long), nor will many land plants survive in saturated soil, as their roots will become oxygen deficient.

Temperate climates offer natural extremes from well below freezing to boiling point (e.g. in hot springs), from 100 per cent humidity to extreme desiccation, from highly acid to highly alkaline. There may also be very salty or windswept environments, those which suffer concentrated heat to those which are permanently shaded. Then there is a middle range of environments which avoid these extremes completely or suffer them only occasionally. Amongst the croppable plants and animals adapted to this middle range we find most of our useful species. Some species thrive at extremes, making them useful for such habitats, but they are not in the majority. Plants which are most abundant in temperate climates prefer, and recognise as fertile, soils which have:

> adequate provision of essential chemical elements
> sufficient water
> a structure which is open enough to admit sufficient air
> optimum alkalinity/acidity (measured as pH)

In addition, all this will be futile, unless they:

> have enough sunlight and dark for their photosynthesis/ transpiration systems to function
> are sufficiently protected from the hostile effects of climate
> are healthy enough, well adapted enough or well protected enough to resist predators

Most developed world farming methods rely for their science on the work of the German agrochemical researcher Justus von Liebig, carried out in the nineteenth century. Liebig measured vital soil chemicals. He concluded that nitrogen (N), phosphorus (P) and potassium (K) were the essential elements for life. Present fertilisers, bags of which are stacked by the truckload in nearly every farmyard, still have N,P,K stamped on the side, with numbers indicating proportions. Liebig's discovery was a great boon for the chemical industries.

Such has been the growth rate of artificial fertiliser application that 20 per cent of the world's human harnessed energy supply will be needed to produce chemical nitrogen by the year 2000 AD. Now it is becoming widely understood that the complex processes of soil life are not simply duplicated by the addition of these chemicals.

Firstly, applying N,P,K alone ignores the value of trace elements in the soil. Trace elements control many of the metabolic functions of plant growth, either directly, or as catalysts (catalysts are things which encourage a reaction). Animals (including humans) who eat food which is deficient in trace elements will become malnourished. The result is ill health, or even death, in extreme cases. These ill-effects can occur even when the diet is plentiful, if sufficiently poor in nutritional value.

Secondly, whilst recognising the importance of these major elements (N, P, K), these fertilisers are applied in quantities which are toxic to microbial life in the soil. These life forms are the natural fertilisers of the soil, and they die in the sudden onslaught of chemicals which in moderate proportions feed them. The old adage is: 'anything is poisonous, it's just a matter of quantity'.

Thirdly, these chemical fertilisers are highly soluble. This ensures that the applied matter will rapidly become available to feed the crop, and that the grower will reap a quick return on investment. It also means that a great quantity of the 'fertiliser' will not be intercepted by the crop at all, but will end up in water supplies and finally in the sea. Excess nitrogen compounds in drinking water are known to be capable of causing cancer, by forming nitrosamines upon ingestion. Whilst low levels of nitrate are beneficial, high levels can be lethal to young animals, including children. This water has probably taken, on average, twenty years to filter through the water table, and the application of chemical fertiliser has dramatically increased in the last twenty

years. We are being poisoned by our farming practices, and it will get worse.

Soil Development Techniques

Our first goal is to make deep, rich, enduring topsoil. Topsoil is the upper layer of 'earth', the living depth of which rarely exceeds 2m. Below this we find subsoil, and below that, maybe gravel resting on bedrock. Topsoil differs from the lower levels in having abundant life in the form of worms, burrowing creatures, bacteria etc. and high humic content. Humus is decayed organic matter.

The nature of the soil may be affected by its type, i.e. clay, silt, sand or any admixture thereof (see Chapter 6: Landscape). Good topsoil has an open structure trapping air. The layers should change imperceptibly through the soil. Acid soils and compacted or heavily tilled soils can form 'pans' – hard layered surfaces between different strata forming barriers to nutrient and root penetration. Ideally, water travels through these materials both upwards and downwards. When the topsoil is saturated with water (usually from October to April in the northern hemisphere) it is travelling downwards from rain infiltration. In the drying months of May to September the atmosphere is drawing it up from the water table.

If you're worried about your soil, get a professional soil analysis done. The essential message here is that the middle path is the safe one. Mid-range soils (neither too acid nor too alkaline) are healthy if they have enough humus and are free from poisonous residues. They will support the greatest natural soil flora and fauna, and the most productive crops. Follow the strategies for soil building and you will have soils like this.

If your soils are not ideal then there are plants adapted to do well on most soils. On polluted soils micro-organisms associated with algae, and reed and rush roots can even break down hydrocarbons such as petrol and diesel wastes, as well as trapping heavy metals. They just need the right placement in your system.

Trees are excellent at sending down roots deep into the soil, absorbing vital elements and spreading them as a mulch through leaf fall. Leafmould is initially acid, but humic acids quickly break down, and are balanced by the high lime content of dead leaves. Therefore they are great helpers in the work of soil creation. The growing tips of roots break up soil compaction. As with many living things there is die-back during the life of the organism as well as at its ultimate demise. This means that decaying roots leave nutrients behind (and well-dug channels) for new roots to follow on. Some herbs (e.g. horseradish, comfrey) root as deeply as trees. Green manure from crops like these can be cut and composted, or retted (i.e. wet rotted) to make liquid manures. A simple method is to cut the leaves and add them to water butts fed from roof-caught rain water. A comfrey liquid manure like this is the ideal feed for potatoes, beans and tomatoes.

We have looked at how no-tillage systems aid fertility. On poor soil a regime of digging combined with soil improvement may work over a limited period, looking to create favourable conditions for abandoning digging in the near future. This can be particularly helpful in creating soil structure in heavy clays by incorporating old building rubble, plaster etc. and in making a humic content in very sandy soils. Applying seaweed and other useful concentrated nutrients will improve impoverished soil.

People call the soil mineral matter, but some one hundred million bacteria, yeasts, moulds, diatoms, and other microbes live in just one gram of ordinary topsoil. Far from being dead and inanimate, the soil is teeming with life. These micro-organisms do not exist without reason. Each lives for a purpose, struggling, cooperating, and carrying on the cycles of nature.

Masanobu Fukuoka

By learning good techniques for mulching, by leaving roots of previous crops intact in the soil, you will create, not natural conditions (that would be meadow or forest), but soils for growing which have natural health.

Trace elements can be added in natural ways, by spreading crushed rock, calcified seaweed, and seaweed itself. If there is no available free harvest of these additives, they are also available in prepared form from specialist suppliers and well-informed nurseries and seed merchants. You do not need to add elements which your soil already has in plentiful supply.

All these methods provide long-term slow release of valuable nutrients into the soil, whilst also aiding structure formation. They need only be scattered on the surface for worms to distribute. The work of Dr Julius Hensel (published in 1894 as *Bread from Stones*) indicated that extremely healthy and productive plants were produced when trace minerals were made available to the soil from crushed rock. In recent years the idea has gained prominence from the work of John Hamaker (*The Survival of Civilisation*) who describes 'remineral-isation' as the only way to fend off a threatening ice age. The availability of calcium to the soil is also important in counteracting the effects of acid rain, and therefore local sources of crushed dolomite, gypsum and basalt are worth finding. The ideal application is glacial alluvium, which is present in the silt in some river valleys if you don't happen to live next to a melting glacier.

196

Specific Soil Improvements

1 Nitrogen

How do you supply nitrogen in an organic system? The simple answer is that you feed the soil, rather than the plant, by building and then maintain a high organic content. Apply manure, and compost (the latter usually only at garden scale). Adding green matter to the soil will help. So, for instance, when old pasture is ploughed in to make way for arable crops, there is the nitrogen yield of the decaying meadow in the soil. At first green manure causes the soil to lose nitrogen. As the microbial and worm life dies and decays in turn, the nitrogen becomes available to the next crop.

Using green manure can be a strategy on its own, but nature has provided us with some special helpers in the effort to refertilise our soils – plants which have the ability to concentrate nitrogen. There are three types of plants which are important here: firstly legumes (the pea family), secondly the alders (a small family of temperate climate trees) and thirdly 'dynamic accumulators' (plants which have the ability to store unusually high concentrations of certain elements in their green matter).

The family *Leguminosae* is a large collection of herbaceous plants, shrubs and trees which have in common seed cases of a pea shape, and the ability to trap nitrogen from the air. They do this by forming special nodules on their roots composed of nitrogen-fixing bacteria. Legume seeds take up 70 per cent of the plant's nitrogen. So if you grow beans, pick the pods, and then put back the remaining green matter, some nitrogen will be gained. The increase is much higher if the whole crop is mulched back onto the field. Contrast this with, for instance, wheat seed, which is mostly starch with very little nitrogen.

You can, however, fool legumes into shedding their root nodules before seeding. They do this in reaction to stress. So, cut the tops off the legumes, graze them with stock, subject them to shade or drought and they'll immediately release nodules into the soil where they will decay, leaving nitrogen-rich compounds. Minimum tillage systems require crop wastes to be returned to the soil.

Legumes will only fix nitrogen if the correct rhizobia (special bacteria) are present in the soil. Many areas will have high rhizobial level. Wild legumes will likely indicate their presence. You can, however, 'inoculate' the soil with sprays containing generic (unspecialised) rhizobia, or buy inoculated seed. It is particularly important with clover to have the correct rhizobium, so if planting foreign clover seed you will need the foreign rhizobia to be added.

The alder family has a similar ability to fix nitrogen from the air by producing

197

root nodules in conjunction with the fungus *Ascomycete frankia*. To make this nitrogen available it is possible to grow the alders with other plants. Alders like wet ground, but will stand other conditions. There may be small benefit from this form of cropping. Better effect will be had from cutting and mulching the leaf matter, which will bring extra nitrogen to the soil. Alders and some legumes can be fed as leaf hay to stock, giving them direct high protein feeds. The milk vetches are so called because of their ability to increase milk yields in stock, notably goats.

'Dynamic accumulator' is the title given to plants which can gather relatively high chemical concentrations to themselves. The queen of the pack is comfrey, which is notable for its rich assembly of vital minerals. Such plants have a special ability to collect and store these substances. The presence of hyperaccumulating plants has been successfully used to prospect for copper, selenium and nickel. To release nutrients from these plants, cut the green leaves and lay them on the ground as a mulch, or let the dead leaves lie when they fall in autumn.

2 Potassium

This mineral is available from wood ash, leaf material and bonemeal. Spread it on the surface or in compost heaps, avoiding too much wet ash which will retard decomposition of compost. Ash is best stored in a watertight bin over the winter and applied after the start of the growing season to avoid premature leaching away of the good stuff in winter rains.

The following accumulate potassium: bracken, carrot leaves, chamomile, chickweed, chicory, coltsfoot, comfrey, dandelion, docks, fennel, mints, mullein, nettles, oak bark, plantains, sowthistle, tansy, creeping thistle, vetches, watercress and yarrow. Chicory, chickweed, comfrey, dandelion, and yarrow would make an animal fodder bed which was prolific in damaged soils. Docks and vetches would be good rehabilitators against compaction and nitrogen deficiency. Beware the difficulty of getting rid of docks, dandelions and comfrey once planted.

3 Phosphorus

Bones, and guano (bird manure) are the best sources. Fish bones are particularly rich in phosphorus. Superphosphate is rock phosphorus combined with lime (to make the phosphorus available) and if you have local rock which bears phosphates, crushed rock could be a source for you. Bracken (which can be applied as ash), buckwheat, caraway, chamomile, chickweed, clovers, dandelion, docks, garlic, lupin, marigold, meadowsweet, mustards, purslane, savoury, sorrel, vetches, watercress and yarrow are all good accumulators of phosphorus.

These are ideal opportunities for multiple function design. Many of these coincide with nitrogen fixers and accumulators, and many are edible salad plants. The sowing of an edible lawn (see Chapter 10: Wilderness) on previously cultivated land needing phosphorus will give soil conditioning and a food crop simultaneously. The lawn could be mown and the cuttings left to lie as a mulch in the growing season.

4 Calcium

Calcium is generally applied to sweeten soil which is becoming acid. It is good at deterring club root, where it is generally applied as lime. Calcified seaweed brings lime with a good supply of trace elements. Crushed rocks are already mentioned above. Note that some plants are lime-hating so do not apply it indiscriminately; this is a bad idea in any case as it upsets the availability of other elements to plants.

5 Magnesium

This is best applied as ground Dolomite, where calcium is present to balance the magnesium and make it available.

6 Sulphur

Sulphur is used principally to adjust soils towards greater acidity. This tends to be more of a problem in arid regions. It is present in coal soot and volcanic ash.

7 Trace elements

Use seaweed or seaweed products as detailed above.

Compost

Mulching is an effective way of composting at the point of usage, but compost heaps can be a good way of converting material which is not easily mulched, such as kitchen waste and turf. A compost heap is, in effect, a slow fire. The whole object is to achieve a chemical balance and good moisture content so that the completed heap will rise in temperature, converting the contents to rich humus and killing annual weed seeds in one fell swoop. The great authority on compost heaps was Lawrence Hills, and any gardener should possess a copy of *Organic Gardening*.

Layer compost material so that the air can get through the heap, and see there is a reasonable mixture of nitrogen-rich material as well as woody or stemmy matter. Once given a good soaking the heap should be covered to trap moisture and heat. In summer the heap will be 'cooked' in a couple of months. In winter six months may be needed. A compost heap which has worked well will have traces of grey-white ash where the heat has reduced vegetable matter. Any matter not sufficiently composted can be put in the next heap.

There are compost tumblers made

199

from rotating barrels which are a great idea for the small city garden, where space is limited, and make it possible to sit in your garden without fruit flies everywhere.

Manure

Different animal and bird manures contain different balances and strengths of various essential elements. I believe the importance of manure is more in its ability to foster earthworms, and I apply manure to feed soil life, which in turn will feed the soil. Manure should be well rotted before being applied to the soil, in which case it will normally contain many worms and worm egg cases, as well as ideal feed stuff for the existing population.

Some contend that manure is too concentrated an intervention for natural ecosystems, and prefer to use vegetative matter directly or mix their manure into compost heaps. Perhaps the real role of interventions like these is in building a living soil, which, when it reaches a certain level of structure, nutrient content and species population, will become self-maintaining, requiring no further additions. For farmers (have you ever tried to compost for 150 acres?) manure is the sensible application, even more sensible if the animals deposit it whilst ranging. The Rothamstead wheat trials, run in the UK since the 1840s, show that manure is a marginally more effective fertiliser in conventional yield terms than the artificial fertilisers in the companion plot.

It used to be a requirement that straw, hay and manure stay on the farm of origin. This ensured that all farms had good supplies of natural fertility, and encouraged the beneficial effects of mixed farming (i.e. arable and stock).

Worm Culture

Many companies have sprung up in the last few years providing starter packs for 'worm composting', on both farm and garden scales. The worms create compost from heaps of organic matter, including kitchen scraps, crop residues, manure, green manure and any other items as bizarre as you are prepared to be adventurous. Research at the Open University has shown that paper and brewer's yeast gives wonderful results at steady warm temperatures. If you feel this kind of diet is a bit like using dope to win the Olympics then there's still hair from your local barber's shop, chipped bark and other stemmy material and all the old waste organics from the fruit and veg. shop on the corner, down to human excrement!

Each material is applied to the top of the worm nursery contents, allowing the worms to live naturally by feeding at the surface. In time all will be reduced to thick brown crumbly humus. When applied to the soil, a rich feed is being

Jean Pain invented a technique for chipping and fermenting green woody material for heat production from which the end product is rich fibrous soil fodder, ideal for mulching. You need adequate supplies of tree/shrub material and space to construct the heap. Mechanical chipping equipment is essential. The chipped material is soaked and piled in heaps which release heat slowly for long periods, sufficient to heat greenhouses, or even produce hot water for domestic purposes. Working mostly in arid areas of France, he developed a system which has great potential throughout the temperate world. (See the booklist.)

added with lots of free new soil diggers. Sufficient of the previous batch is kept to inoculate the next with worms. There is no wastage in this technique.

Extending Fertility

The pattern of fertility can be applied to any enterprise: the future sales of a business, the success of a club, the energy efficiency of a building, are all maximised, not by attention to the end result, but by ensuring that the structure from which that springs is developed in a self-regenerating way.

If this book inspires you to create your own Permaculture, or helps you add dimensions to the one you already enjoy, there will be nothing more important for you to do than increase the fertility of your community. The soil is a good place to start.

18 WATER

Since living processes depend on water, a good understanding of its action in the landscape is a requirement for any healthy land use.

Where's All the Water?.

How inappropriate to call this planet Earth, when it is clearly Ocean.

Arthur C Clarke

Water is the most important resource in the management of the human environment. Yet in Britain we have regarded water as something of a nuisance throughout recent history. We are notoriously damning of our 'wet' climate, and our major attention to this life-giving substance seems to have been how to get rid of it. World industrial and domestic per capita consumption is probably the highest it has ever been. We cannot sustain this profligate attitude.

The fragility of the world's water cycle is shown in the figures above.

The oceans of the world hold about 3.5 per cent of salts in solution, and so are largely unusable. Water with under 1 per cent salts in solution is classified as brackish. It can be used for irrigation if diluted with less salty water, but in time the salts build up and ruin the soil. Three-quarters of the world's fresh water supply sits frozen in Greenland and Antarctica. Fresh water in lakes, rivers and known underground reserves, in other words the water available for

Sea & Oceans	97.2	%
Ice Sheets/Glaciers	2.15	%
Groundwater	0.62	%
Freshwater lakes	0.009	%
Inland seas, salt lakes	0.008	%
Soil water	0.005	%
Atmosphere	0.001	%
Streams	0.0001	%

human consumption, amounts to about 0.05 per cent of all the water on Earth. This tiny proportion is actually quantified at 500,000 cubic kilometres, or 125 million litres for every one us. However, most of this needs cleansing before it is drinkable. Also, it is not evenly spread out where the people are concentrated.

The atmosphere is surprisingly dry. If all the water in the air fell as rain evenly over the planet's surface, it would only amount to 15mm of rainfall. The water stored in the planet's biomass is a tiny proportion of the whole, but is the vital medium which makes life on Earth possible in its present forms.

What Water Does

In the USA present average usage of water is around 400 litres per person per day, and 80 per cent of that is used for waste disposal. In other words, massive effort is used to cleanse fresh water, only to repollute four-fifths of it. Present trends show usage of as much as 600 litres per person per day by 2000 AD. Population is growing, usage per head is increasing, and industrial and domestic waste needing disposal is increasing. Major cities are finding it hard to match supply to demand. Los Angeles draws water from up to three hundred kilometres away. Over-harvesting of underground water leads to aquifer collapse and the salting of water tables,

preventing further usage. In dry summer weather, partially-treated sewage effluent forms 25 per cent of the water in the Thames (England), or a dilution of only 3:1.

Half of water usage in the developed world is for industrial processes. Between a third and two-fifths is for agricultural purposes, and only a tenth, or a little over, is used in municipal and domestic situations. Irrigation has been shown to increase crop yields in half the growing seasons tested in most of England. In the drier localities the figure is nearer nine out of ten. So agricultural usage can be justified by increased crop weights, yet water supplies are already severely stretched.

In living organisms water assumes differing vital forms. Its main function in large multi-cellular organisms (like us) is to transport nutrients and waste products around. Many organic processes have to take place in a watery environment. Evaporation of water from surface cells is a mechanism whereby living forms can cool themselves. Many organisms have intricate systems for conserving their moisture content.

Hydrological Cycle

All the rivers run into the sea, yet the sea is never full; unto the place from whence the rivers come thither they return again.

The Bible: Ecclesiastes 1:7

203

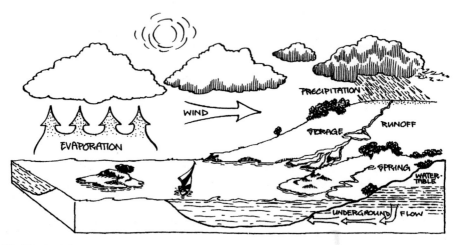

36 The hydrological cycle

The ceaseless flow of water around the globe is known as the hydrological cycle. Evaporation occurs when water vaporises from the sea and the land. Precipitation is the main way in which this water returns from the atmosphere to the Earth's surface. Rainfall on large landmasses is 90 per cent derived from the sea. Technically speaking, we should also consider sublimation. This is where ice turns straight to water vapour, without passing through a liquid stage. We see this when sunlight 'burns off a frost'. Another source of atmospheric water is transpiration. This is the process by which plants release water vapour from their leaf pores.

Water condenses from vapour to liquid, usually as dew. Frost is solid deposition. Precipitation (rain, snow, hail) is how the majority of atmospheric water returns to the land and sea. About a third more water is precipitated on land than evaporates or is transpired from it. The difference is the amount of water which runs back from the land to the sea through rivers and glaciers, and that which travels through infiltration into the soil and then flows back out to sea underground. The cycle is relatively constant.

At each stage of evaporation and condensation, the water leaves behind impurities, so evaporated sea water is fresh water. The salts are left behind in the sea.

Capturing It

Water enters a managed system in a number of ways. Precipitation, condensation and deposition are affected by the weather, the nature of ground surface, and microclimates. Thus extensive evergreen forests offer vastly more surface area for condensing maritime fogs than bare hillsides. Corrugated iron roofs are ideal surfaces for making condensation collection points because of their large surface area and rapid cooling properties.

There are also ground flows on the surface (streams and rivers) and underground, such as the streams which eat away below chalk landscapes. Groundwater is also moving through saturated bedrock or cracks in the subsurface below our feet.

Soil holds moving water and growing plants and trees store it. Plants and trees extract and pump water from the soil and rock below, converting it into plant cell matter, and transpiring it into the atmosphere. Plants also intercept rainfall, and trees absorb significant amounts of throughflow before it reaches the ground.

These sources can all be tapped, and we can construct reservoirs of our own. Dams, roofs and roadways have already been considered as collectors. We can also manage the existing landscape in ways which will encourage the water to infiltrate. Planting more trees reduces run-off, and intercepts more of the available atmospheric water vapour. Building deep soils with high humic content creates ground reservoirs.

Using It

We need to use the water we have as effectively as we can while it remains within our managed environment. This means being aware of water quality at each stage as it passes through. Appropriate water usage means taking water of only sufficient quality to meet the present need. Why flush the toilet with tap water when used washing water is quite good enough? Why use four gallons of water to flush away half a pint of pee in the first place?

And why throw water away because we have used it once? Why not construct biological systems of management which cleanse effluent water, and return it higher up the system for another trip round the cycle?

Recycling It

In nature water runs through rocks, uses the web of life in the soil, has specific creatures which cleanse water, uses evaporation, and has wetlands to help. In each of these processes particles are filtered from the water and chemical changes take place which return the water to a clean usable form. As anyone who has drunk distilled water will know, pure water is unpalatable. Water that is good for human usage has a balanced mineral content.

We can create processes which mimic these natural cleansing actions. Rainwater collected from roofs is stored in water butts. A little crushed limestone in the bottom counteracts the natural acidity of rainwater, and helps keep the water pure. Outflow through gravel beds or filters made of charcoal is a natural way of precipitating particulate impurities, and adding a little mineral content. Evaporation can be used with solar stills – sunpowered water cleansing. The most promising process is the wetland approach, covered below.

Sanitation

Water cleanses out domestic and industrial waste very effectively. Water is plentiful, easy to transport and, in diluting waste products, it makes it much easier to dispose of them. What is not so desirable is the way in which we use water to carry out the cleansing function, and then happily watch it all glub down the drain as if the problem ended there.

Often the 'flushing' syndrome has simply been used to transport the problem elsewhere. There are few major rivers in Europe where a sensible person would dare swim these days. These water courses are foul with effluent from the drains of homes and factories. Clean water is made, it doesn't just come out of the tap.

We need water for washing which is sufficiently clean, but needn't be the same standard as water for drinking. Homes which have cold water tanks accumulate very undesirable pollution. Anyone who has ever investigated a water tank in a loft will have been appalled at the rubbish which collects in the bottom. Plumbers will confirm that this material can be actually corrosive – definitely not water for drinking! 'Clean' water is a relative concept.

To reduce domestic water consumption, use showers in preference to baths, compost rather than flush toilets, and wash less often or using less water.

To keep water in mains supplies at desirable quality, most water authorities now add various chemicals. Acidity and alkalinity are controlled by adding substances like sulphuric acid. Chlorine is used as a disinfectant, because it is soluble, and does not change its composition in the pipes. It is also a poison. Yet it is effective in combating bacterial growths. Where do you draw the line as to what is sanitary and what isn't? The more we take responsibility for our own supplies and effluent, the better.

Pumps

Water in a system runs downhill, however conservative of usage we are. Pumping it back uphill is another part of recycling. We looked at ram pumps in Chapter 12 (energy) – pumps which use the force of flowing water to raise a proportion of the flow. There are also wind-driven water pumps. Draught animals have been used to power pumps over many centuries. There are also various hand pumps available.

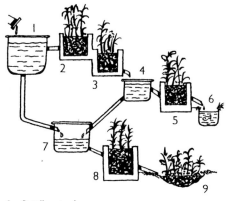

1 Settling tank
2 Reed bed 1 (*Phragmites* spp.)
3 Reed bed 2 (*Phragmites, Iris* spp,
   Schoenoplectus)
4 Settling junction
5 Reed beds 3 (*Iris, Acorus, Carex,
   Sparganium*)
6 Fish tank (*Typha* spp)
7 Sludge holding tank
8 Sludge reed bed 1 (*Phragmites*)
9 Sludge bed (*Iris, Typha*)

Reed Beds

The plants which do well in wetland
environments (willows, alders, reeds,
irises and rushes, for example) all have
root systems which can survive in
anaerobic conditions – situations where
they are starved of oxygen. They do so
by association with bacteria and
microbes which like those conditions.
We have similar creatures working away
in our guts helping us digest food.

These microbes have the capacity to
digest and break down substances which
oxygen-loving lifeforms find toxic.

However, given a plentiful diet of rich
available food they will pass the toxins
by. The secret in removing such waste
through natural systems is to make sure
that the root structures have to 'eat' the
toxins, because there are no alternatives.
This means careful separation of effluent
into levels of toxicity. If we dump heavy
metals into the sewage system it will be
difficult to retrieve them. If sewage and
industrial output are separated, then all
will be well. Rainwater should also be
kept separate from sewage, so as not to
flood the beds and ruin their capacity to
cope.

Biological cleansing is best done in
stages – effluent enters a bed where
solids are removed, and liquids partially
cleansed. Liquid outflow is treated in a
secondary lagoon. A third stage cleans
the water so that it is adequate for fish
stocks, and the outflow from that will be
of usable quality. Running through

The Camphill Trust is a series of
communities integrating people
with mental disabilities with able
people in meaningful work. Their
community in Gloucestershire
recycles all its own sewage and
water wastes through a series of
enchanting water gardens designed
by Uwe Burke, who is now teaching and designing such systems
full-time – a great example of
turning liabilities into assets.

waterfalls for aeration completes the process. There are a growing number of skilled practitioners who can help communities establish biological water cleansing systems which are safe, and give really clean water output – far more so, in fact, than that from present municipal systems.

Sacred Water

Such is the life-giving quality of water that it has often assumed a sacred quality in past cultures. Europe is dotted with 'Holy Wells' which were revered for their properties. Some were thought to heal people of diseases, or to have patron saints who restored sight to the blind. Where high mineral content affects the water there may indeed be health-giving properties, and given the popularity of bottled spring water, many present-day folk agree.

The former respect for sources of pure clean water rightly recognised that without these, there was simply no possibility of life. Millions have died in Africa and Asia this century as water has given out. That we live in cool climates does not mean that we are free of ever returning to the situation in which good water is rare. Our own water courses are telling us the dangers. Perhaps it is time to restore the sanctity of water, before we forget.

19 ENDPIECE

Permaculture works by managing resources systematically. The concepts and techniques in this book have been introduced to show a scale of priorities, and to encourage you that it is a way of thinking which is available to guide the actions of any person. Using Permaculture is a way of taking personal responsibility for greening the planet.

Design Sequence

Ultimately, Permaculture is a way of designing. That's just a word that means consciously choosing where you put things. You can use these methods when working with others, or equally well, just to make your own life easier. Here is a useful sequence for designing anything.

1 Assess the Boundaries

A detailed examination of the perimeter reveals unused resources. It tells you how often the people get that far out from the centre, whilst giving a good idea of overall scale. It highlights limitations as to what can be done with the centre when the boundary is poorly maintained in some way. Don't judge, just observe.

2 Record Resources

Examine the whole in detail, noting all resources, and how energy flows through the system. At this stage learn how the physical layout of the site or system affects its performance. What financial and skills resources are there? Do the users of the system have 'sacred sites'? What can you observe about how people and animals move about and use the area? Maps are handy at this stage.

3 Examine and Evaluate

What needs and outputs do all the parts of the system have? How well do they interact together? Are there wasted resources, or conspicuous shortages?

4 Design

Now there is sufficient information to think about placing things differently.

What can be done with the assets available to increase yield?

5 Implementation

Make sure that what is suggested can realistically be done. Who's going to do the work, have they the necessary time, skills, tools and money to do it all?

6 Maintenance

An average design will have 20 per cent labour breaking new creative ground and 80 per cent labour tied up in keeping things going. A good design will reverse the flow, reducing maintenance to 20 per cent, and freeing 80 per cent of the available labour time for creative improvement. How much maintenance is required, who's going to do it, and have they got the necessary resources?

Design Checklist

If a designer is responsible . . . it is no good him stating afterwards that he was given the wrong information. Part of his job is to query any conditions about which he has the slightest suspicions, even if they are outside the area of his expertise.

Gordon L Clegg
The Selection of Design

Here's a useful checklist to make sure nothing is forgotten.

- Who are we designing for?
- What are their unmet needs?
- What resources do they have?
- What outputs are they not using?

- What are the limits of the site?
- Have we a map?
- Do we know compass directions, contour shapes, and heights?
- Do we have weather records?
- What does the sun do in relation to the site across the seasons?
- What does the wind do here?
- How much does it rain or snow, and when?
- Is there frost and fog on this site?

- Who is responsible for maintaining boundaries?
- Do the users own the site, rent it, or borrow it?
- What rights of way are there?
- Is access adequate?
- How does the site affect neighbours and vice versa?
- Where is the nearest village or town?
- Are the shops nearby, and if not how can we get stores when needed?

- What buildings are there?
- Do they serve the purposes needed, and can they be changed if not?
- How can they be made more energy efficient?
- Can the system be made more efficient by moving jobs about?
- What energy sources are there?

- Can more renewable energy be harnessed here?
- What transport system is used?
- Is it adequate? Could a 'softer' system be used?

- What water is there on the site?
- Can it be made to cycle further to yield more?
- Is water of adequate quality on entering and leaving the system?
- How can its quantity or quality be improved?

- What crops are grown on the site?
- What is the soil type?
- What is the underlying geology?
- What is the condition of the soil?
- What species do well on this site?
- What others might yield more or offer more variety?
- Is there good stacking of yields?
- How diverse are they?
- What stock is there here, and is it the best mixture of breeds for the site?

I'M SURE WE'VE FORGOTTEN TO ASK OURSELVES SOMETHING...

- Can maintenance of crops be reduced?

- What craft skills are used here?
- If more are needed, are they available locally?
- Are tools adequate for the job?
- Is training needed to enable the people to have more control?
- What materials are imported to the site?
- Could they, or substitutes, be provided from the site?
- What products are exported from the site?
- Do they bring the best return they could?

- Is the surrounding community supportive and co-operative?
- Are the site users supportive of their neighbours?
- What resources are there in the immediate community which could improve life?
- How could people on this site enhance their surrounding area?

- Is wilderness given a place here?
- Is there room for more of it?

- Are financial resources adequate?
- What external sources of trade skills and funding could help?
- Could new structures be developed to make things work better?

- Where am I short of knowledge in answering these questions?
- How can I learn more?
- Is what I am suggesting the least level

of intervention needed to achieve the stated aims?
- Is it practicable to implement my suggestions?
- Can the system be maintained once changed in the way I suggest?

Commitment to Succeed

Debate rarely changes the world for the better. Considered action may do so. The changes needed to rescue our planet from environmental destruction are within the capability of ordinary people. They only require us to make the commitment to succeed. Anyone can take responsibility for shaping the future. All we need to do is define an area we want to tackle, and decide that that's our goal. Remarkable things can be achieved.

Where Next?

There is little point in spending your life trying to persuade other people they are wrong. If there is a better way of doing things, and you know what it is, then do it. If it really is better, then other people will be pleasantly surprised, and will want to try it too.

What would you like to change for the better in the world? Pick things which are within your capabilities. Make a commitment that this is your goal. Then do it. It need only be one thing, and

only you will know what the right thing is for you. It can be simple or complex, quickly over, or lasting your lifetime. What will it be? 'Reduce my energy consumption by 20 per cent in the next three months'? 'Grow half my own food next year'? 'Organise a street party'? 'Green the planet'? It's your choice.

Adding to Permaculture

It is open to anyone to add to the store of knowledge which we name Permaculture. There is no controlling bureaucracy. The name describes a process, and that process will be different at different times and in different cultures.

Feel free to make your own contribution to spreading the idea. Forests, our natural model, are delightfully anarchic in the way in which they blossom, mature, die back and invade and reinvade themselves and their perimeters with life in all its forms. Permaculture should be alive, and if it didn't grow and change under your touch, it would not be a durable offering.

Useful Contacts

The way forward is often not alone. It often means gathering more information before proceeding with an idea, or finding fellow travellers to make the journey pleasanter. Making your own list of useful contacts can be a good experience. The list given at the back of this book is a small one, which hopefully gives some starting points. I hope that this book has given you some answers. I am sure it will have raised many questions. To the reader that has made it this far I give my thanks for their attention, and wish them well in their future part in the voyage of Planet Earth.

APPENDIX: SPECIES LISTS

Biological solutions to human needs require us to develop our understanding of the needs and uses of available species. Species knowledge is a pleasurable and necessary way of deepening our contact with nature, and of understanding how to increase biomass whilst getting what we want in life. Species variety gives an inkling of the staggering complexity of life on Earth.

Botanical Names

Plants, by convention, have Latin names. You don't have to be a Latin scholar to use them. Common names are open to confusion so the international standards for biological names allow us to be specific without fear of misunderstanding.

The base level of this naming system is the species with at least two parts to its name. First is the 'generic name', indicating to which 'genus' (or group) the plant belongs. Second is the 'specific epithet'. Latin names are normally written in italics or underlined, with a capital letter to start the generic name, and the rest of the name in small letters. So *Salix alba* is the white willow. Here the Latin is a translation of the common name. Sometimes this may not be so, and the names may have little relation, so *Carpinus betulus* is the hornbeam. Here the Latin *betulus* indicates that the leaves are 'beech-like', from the Latin for beech, *betula*. After a while you notice familiar specific epithets, such as *variegata*, meaning variegated, or two-coloured.

Sometimes there is a third name, which indicates a sub-species, so *Pyrus salicifolia pendula* is a weeping willow-leaved pear. This is a sub-species of the willow-leaved pear. Some plants are 'cultivars'; that is, they are sub-species derived by human selection and propagation. So 'James Grieve' is an apple cultivar. If you see a name like *Colutea x media* (a bladder senna) it indicates that the plant is a hybrid. Hybrids are genetically crossed between two plants within a genus. F1 hybrids are a particularly vigorous but sterile form of hybrid used for annual crops. Sometimes you see 'syn.' which means that the name is a synonym, indicating that the plant was formerly known by another name. If you see *Quercus* spp. it indicates that the plant is being spoken about in a general way to include various species, here 'the oaks'. Sometimes the authority is quoted, so *Arbutus unedo* (L) means that the strawberry tree was so named by Linnaeus, the founding father of botanical nomenclature. Less well-known authorities are written in full.

Genera are themselves subdivisions of 'families', so when you see *Colutea x media (Leguminosae)* it is telling you that bladder senna is a member of the pea family, or 'the legumes'.

Animal names are made on a similar basis. The 'kingdoms' of plants, animals, fungi, bacteria and single-celled creatures overlap. Each 'kingdom' breaks down into classes, each class into families, each family into genera, and then genera into species. An intimate understanding of this is not necessary to be a successful grower.

All species here are economically useful. A fuller list by the author is available from Ecologic Books (address in back of book).

Species Lists: Trees

Trees are a great asset in any landscape, adding a vertical dimension, increasing the water cycle, mining nutrients, giving us timber and other tree crops: useful saps, barks, nuts and flowers. They are home to many species of wildlife, and so form a vital function in the food chain. Because of all these uses, trees have strong cultural associations for people, being revered in all indigenous societies.

Careful selection is needed to make the crop as bountiful as possible. The following list is the most common trees which will do well in cool climates. They are not all equally hardy, and some are fussy about types of soil they prefer.

Trees are either deciduous (dropping their leaves in winter time) or evergreen (keeping continuous leaf-cover which they replace on an ongoing basis). Most

Key to usage:

A = Animal fodder
C = Soil conditioner (green manure, legumes etc.)
E = Edible leaves
F = Fibre crop
H = Hedging species
I = Edible inflorescence (flowers)
M = Medicinal
N = Edible nuts/fruit
P = Pioneer
R = Edible root
S = Edible sap
T = Timber crop (large wood)
W = Wood crop (small wood)
X = Poisonous in whole or part

evergreens are conifers (cone-bearing), although there are exceptions like holly and holm oak. A few conifers are deciduous – the larches and the dawn redwood.

Tree species native to Britain, Ireland and continental Europe

European silver fir	*Abies alba*	T,W
Field maple	*Acer campestre*	H,W
Sycamore	*Acer pseudoplatanus*	S,T,W
Common horse chestnut	*Aesculus hippocastanum*	A,N,W
Common alder	*Alnus glutinose*	A,C,W
Silver birch	*Betula pendula*	P,S,T,W
Pea tree	*Caragana arborescens*	C,W
Hornbeam	*Carpinus betulus*	W,T
Sweet chestnut	*Castanea sativa*	A,N,T,W
Hazel	*Corylus avellana*	A,H,N,P,W
Hawthorn	*Crataegus monogyna*	E,H,N,P,W
Quince	*Cydonia oblonga*	N,W
Spindle tree	*Euonymus europaeus*	W
Beech	*Fagus sylvatica*	A,E,H,N,T,W
Alder buckthorn	*Frangula alnus*	W
Ash	*Fraxinus excelsior*	A,N,T,W
Holly	*Ilex aquifolium*	H,W
English walnut	*Juglans regia*	A,E,N,T,W
Juniper	*Juniperus communis*	N,P
Common laburnum	*Laburnam anagyroides*	C,H,P,W,X
European larch	*Larix decidua*	T,W
Bay	*Laurus nobilis*	E,H
Crab apple	*Malus sylvestris*	H,N,W
Norway spruce	*Picea abies*	E,T,W
Corsican pine	*Pinus nigra var maritima*	T,W
Scots pine	*Pinus sylvestris*	T,W
London plane	*Platanus x hispanica*	T,W
White poplar	*Populus alba*	P,W
Wild cherry	*Prunus avium*	N,T,W
Cherry plum	*Prunus cerasifera*	H,N,W
Damson	*Prunus domestica*	H,N,W
Blackthorn	*Prunus spinosa*	H,N,W
Wild pear	*Pyrus communis*	A,N,T,W

Oaks	*Quercus spp*	A,N,S,T,W
Willows	*Salix spp*	A,H,P,W
Elder	*Sambucus nigra*	A,H,I,N,P
Whitebeam	*Sorbus aria*	A,N,T,W
Rowan	*Sorbus aucuparia*	A,H,N,P,T,W
Yew	*Taxus baccata*	H,T,W,X
Common Lime	*Tilia x europaea*	A,I,T,W
Elms	*Ulmus spp*	A,T,W
Guelder Rose	*Viburnum opulus*	A,N,W

Some other tree species native to North America

Grand fir	*Abies grandis*	T,W
Noble fir	*Abies procera*	T,W
Maples	*Acer spp*	S,T,W
Snowy mespil	*Amelanchier laevis*	A,H,N,W
Hickories	*Carya spp*	A,N,T,W
Indian bean tree	*Catalpa bignonioides*	A,T,W
Hackberry	*Celtis occidentalis*	A,N,W
Lawson cypress	*Chamaecyparis lawsoniana*	H
Yellow wood	*Cladrastis lutea*	T,W
Leyland cypress	*x Cupressocyparis leylandii*	H
Monterey cypress	*Cupressus macrocarpa*	H,W
Persimmon	*Diospyros virginiana*	A,N,W
Honey locust	*Gleditsia triacanthos*	A,N,W
Kentucky coffee tree	*Gymnocladus dioica*	N,W
Butternut	*Juglans cinerea*	A,N,T,W
Black walnut	*Juglans nigra*	A,N,T,W
Tulip tree	*Liriodendron tulipfera*	T,W
Ironwood	*Ostrya virginiana*	T,W
Sitka spruce	*Picea sitchensis*	T,W
Lodgepole pine	*Pinus contorta var latifolia*	T,W
Cottonwood	*Populus deltoides*	W
Douglas fir	*Pseudotsuga menziesii*	T,W
Black locust	*Robinia pseudoacacia*	C,W
California bigwood	*Sequoiadendron giganteum*	T,W
White cedar	*Thuja occidentalis*	H,W
Hemlocks	*Tsuga spp*	T,W

Other exotic tree species (* = less hardy)

Monkey puzzle	*Araucaria araucana*	N,T,W
Cedars	*Cedrus spp*	T,W
Gums	*Eucalyptus spp*	M,P,W
Fig	*Ficus carica**	N
Maidenhair tree	*Ginkgo biloba*	W
Dawn redwood	*Metasequoia glyptostroboides*	T,W
Mulberry	*Morus spp*	A,N,W
Raoul (Southern beech)	*Nothofagus procera*	T,W
Apricot	*Prunus armeniaca**	N,W
Almond	*Prunus dulcus**	N,W
Peach	*Prunus persica**	N,W

Species Lists: Wild Perennials and Annuals

Wild plants are a largely untapped food source.

Green herbs are largely edible; however, as with any wild gathering, there's always the risk of eating something poisonous. Umbels are particularly hard to tell apart, and have some of the most poisonous plants as members of the family. Do not eat anything unless you are sure of its identity. The responsibility for getting this right is yours alone. Learn with a knowledgeable companion for best results.

Shrubs

Barberry	*Berberis vulgaris*	H,N
Japanese quince	*Chaenomeles japonica*	H,N
Dogwood	*Cornus sanguinea*	H,W
Crowberry	*Empetrum nigrum*	N
Oregon grape	*Mahonia aquifolium*	A,H,N
Bog myrtle	*Myrica gale*	C,E,P
Currants	*Ribes spp*	H,N
Gooseberry	*Ribes uva-crispa*	H,N
Rose	*Rosa spp*	A,H,I,N,P
Raspberry	*Rubus idaeus*	E,H
Broom	*Sarothamnus scoparius*	A,C,H,I,P
Spanish broom	*Spartium juncium*	C,H,X
Gorse	*Ulex europaeus*	A,C,H,I,P

219

American blueberry	*Vaccinium angustifolium*	N
American cranberry	*Vaccinium macrocarpon*	N
Bilberry	*Vaccinium myrtilis*	N

Climbers

Siberian Kiwi fruit	*Actinidia arguta*	N
Ivy	*Hedera helix*	A,X
Hop	*Humulus lupulus*	E,I,M
Blackberry	*Rubus fruticosus*	E,H

Herbs

Yarrow	*Achillea millefolium*	E,M
Ground elder	*Aegopodium podagraria*	E,P
Garlic mustard	*Alliaria petiolata*	E
Ramsons	*Allium ursinum*	E,R
Dill	*Anethum graveolens*	E,I,N
Chervil	*Anthriscus cerefolium*	E
Horseradish	*Armoricia rusticana*	E,R
Burdock	*Arctium minus*	E,R
Tarragon	*Artemisia dracunculus*	E
Orache	*Atriplex patula*	E
Winter cress	*Barbarea vulgaris*	E
Daisy	*Bellis perennis*	I
Borage	*Borago officinalis*	A,E,I,M
Rape	*Brassica napus*	E,R
Hairy bittercress	*Cardamine hirsuta*	E
Chamomile	*Chamaemelum nobile*	I,M
Fat-hen	*Chenopodium album*	E,P
Chicory	*Chicorium intibus*	R
Fennel	*Foeniculum vulgare*	E,N
Wild strawberry	*Fregaria vesca*	N,P
Dead nettle	*Lamium spp*	E,I
Lovage	*Ligusticum scoticum*	E
Mallow	*Malva sylvestris*	E,I,N
Balm	*Melissa officinalis*	E,I
Mints	*Mentha spp*	E
Sweet cicely	*Myrrhis odorata*	E,R
Evening primrose	*Oenothera erythrosepala*	A,E,I,M

Marjoram	*Origanum vulgare*	E,I
Wood sorrel	*Oxalis acetosella*	A,E
Salad burnet	*Poterium sanguisorbum*	E
Primrose	*Primula vulgaris*	E,I
Rosemary	*Rosmarinus officinalis*	M
Sorrel	*Rumex acetosa*	E
Chickweed	*Stellaria media*	A,E
Comfrey	*Symphytum officinale*	A,C,E,F,M
Dandelion	*Taraxacum officinale*	E,I,R,M
Wild Thyme	*Thymus drucei*	E,I
Salsify	*Tragopogon porrifolius*	R
Red clover	*Trifolium pratense*	A,C,E,I
Stinging nettle	*Urtica dioica*	C,E,F
Cornsalad	*Valerianella locusta*	E
Sweet violet	*Viola odorata*	I

In some countries, like Britain, it is technically illegal to pick wild plants on someone else's land without permission. In general, digging up wild plants is a very bad idea, unless they're something which is extremely common. There is no reason why you can't collect seed and grow on all these useful plants in your own plot for your own usage.

Species List: Fungi

Some fungi are acutely poisonous, so no-one should go mushroom gathering without knowing what they're doing. Use a proper illustrated guide, and preferably learn alongside an experienced person. Remember: if in doubt, don't eat!

Field mushroom	*Agaricus campestris*	E
Honey fungus	*Armillariella mellea*	E
Cep	*Boletus edulis*	E
Chanterelle	*Cantharellus cibarius*	E
Shaggy inkcap	*Coprinus comatus*	E
Horn of Plenty	*Craterellus cornucopoides*	E
Beefsteak fungus	*Fistulina hepatica*	E
Giant puffball	*Langermannia gigantea*	E
Parasol mushroom	*Lepiota procera*	E
Field blewit	*Lepista saeva*	E
Morel	*Morchella esculenta*	E
Oyster mushroom	*Pleurotus ostreatus*	E

Species List: Domestic Plant Crops

Onions/garlic/chives	*Allium spp*
Angelica	*Angelica archangelica*
Celery/celeriac	*Apium spp*
Asparagus	*Asparagus officinale*
Oats	*Avena sativa*
Bamboo shoots	*Bambusa spp*
Beets	*Beta vulgaris spp*
Mustard	*Brassica alba*
Pak choi	*Brassica spp*
Turnip	*Brassica spp*
Kale	*Brassica spp*
Cauliflower	*Brassica spp*
Cabbage	*Brassica oleracea spp*
Brussels sprouts	*Brassica oleracea gemmifera*
Marigold	*Calendula officinalis*
Sweet pepper	*Capsicum annuum*
Chicory	*Cichorium intybus var foliosum*
Winter purslane	*Claytonia perfoliata*
Coriander	*Coriandrum sativum*
Cucumber	*Cucumis sativus*
Marrow/squash	*Cucurbita spp*
Globe artichoke	*Cynara scolymus*
Carrot	*Daucus carota*
Buckwheat	*Fagopyrum spp*
Florence fennel	*Foeniculum vulgare var azoricum*
Jerusalem artichoke	*Helianthus tuberosus*
Barley	*Hordeum distichon*
Lettuces	*Lactuca spp*
Garden cress	*Lepidium sativum*
Tomato	*Lycopersicon esculenta*
Alfalfa	*Medicago sativa*
Parsnip	*Pastinaca sativa*
Parsley	*Petroselinum crispum ssp*
Beans	*Phaseolus spp*
Peas	*Pisum sativum ssp*
Purslane	*Portulaca oleracea*

Radish	*Raphanus sativa ssp*	
Rhubarb	*Rheum rhabarbarum*	
Rye	*Secale cereale*	
Aubergine	*Solanum melongena*	
Potato	*Solanum tuberosum*	
Spinach	*Spinacea oleracea*	
New Zealand spinach	*Tetragonia tetragonioides*	
Nasturtium	*Trapeolum majus*	
Fenugreek	*Trigonella foenum-graecum*	
Wheats	*Triticum spp*	
Broad beans	*Vicia faba*	
Sweet corn	*Zea mays*	

Species List: Legumes for Use in Temperate Climates

Peanut*	*Arachis hypogae*	R
Pea Tree	*Caragana viscosa*	
Bladder Senna	*Colutea arborescens*	
Crotolaria (US)	*Crotolaria ssp*	
Brooms	*Cytisus ssp*	A,I
Lablab (US)	*Dolichos lablab*	
Goat's Rue	*Galega officinalis*	A
Brooms & greenweeds	*Genista ssp*	
Honey Locust (US)	*Gleditsia triacanthos*	A,S
Soy Bean	*Glycine max (syn Soya max)*	A,N
Licorice	*Glycyrrhiza lepidota*	R
Pigweed (US)	*Hoffmansegia densiflora*	
Indigo	*Indigofera heterantha*	
Laburnums	*Laburnum ssp*	X
Peas & vetchlings	*Lathyrus ssp*	N
Desmodium (US)	*Lespedeza bicolor*	
Birdsfoot trefoils	*Lotus ssp*	
Lupines	*Lupinus ssp*	
Medicks & lucerne	*Medicago ssp*	A
Melilots	*Melilotus ssp*	A,I

* Does not stand hard frost; can be grown as annual or greenhouse plant.
(US) Recommended for certain conditions in US. Herbaceous plants unproven in UK.

Restharrows	*Ononis ssp*	
Bird's Foots	*Ornithopus ssp*	
Milk Vetches	*Oxytropis ssp*	A
Runner & dwarf beans	*Phaseolus ssp*	N
Field Bean (US)	*Pisum arvensis*	A,N
Garden Pea	*Pisum sativum*	N
Black locust (US)	*Robinia pseudoacacia*	
Colorado River Hemp (US)	*Sesbania macrocarpa*	
Spanish Broom	*Spartium junceum*	X
Velvet Bean (US)	*Stizolobium deeringianum*	
Asparagus Pea	*Tetragonolobus purpureus*	N
Thermopsis (US)	*Thermopsis gracilis*	
Trefoils & clovers	*Trifolium ssp*	A,I
Fenugreek	*Trigonella foenum-graecum*	E
Gorses	*Ulex ssp*	A,I
Vetches & tares	*Vicia ssp*	A,N
Broad Bean	*Vicia faba*	A,N
Wisterias	*Wisteria ssp*	

Freshwater Fish

		Best Habitat
Common bream	*Abramis brama*	Bottom feeder
Eel	*Anguilla anguilla*	Bottom feeder
Crayfish	*Austropotamobius pallipes*	Chalky bottoms
Crucian carp	*Carassius carassius*	Swampy lakes
Common carp	*Cyprinus carpio*	Bottom feeder
Pike	*Esox lucius*	Open water
Chub	*Leuciscus cephalus*	Swift rivers
Dace	*Leuciscus leuciscus*	Swift rivers
Signal crayfish	*Pacifastacus leniusculus*	Chalky bottoms
Perch	*Perca fluviatilis*	Mobile
Rainbow trout	*Salmo gairdneri*	Fast streams
Salmon	*Salmo salar*	Fast rivers
Trout	*Salmo trutta*	Fast streams
Rudd	*Scardinius erythrophthalomus*	Mid & surface
Tench	*Tinca tinca*	Slow water

Perch, brown trout and pike are predatory of other fish. Some other fish were formerly prized food, such as stone loach (*Noemacheilus barbatulus*), whilst some of the above are little eaten today (rudd, for instance). No managed water system will work effectively without all the other creatures which make up the fishes' food chain, such as flies, larvae, beetles, worms and so on. The appropriate species for building a self-governing water ecosystem will depend on the locality and the stocking of the water.

See references in the booklist for lists of water plants and shellfish.

Salt Water Fish

Whales and dolphins (which are mammals, not fish) have high economic value. We could also say that one of the commitments we make to restoring wilderness is for no-one on planet Earth ever to make economic use of a whale or dolphin again.

Herring	*Clupea harengus*
Conger eel	*Conger conger*
Bass	*Dicentrarchus labrax*
Cod	*Gadus morhua*
Halibut	*Hippoglosus hippoglossus*
Haddock	*Melanogrammus aeglefinus*
Whiting	*Merlanguis merlanguis*
Lemon sole	*Microstomus kitt*
Common octopus	*Octopus vulgaris*
Plaice	*Pleuronectes platessa*
Skate	*Raja batis*
Mackerel	*Scomber scombrus*

Species Lists: Wild Stock

The following animals, wild in temperate areas could be said to have economic uses.

Deer:	
Elk	*Alces alces*
Roe deer	*Capreolus capreolus*
Fallow deer	*Cervus dama*
Red deer	*Cervus elaphus*
Sika deer	*Cervus nippon*

225

Chinese water deer	*Hydropotes inermis*
Muntjac	*Muntiacus reevesi*
Reindeer	*Rangifer tarandus*
Other large mammals:	
Bison	*Bison bonasus*
Wild cattle	*Bos bovis*
Wild goat	*Capra aegagrus*
Wild boar	*Sus scrofa*
Smaller mammals:	
Hedgehog	*Erinaceus europaeus*
Brown hare	*Lepus capensis*
Rabbit	*Oryctolagus cuniculus*
Amphibians:	
Edible frog	*Rana esculenta*
Common toad	*Bufo bufo*

Birds: the following wild birds are considered edible. In times past a much wider range of fowl have been eaten (e.g. the rook, *Corvus frugilegus*). This doesn't give you the right to go and shoot all you see for the pot, since wildlife is generally protected by law. It does, however, give an indication of the diversity of fowl which can be stocked into the countryside as self-foraging food.

Many other species have edible eggs, but again there are laws protecting most of these from collection.

Red legged partridge	*Alectoris rufa*
Duck	*Anas platyrhynchos*
Goose	*Anser anser*
Stock dove	*Columba oenas*
Wood-pigeon	*Columba palumbus*
Quail	*Coturnix coturnix*
Snipe	*Gallinago gallinago*
Red grouse	*Lagopus lagopus*
Ptarmigan	*Lagopus mutus*
Black grouse	*Lyrurus tetrix*
Partridge	*Perdix perdix*
Pheasant	*Phasianus colchicus*
Woodcock	*Scolopax rusticola*
Doves	*Streptopelia spp*
Capercaillie	*Tetrao urogallus*

Species List: Domestic Stock

Birds:

Ducks

Geese

Guinea fowl

Hens

Peacocks

Pigeons (Squabs)

Quail

Turkeys

Fish:

Carp

Channel catfish

Crayfish

Rainbow trout

Salmon

Trout

Animals:

Bison/buffalo

Cattle

Deer

Edible frogs

Goats

Guinea pigs

Horses

Llamas

Pigs

Rabbits

Reindeer

Sheep

Snails

BOOKLIST

Dates are latest editions referred to by the author.

Individual Development

Feminism & Linguistic Theory 195pp Deborah Cameron (Macmillan, Basingstoke, England, 1985)

Fundamentals of Co-Counselling Manual 54pp Harvey Jackins (Rational Island Publishers, Seattle, 1982)

Future Shock 517pp Alvin Toffler (Pan Books, London, 1971)

Games People Play Eric Berne (Grove Press, New York, 1967)

I am right – You are wrong 293pp Edward de Bono (Viking, London, 1990)

I'm OK – You're OK 269pp Thomas A Harris MD (Pan Books, London, 1979)

Small Change – A Pocketful of Practical Actions to Help the Environment 79pp Marianne Frances (Centre for Human Ecology, Edinburgh, 1989)

Walden 294pp Henry David Thoreau (Everyman/JM Dent, London, 1908)

A Whack on the Side of the Head 196pp Roger von Oech (Warner Books, New York, 1990; Thorsons, London, 1990)

Community Development

Capital City 264pp Hamish McRae & Frances Cairncross (Methuen, London, 1985)

The Common People 445pp J F C Harrison (Fontana, London, 1984)

Community Organising – You've never really tried it 68pp James Pitt & Maurice Keane (J & P Consultancy, Birmingham, England, 1984)

Inequalities in Health 240pp Sir Douglas Black & others (Penguin, Middlesex, England, 1983)

Interest and Inflation-Free Money 87pp Margrit Kennedy (Permakultur Institut, Steyerberg, Germany, 1989)

The Permaculture Plot 52pp edited by Simon Pratt (Permaculture British Isles, Buckfastleigh, England, 1991)

Reviving the City 278pp Tim Elkin, Duncan McLaren (Friends of the Earth, London, 1991)

A Rural Manifesto for the Highlands 30pp (The Scottish Green Party, Duartbeg, Sutherland, 1989)

Global Concerns

Ecologistics 112pp Patrick F Howden (Self published: Truro, Cornwall, UK, 1979)

Gaia: A new look at life on Earth 154pp J E Lovelock (Oxford University Press, 1987)

Geological Structures 250pp John L Roberts (Macmillan Field Guides, London, 1989)

I Can't Stay Long 230pp Laurie Lee (Andre Deutsch, London, 1975)

Meteorology – The Atmosphere and the Science of Weather 502pp Joseph M Moran & Michael D Morgan (Macmillan, New York, 1986)

Radical Technology 304pp edited by Godfrey Boyle, Peter Harper (Wildwood House, London, 1976)

The Tao of Physics 455pp Fritjof Capra (Flamingo, London, 1979)

Design Skills

Designing and Maintaining Your Edible Landscape Naturally 370pp Robert Kourik (Metamorphic Press, Santa Rosa, California, 1984)

The International Permaculture Species Yearbook 144pp Edited by Dan Hemenway (Self published, Orange, Ma, USA, 1986)

Permaculture One 127pp Bill Mollison, David Holmgren (Tagari Press, Tyalgum, Australia, 1990)

Permaculture Two 150pp Bill Mollison (Tagari Press, Tyalgum, Australia, 1979)

Permaculture – a Designer's Manual 576pp Bill Mollison (Tagari Publications, Tyalgum, Australia, 1988)

The Selection of Design 84pp Gordon L Clegg (Cambridge University Press, England, 1972)

The Timeless Way of Building 550pp Christopher Alexander (Oxford University Press, New York, 1979)

Energy

Another Kind of Garden 58pp Ida & Jean Pain (Self published, Villecroze, France, 1972)

A Chinese Biogas Manual 135pp translated by Michael Crook, edited by Ariane van Buren (Intermediate Technology Publications, London, 1983)

Energy – a guidebook 345pp Janet Ramage (Oxford University Press, Oxford, 1986)

The Generation of Electricity by Wind Power 338pp E W Golding (E & F.N. Spon, London, 1955 revised 1976)

Solar Prospects – The Potential for Renewable Energy 190pp Michael Flood (Wildwood House/Friends of the Earth, London, 1983)

Stoves, Hearths and Chimneys 192pp Keith Williams (David & Charles, Newton Abbot, Devon, 1987)

Sun Power 259pp J C McVeigh (Pergamon Press, Oxford, 1983)

Gardening

Bread from Stones 51pp Dr Julius Hensel (Health Research, Mokelumne Hill, Calif., reprint 1977)

Companion Planting 128pp Gertrud Franck (Thorsons, Wellingborough, England, 1983)

The Forest Garden 24pp Robert Hart (Institute for Social Inventions, London, 1990)

The Formation of Vegetable Mould (Through the Action of Worms With Observations on their Habits) 152pp Charles Darwin; Intro by Sir A Howard (Faber & Faber, London, 1945)

Mushrooms in the Garden 152pp Hellmut Steineck (Mad River Press, Eureka, California, 1984) (originally *Pilze im Garten* Eugen Ulmer, Stuttgart, 1981)

The No-Work Garden Book 188pp Ruth Stout & Richard Clemence (White Lion Publishers, London, 1976) (Originally: Rodale Press USA, 1971)

Organic Gardening 240pp Lawrence D Hills (Penguin, London, 1977)

The Victorian Kitchen Garden 160pp Jennifer Davies (BBC Books, London, 1987)

Orchards

Cultivated Fruits of Britain 349pp F A Roach (Basil Blackwell, Oxford, 1980)

The Fruit Garden Displayed 223pp Harry Baker (Cassell Ltd/The Royal Horticultural Society, London, 1986)

The Good Fruit Guide 90pp Lawrence D Hills (Henry Doubleday Research Association, Essex, England, 1984)

The Hillier Colour Dictionary of Trees and Shrubs 323pp Hillier Nurseries (David & Charles, Newton Abbot, England, 1988)

Farming

Agriculture 174pp Rudolph Steiner (Bio-
Dynamic Agriculture Association, London,
1984)

The Farmer, The Plough & The Devil 259pp
Arthur Hollins (Ashgrove Press, Bath,
England, 1986)

Farmers of Forty Centuries 441pp F H King
(Rodale Press, Emmaus, Pennsylvania, 1911)
(modern reprint available)

Forest Farming 207pp J Sholto Douglas &
Robert A de J Hart (Intermediate
Technology Publications, London, 1984)

The Harmonious Wheatsmith 28pp Edited by
Mark Moodie (Self published, Newnham on
Severn, England, 1991)

Natural Way of Farming 260pp Masanobu
Fukuoka (Japan Publications, Tokyo, 1985)

*New Energy Creation & Conservation Policy to
Benefit Farming* 35pp Bruce Marshall (Self
published, West Linton, Scotland, 1990)

One Straw Revolution 181pp Masanobu Fukuoka
(Rodale Press, Emmaus, 1978)

The Organic Food Guide 126pp edited by Alan
Gear (Henry Doubleday Research
Association, Braintree, 1983)

Prodfact 1988 424pp Daphne MacCarthy (British
Food Information Service, London, 1988)

Tree Crops – A Permanent Agriculture 408pp J
Russell Smith (Island Press Conservation
Classics (Reprint), 1987)

Water for Every Farm 248pp P A Yeomans
(Second Back Row Press, Katoomba,
Australia, 1981)

Trees

Green Woodwork 208pp Mike Abbott (Guild of
Master Craftsmen, Lewes, England, 1989)

The International Book of Trees 288pp Hugh
Johnson (Mitchell Beazley, London, 1973)

Silviculture of Broadleaved Woodlands 232pp Julian
Evans (HMSO (Forestry Commission),
London, 1984)

Trees in Britain, Europe & North America 223pp
Roger Phillips (Pan Books, London, 1978)

Trees, Woods and Man 272pp H L Edlin
(Collins, London, 1978)

Plants

The Book of Bamboo 340pp David Farrelly (Sierra
Club Books, San Francisco, 1984)

Food for Free 240pp Richard Mabey (Collins,
London, 1989)

Grasses, Ferns, Mosses & Lichens 191pp Roger
Phillips (Pan Books, London, 1980)

Mushrooms 288pp Roger Phillips (Pan Books,
London, 1985)

Plants & Beekeeping 236pp F N Howes (Faber &
Faber, London, 1979)

Wild Food 159pp Roger Phillips (Peerage Books,
London, 1988)

Animals

Backyard Dairy Book 111pp Andrew Singer & Len
Street (Prism Press, Bridport, England, 1978)

Ducks and Geese at Home 51pp Michael &
Victoria Roberts (Domestic Fowl Trust,
Evesham, England, 1985)

Highland Animals 110pp David Stephen
(Highland & Islands Development Board,
distributed by Collins, Glasgow, 1974)

Water Management

Backyard Fish Farming 170pp (Paul Bryant, Kim
Jauncey, Tim Atack) (Prism Press, Bridport,
England, 1986)

Land Use & Water Resources 246pp H C Pereira
(Cambridge University Press, Cambridge,
1973)

Sacred Waters 232pp Janet & Colin Bord
(Granada, London, 1985)

Sand Dunes 108pp Compiled by Alan Brooks
(British Trust for Conservation Volunteers,
Wallingford, England, 1986)

Taming The Flood 307pp Jeremy Purseglove
(Oxford University Press/Channel 4, Oxford,
1988)

Waterland 310pp Graham Swift (Picador,
London, 1984)

Water Life of Britain 335pp Ed. Frances Dipper,
Anne Powell (Reader's Digest Field Guides,
London, 1985)

Waterways and Wetlands 186pp Compiled by
Alan Brooks (British Trust for Conservation
Volunteers, Wallingford, England, 1987)

USEFUL CONTACTS

Permaculture

BCM Permaculture Association
London WC1N 3XX
office@permaculture.org.uk
www.permaculture.org.uk

Global Ecovillage Network
www.ecovillage.org

Permaculture Activist
PO Box 1209, Black Mountain,
NC 28711 USA
pcactivist@mindspring.com
www.permacultureactivist.net

Permaculture International
www.permacultureinternational.org

Permaculture Magazine
The Sustainability Centre, East Meon,
Hampshire GU32 1HR, UK
info@permaculture.co.uk
www.permaculture.co.uk

Permaculture Research Institute
www.permaculture.org.au

Details of many other useful contacts can be obtained from these addresses.

Books

Permanent Publications
The Earth Repair Catalogue
www.permaculture.co.uk

Useful Organisations

BTCV (British Trust for Conservation Volunteers), 36 St Mary's Street, Wallingford, Oxfordshire OX10 0ED, UK. www.btcv.org.uk

CAT (Centre for Alternative Technology), Machynlleth, Powys, Wales SY20 9AZ, UK. www.cat.org.uk

Ecology Building Society
7 Belton Road, Silsden, Keithley, West Yorkshire BD20 0EE, UK. www.ecology.co.uk

HDRA (Henry Doubleday Research Association), Ryton Organic Gardens, Coventry CV8 3LG, UK. www.hdra.org.uk

Soil Association
40-56 Victoria Street, Bristol BS1 6BY, UK. www.soilassociation.org.uk

Women's Environmental Network
PO Box 30626, London E1 1TZ, UK. www.gn.apc.org/wen

INDEX

access 50, 87, 127-8, 205, 210
acidity/alkalinity 124, 151, 167, 181-5, 191, 193, 195-201, 202, 204-5
added value 179
additives 109, 119, 174-6, 192
'adult' 58
advertising 42
aesthetics 31
Africa 102, 116, 208
age 42, 102, 108, 110
Age Exchange 42
agriculture (*see also* farming) 27, 33, 67, 71, 76, 77, 121, 157, 171-80, 189-90, 203
agro-forestry 177
aid 102
AIDS 29
aikido 68
air 30, 37, 65-6, 93, 97, 110, 129, 134-5, 147, 149, 176, 181, 193, 195, 197, 202-4
aircraft 42, 135, 139, 157
Alinsky, Saul D. 102
Alexander, Christopher 74-5
allotments 109-114
alternative/appropriate 26
Antarctica 202
anthroposophy 68
apples 159-66
aquaculture 175, 179-80, 181-5
architecture 40, 47, 74, 83-4
arts 37, 43, 107, 111
Ashram Acres 112
Asia 42, 102, 115, 208
assets 60, 75-6, 87, 183, 189

babies 31, 37, 190
banks 46, 51, 55, 85, 105, 170, 172
barter 53

beds (garden) 150-3
berm 94-5, 128
bicycles 87, 106, 139, 142-3
biennialism 163-5
biodynamics 68
biomass 138
biotechnics 67
birds 69-70, 117-8, 127, 138, 158, 180, 185, 226
Birmingham, England 112
birth control 29
Black Report 26
blackberries 70, 118, 167, 184
Bone, Eric 58
Bonfils, Marc 178-9
de Bono, Edward 191
boundaries 84-99, 116, 209
brainstorming 59
bracken 117, 149, 198
brassicas 149, 154, 170
Brazil 143
break-even point 56
Breakthrough Trust 108
Britain 38, 112, 116, 123, 134, 140, 185, 202
British Columbia 55
Buddhism 27, 75
building 66, 69, 74, 83-100, 121, 137, 200, 210
   materials 84, 93-5, 98, 124, 177, 180, 196
   timeless way of 74
Burke, Uwe 207
Burkina Faso 30
butterflies 56, 70, 117

Camphill Trust 207
Canada 55, 66, 116, 119, 164, 183
capital 45-56, 57, 86, 190
celebrations 38, 107, 130
Centre for Alternative Technology 53

change 43, 58, 59, 73, 79
Channel Islands 55
chickens *see* hens
'child' 58
childbirth 71, 107
children 31, 41-2, 43, 46, 51, 92, 99, 108, 194
China 42, 86, 110, 111, 155, 177, 185
Christianity 27
cities 95, 98, 99, 105-8, 109-14, 117, 125, 154, 179, 199, 203, 210
clay 124, 148, 184, 195-6
climate (*see also* weather) 27, 29, 30, 64-9, 121, 164-6, 181, 202-4
  macro 64-6, 89, 177
  micro 66-7, 89, 117, 121, 151, 177, 204
clothing 29, 31, 43, 57, 84, 91, 150
coal 96, 131, 199
coasts 64-5, 125-6, 134
co-counselling 58
coinage 49
colloids 148
comfrey 70, 118, 195
communications 42, 50, 103, 107-8, 120
community 21, 32, 37, 42-3, 47, 52, 55, 59, 62, 78, 85, 100-8, 111, 138, 178, 189, 191, 201
companion planting 153
competition 43, 44, 47, 63, 70
compost 76, 86, 132, 149, 173, 183, 196-201, 206
computers 50, 55, 103, 112
condensation 93, 128
consumer groups 38, 79, 112
consumption 20, 21, 25, 26, 30, 41, 73, 79, 91, 92, 98, 102, 140, 202
contour 86, 121-2, 126, 173, 177
cooking 90, 92, 96-8, 107, 129, 156, 164, 192
cooperation 27, 61, 101, 196
core model 64
creativity 59
creosote 97
cultivars 159-70
culture 38, 39, 43, 106-8, 113-4, 139, 212
currency 47, 105
curves 63, 177
curtains 95
customs 37
cut and come again 156
Czechoslovakia 115

DNA 192-3
dams 125-6, 127, 134, 205
dawn chorus 44, 69
death 107, 116, 139, 147, 189, 192, 194, 196
decision making 105
deer 160, 169, 175, 182, 225-6
Denmark 135, 164
density 65, 89
depressions 65

deserts 27, 30, 65, 87, 115, 125, 172, 189, 190
designing 78-80, 84, 102, 121, 129, 177, 189-90, 209-13
dimensions 77
direction 41, 79, 88, 136, 191, 210
disability 31, 51, 87, 108, 110
discharge 58-9
disease 71, 93, 108, 150, 157, 175, 176, 182, 194, 199
disposable income 26
diversity 75, 125, 177-8, 179
do nothing 27, 75, 92, 116-7, 149-50, 171-2
domestic appliances 91-2
doorstep 62, 79
dowsing 68
draughts 92-3, 97
dripline 169-70
ducks 168, 179, 183
dynamic accumulators 155-6, 198

earthworks 127-8
earthworms 147, 148-51, 172-3, 189-90, 195-201
East Anglia, England 185, 189
Ecology Building Society 52
economics 29, 32, 40, 85, 101, 106, 139, 172, 174-5, 191
ecotone 68-9
edge 67-9, 78, 117, 151-3
edible landscaping 156
education 83, 115
electricity 95-8, 126, 130, 185-6
energy 30, 91-3, 96-9, 129-143, 200
  demands 32, 84, 88, 91, 191, 194
  expenditure 40, 127
  flows 32, 63, 65, 67, 68, 121-3, 131-2, 176, 191-2, 209
  human 83
  savings 92-8, 192
  traps/stores 78, 79, 87, 125, 133, 183
entropy 129
epiphytes 78
espalier 161-2
equator 65
ethical investment 52
ethics 20, 26-7, 29, 47, 108, 139
Europe 38, 43, 85, 101, 115, 119, 139, 157, 172, 206
evaporation 64, 149, 204-5
exotics 156-7

faeces 37, 86, 98, 117, 137, 158, 169, 176, 179, 181, 200
fan-trained 161-2
farming (*see also* agriculture) 29, 30, 45-6, 76, 103, 111-3, 119, 125, 138, 171-80, 182, 189, 200
  city 111-2
fear 43, 49, 56, 105, 107

feathering 134
fences *see* boundaries
fertility 111, 172, 176-7, 183, 189-201
fibre 154, 184
filters 185, 206
finance 52, 190, 209
fire 87-8, 94, 123
fish 175, 179-80, 181-5, 193, 207-8, 224-5
flywheel effect 79
foggage 173-4
food 29, 37, 45, 57, 69, 71, 80, 84, 92, 109-13,
    118-9, 129, 137-8, 153-8, 175, 181, 190, 192
  chain 63, 137, 181-2
forest 27, 29, 31-2, 69, 77-8, 88, 112, 115-7, 123,
    128, 138, 161, 169, 196, 205, 212
  gardens 169-70
foxes 70, 137, 158
France 66, 115, 200
freedom 38
Freud, Sigmund 58
friends 61, 84
Friends Provident 52
frost 89-90, 123, 161, 164, 168, 169, 204
fruit 159-70
fuel 84, 92, 96-8, 130-2, 138-9, 143, 149, 176,
    191, 192
Fukuoka, Masanobu 178-9, 196
function 76, 87, 138, 154, 199, 203, 206
fungi 99, 118, 173, 193, 221
furniture 84, 95

game 115, 175, 190
gardening 20, 26, 67, 79, 99, 109-11, 117-9, 138,
    140, 147-58
garlic 70, 198
gas 96, 143, 176, 181
geotextiles 127
geese 99, 168
Germany 94, 112, 140, 168
Giant's Causeway 124
gift 52, 75
glasshouses 87, 93-5, 98-9, 158
global warming 87
goats 116, 150, 158, 198
gold standard 49
government (*see* politics) 25, 32, 55, 98, 140, 172
grafting 159-70
grain 77, 134-5, 172, 176-9, 200
grassland 69, 70, 118-9, 121, 126, 128, 168, 169,
    171, 173-6, 196, 199
Great Lakes 32
green
  Guerrillas 111
  money 54
greenhouse effect 27, 29
Greenland 202
growing season 66, 89-90

guilds 153
guinea fowl 99

Hamaker, John 196
happiness 26, 32
Harris, Thomas 58
Hart, Robert 169-70
harvest 41, 67, 77, 113, 117-9, 136, 164, 167, 172,
    179, 185, 190-2, 203
health 26, 28-9, 32, 38-9, 45, 71-2, 83, 85, 91,
    130, 142, 167, 175, 190, 208
heat
  loss 87, 88-99,
  stores 64, 94, 97, 137, 199
heating 92-9, 130-1, 158
hedging 76, 99, 167, 174, 189
Helsinki 111
hemispheres (*see* north/south) 65-6, 88, 163-4
Henry Doubleday Reasearch Association 157
hens 30, 90, 132, 137, 141, 168, 175
Hensel, Julius 196
herbs 118, 155-6, 170, 174, 195
hierarchies 29, 39, 43
Holland 134
Hollins, Arthur 174
homes 47, 83, 123, 138, 140, 206
Hong Kong 110
horses 127, 139, 142, 150, 174
horse latitudes 65
housing *see* homes
Howden, Patrick 192
human
  needs 37, 40, 50, 57, 58, 60, 70, 80, 83-5,
    103-4, 113, 202-3
  outputs 37, 41, 80, 83-5, 86, 103-4, 137
humidity 65, 128, 193
humus 124, 128, 147-9, 171, 172-4, 190, 195-201,
    205
hydrological cycle 204-5

ICOM 53
immune system 26, 71
India 139, 140
insects 90, 118, 147-53, 158, 162, 168-70, 176,
    181-5, 200
insulation 92-3
interest 55
internal combustion engine 42, 130, 138
intervention 71, 150, 189
  minimum 75, 99, 157, 192, 211-2
Inuit 75, 191
investment 45, 53, 105, 116, 123, 135, 171-2, 194
irrigation 126
Islam 27

Japan 43, 85, 102, 134, 155
judo 68

Kent, England 169
Kielder Forest 128
kitchens 87, 92, 148, 199
knowledge 50, 60, 69

land 29, 30, 171
  ownership 46, 59, 61, 109-10, 175
  scape 37, 64-5, 67, 88-91, 120-8, 136, 192, 205
language 38-9, 43, 58, 60, 73, 103, 107-8, 121
larders 87
Latin America 42
lawns see grassland
leadership 20, 43-4, 105
leaves 64, 70, 88, 148, 156, 195, 198-201
legumes 116, 149, 155, 156-7, 169, 172-3, 174,
  178-9, 196-8, 223-4
LETS 54-5
liabilities 75-6, 183
libraries 61
Libya 189
Liebig, Justus von 193-4
life expectancy 42
lighting 92, 96, 133
listening 60
loam 124, 184
loan trusts 52
local control 79, 103-6, 125, 179
love 83, 107, 170
Lovelock, James 192
lunar cycles 67-8

maintenance 90, 151, 185, 210
maize 65
manure see faeces/urine
maps 120-1, 209
maritime see sea
materialism 25, 26, 30, 44
men 92
menstruation 67
Mercury Provident 52
minerals (in soil/air/water) 86, 116, 150, 173, 181,
  183-4, 193-200, 206
momentum 79
money 13, 32, 41, 45-56, 59, 103-4, 110, 177-8
monoculture 77, 176, 178, 182, 189-91
moon 67-8, 131
Moscow 66, 164
motor car 30, 85, 105-6, 130, 141, 185
mulching 137, 148-9, 154-5, 169, 171, 196
multi-racial 43
mycorrhizae 173

nature 22, 29, 31, 41, 60, 63, 72, 73, 78, 115-9,
  136, 196
Neighbourhood Energy Action 95
neighbours 61, 79, 85, 101, 106, 157, 161, 193
nettles 70, 154

New Forest, England 169
New Zealand 55, 66, 157
Newcastle, England 66
niches 69-70, 78, 116, 119, 158, 183
night/day 38, 69-70, 131
no-lose scenario 55
north/south 22, 28, 66, 93, 113-4
North Sea 32
nuclear power 21, 143
nursing 37
nuts 118, 160-70

offers and requests 51
oil 96, 131, 167
oral tradition 107-8
orchards 90, 112, 123, 159-70, 176
Oregon Experiment 74
organic growing 32, 109, 112, 147, 158, 173-5,
  195-201
Owen, Robert 101
ozone layer 33

Pain, Jean 200
pannage 169
parasites 37
'parent' 58
parents 37, 43, 87
pasture see grassland
pattern 20, 31, 41
  behavioural 73-80, 107, 190
  language 74
  global 65
  physical 63-72, 112
pay-back period 92
peace 27, 83-4, 109
Pearson, David 83
peat 124, 149
people care 29, 37-44
perennials 32, 153-4, 177
permission 43
pigs 90, 142, 150, 158, 169, 175
pines 88, 156, 169, 190
pioneers 78, 117, 127, 149
placement see position
plains 65
Poland 140
poles 65, 66
politics (see also government) 38, 44, 101-2
pollution 22, 25, 32, 38, 40, 79, 102, 110-4, 116,
  138, 140, 191, 194, 209-10
ponds 69, 88, 136, 175, 181-5
population 28-9, 41-2, 101, 111, 115, 179, 190,
  203
position 20, 32, 66, 84, 87, 90-1, 93, 97, 121, 123,
  149, 182-3, 195, 209-10
potatoes 148, 196
poverty 26, 101, 113, 140

precipitation 64-5, 85, 88, 125-6, 128, 137, 181, 190, 196, 203-5
predators 68, 70-2, 80, 87, 90, 116, 149, 156-7, 169, 193
pre-selling 53
pressure (atmospheric) 65, 129
productivity 67-9
professionalism 39, 47, 69, 102, 126, 208, 210
profit 46, 79, 138, 172, 179, 189-91
pruning 75, 91, 161-2

quality 74, 159, 184

rabbits 70, 116, 158, 190
racism 43, 73, 113
radio 42, 103
railways 50
rain see precipitation
rain shadow 65
ram pumps 134, 206
recession 13, 50, 101
recycling 79, 86, 95, 98, 113, 148, 176, 183-4, 192-3, 205-6
reductionism 50
reeds 113, 180, 182, 195, 207-8
reflection 67
relationships 75, 90, 130, 181, 190
relaxation 83, 100, 139, 190, 191
religion 43
REMAP 69
remineralisation 196
resource management 21, 27, 29, 32, 40, 50-1, 75, 117, 139, 205, 209
retro-fitting 95
return (on capital) 46, 194
risk management 49, 55, 75, 88
roads see access
Rochdale, England 101
rocks 64, 120-5, 132, 155, 195, 196, 205
Romans 159, 189
roots 64, 78, 111, 118-9, 127, 128, 130, 149, 154, 156, 160, 169, 171, 193, 195
rotation 149-50, 176-7
Rothampstead trials 200

salads 87, 110-2, 153, 156, 170
Sami 191
sand 124, 195
sanitation 85, 206
Scandinavia 94, 158
schools 78, 138
science 27, 50, 57, 60, 67, 83, 190, 192-3
Scotland 89, 115, 156-7, 190
sea 64, 88, 89, 121, 125, 128, 136, 138, 172, 181, 182-3, 194, 199, 202-4
seasons 64-5, 66, 67, 70, 88-9, 93, 107, 121, 135, 147, 150, 155, 160, 178-9, 195

security 83, 88, 99, 108, 125, 178
seed funding 52
seeds 153, 157, 159, 169, 171, 174, 178-9, 196
savers 157
Segger, Pete 192
self
    employment 41
    sufficiency 21, 106
sewage 85-6, 113, 203, 206-8
shade see sun
shade tolerance 66
sheep 70, 116, 126, 142, 158, 168, 174, 175, 190
shelter 37, 57, 80
shops 85, 98, 103-4, 110, 138, 179
Shropshire, England 170, 174
slope 120-8, 163, 173, 184
skills 31, 39-44, 46-7, 50, 55, 59, 69, 190
smallholding 47, 90, 179
social
    credit 55
    structures 37, 44, 101-8, 191
soil 120-5, 130, 147-53, 161, 189-201
    compaction 71, 126-7, 151, 171
    conditioning 76, 116-7, 150-6, 169, 172-3, 183, 195-200
    erosion 27, 115, 126-7, 128, 148, 172, 184, 190
    nutrients 65, 111, 116, 169, 183-4, 196-200
solar
    charts 66
    gain 66, 76, 87, 89, 92-9, 130-1, 136-7, 177
Somerset, England 169
Spain 115
special needs 108
species 29, 70, 80, 119, 154, 162, 181, 184, 193, 215-227
spirals 67, 69
    of intervention 71-2
springs 85, 122, 208
stacking 76-7, 168, 177-8
standard of living 17, 25, 27, 142
Steiner, Rudolph 68
stock
    animals 47, 76, 80, 94, 115-7, 126, 138, 143, 153, 158, 168-70, 172-80, 184, 185, 193, 198, 206
    for grafting 159-70
    valuables 45, 50, 57
stocktake 57-62
stoves 96-9
streams/rivers 66, 173, 189, 203-5
structures 66-7, 74, 88-100, 121, 125, 183-5
success 55-6, 212
succession 31, 78, 116-7, 149-50, 155, 169, 183
succulents 88
sun 193, 204, 210
    sector 66
    vs. shade 22, 66, 87-9, 92-4, 123, 167, 193

surplus 30, 51, 62
sustainability 32, 79, 171, 176, 189
swales 128, 173
Sweden 98, 140, 141
Swift, Graham 185
Switzerland 112
synthesis 44

tannin 168
Taoism 27
taxonomy 215-6
technique 32, 171
technology 20, 26, 60, 91-4, 103, 111, 136, 142, 192-3
telephone 50, 103
television 42, 123
temperate 65, 78, 87-90, 119, 167, 181, 193
template 80
tenancy 46, 84, 109-10
terracing 128, 173
tessellation 67
Thoreau, Henry David 83, 171
tides 67, 179, 185
Tierra del Fuego 66
tillage 126-7, 132, 137, 147-8, 158, 171-2, 196
time management 83-92, 98, 110, 140, 191
toilets 86, 205
tomatoes 65, 196
tools 45, 47, 48, 50, 57, 61, 80, 90, 91, 103, 211
Toronto 66
towns see cities
trace elements 194-200
tractors 127, 132, 142
trade 45-56, 57, 103, 109, 112-3, 139-40, 192
training 40, 50-1, 55
transactional analysis 58
transport 80, 84, 85, 87, 105-6, 112, 113, 127, 129, 131, 138-9, 140-2, 171, 191, 211
travel see transport
trees 30, 63, 64-8, 76, 112, 116-7, 154, 173, 177, 182, 191, 195, 205
    fruit 159-70
    spacings 77, 169-70
triploid 162-3
tropics 65, 78
turbidity 122
turbulence 65-6, 126, 184
Tyneside, England 112

United States of America 38, 79, 94, 98, 101, 106, 111, 112, 115-6, 119, 123, 135, 140, 165-6, 169, 190, 203
urine 37, 86, 98, 137, 205

valleys 121-2, 125-6, 196
vegetables 90, 110-2, 137, 153-8, 176, 192
vegetarianism 47, 175
viewpoints 100
Village Homes 111
voles 70

walls see boundaries
war 28-9, 73, 107, 110, 140, 190
waste 86, 95, 98, 129, 132, 137, 148, 178, 195, 206
wasteland 44, 110-3
water 27, 28, 30, 64-6, 67, 69, 80, 84, 85, 120, 122-3, 124, 127, 160, 172, 181-5, 193, 194, 202-8
    power 131-4, 206
    table 122-3, 128, 195, 203
    wheels 133
wealth 45, 47, 55, 79, 103-4, 113, 116, 140
weather (see also climate) 64, 123, 125, 204
weeds 31, 76, 118-9, 147, 149, 155-6, 171, 183, 197-200
wetlands 69, 113, 126
wheat see grain
wholeness 38, 83-4, 191
wilderness 29, 79, 113, 115-9, 150, 167, 175, 191, 225-6
wind 64-5, 68, 88-9, 123, 126, 181, 193
    mills 126, 132, 134-6
    power 131-6
windbreak 68, 76, 88, 168, 177
women 41, 67, 73, 92
wood 94, 131, 165-8, 198
    fire 28, 76, 96-8, 118, 170, 176
    houses 88
    land 69, 88, 117, 167, 169, 173
    working 41, 177
Woodbridge, Kevin 93
work 20, 22, 30, 37-42, 45-6, 54, 57, 69, 76, 83, 90-2, 113, 136, 158, 171

yield 45, 46, 67, 75, 77-9, 117-9, 128, 132, 137, 153, 172, 176, 179, 190-2, 200

zenith 67,
zones 90-1, 113, 129, 182-3